AF238873

Markus Ludwigs / José Hernán Muriel Ciceri / Annika Velling (eds.)

Digitalization as a challenge for justice and administration

Abhandlungen zum Öffentlichen Recht

Herausgegeben von

Markus Ludwigs, Laura Münkler, Ralf P. Schenke, Stefanie Schmahl

Band 1

Das Öffentliche Recht ist in allen seinen Facetten ein dynamisches Rechts-gebiet. Die „Abhandlungen zum Öffentlichen Recht" tragen den Entwicklun-gen des deutschen, europäischen und internationalen Öffentlichen Rechts in seiner gesamten Breite und in seinen Verbindungen zu den Grundlagen Rechnung.

Markus Ludwigs / José Hernán Muriel Ciceri /
Annika Velling (eds.)

Digitalization as a challenge for justice and administration

La digitalización como reto para la justicia y la administración

Digitalisierung als Herausforderung für Justiz und Verwaltung

Würzburg
University Press

Impressum

Julius-Maximilians-Universität Würzburg
Würzburg University Press
Universitätsbibliothek Würzburg
Am Hubland
D-97074 Würzburg
www.wup.uni-wuerzburg.de

© 2023 Würzburg University Press
Print on Demand

Cover: Holger Schilling

ISSN 2941-2854 (print)
ISSN 2941-2862 (online)
ISBN 978-3-95826-200-3 (print)
ISBN 978-3-95826-201-0 (online)
DOI 10.25972/WUP-978-3-95826-201-0
URN urn:nbn:de:bvb:20-opus-301717

Preface

Digitalization is one of the global challenges for justice and administration. The complex legal issues arising in this context and the manifold effects in the various legal systems were the subject of an online conference organized on March 22, 2022 by Prof. Dr. *Markus Ludwigs* and Ms. *Annika Velling* of the Julius-Maximilians-University of Würzburg together with Prof. Dr. *Hernán Muriel* of the Tecnológico de Monterrey in Mexico. This multilingual research volume documents the results of presentations given by speakers from four continents in this context. They addressed central issues of this highly relevant subject from African, Japanese, U.S., Swiss, Latin American and German perspectives. The spectrum of topics touches on all three areas of law and ranges from fundamental questions of administrative automation, the digitalization of procedural law and the regulation of artificial intelligence to special problems in the area of marriage contract law.

We would like to express our special thanks to the speakers who discussed their contributions in an engaged manner during the symposium and presented their research results on this basis. Valuable support in the editorial supervision of the manuscripts was provided in particular by the student assistants of the Chair of Public Law and European Law in Würzburg. Ms. *Anna Blösch* and Ms. *Charlotte Lorenz* deserve special mention. At the Tecnológico de Monterrey, Ms. *Marilupe Mirón Toruño* was involved in the formatting of the contributions in accordance with the format templates. The publication of the volume was generously aided by a printing cost grant from the Hanns-Seidel-Stiftung. We would like to thank the publishers Würzburg University Press, namely Ms. *Claudia Schober* and Mr. *Manuel Beck*, for their uncomplicated cooperation and excellent support of this volume.

Würzburg and Puebla, December 2022

Prólogo

La digitalización es uno de los retos globales de la justicia y la administración. Una conferencia en línea organizada por el Prof. Dr. *Markus Ludwigs* y la Sra. *Annika Velling* de la Julius-Maximilians-Universidad de Würzburg junto con el Prof. Dr. *Hernán Muriel* del Tecnológico de Monterrey en México, el 22 de marzo de 2022, estuvo dedicada a las complejas cuestiones jurídicas y a los diversos efectos en los diferentes sistemas jurídicos que surgen en este contexto. Este volumen de investigación multilingüe documenta los resultados de presentaciones realizadas en este ámbito por ponentes de cuatro continentes. Las contribuciones abordaron cuestiones centrales de este tema de gran actualidad desde las perspectivas africana, japonesa, estadounidense, suiza, latinoamericana y alemana. El espectro de temas toca las tres áreas del derecho y abarca desde cuestiones fundamentales de la automatización administrativa, la digitalización del derecho procesal y la regulación de la inteligencia artificial hasta problemas especiales en el ámbito del derecho contractual matrimonial.

Queremos expresar nuestro especial agradecimiento a los ponentes que discutieron sus contribuciones de forma comprometida durante el simposio y presentaron los resultados de sus investigaciones sobre esta base. El valioso apoyo en la supervisión editorial de los manuscritos fue proporcionado en particular por los estudiantes asistentes de la Cátedra de Derecho Público y Derecho Europeo de Würzburg. Mención especial merecen las Sras. *Anna Blösch* y *Charlotte Lorenz*. En el Tecnológico de Monterrey, la Sra. *Marilupe Mirón Toruño* ayudó a formatear las contribuciones según las especificaciones de formato. La publicación del volumen fue financiada con una subvención para gastos de impresión, de la cual agradecemos a la Fundación Hanns-Seidel. Nos gustaría agradecer a la editorial de la Universidad de Würzburg, concretamente a la Sra. *Claudia Schober* y al Sr. *Manuel Beck*, por su cooperación sin complicaciones y su excelente apoyo de este volumen.

Würzburg y Puebla, diciembre de 2022

Vorwort

Die Digitalisierung zählt zu den globalen Herausforderungen für Justiz und Verwaltung. Den sich dabei ergebenden komplexen Rechtsfragen und vielfältigen Auswirkungen in den unterschiedlichen Rechtskreisen widmete sich eine Online-Konferenz, die am 22. März 2022 durch Herrn Prof. Dr. *Markus Ludwigs* und Frau *Annika Velling* von der Julius-Maximilians-Universität Würzburg gemeinsam mit Herrn Prof. Dr. *Hernán Muriel* von der Tecnológico de Monterrey in Mexiko organisiert wurde. Der vorliegende multilinguale Forschungsband dokumentiert die Forschungsergebnisse von in diesem Rahmen gehaltenen Referaten der aus vier Kontinenten zugeschalteten Vortragenden. Diese widmeten sich zentralen Fragestellungen der hochaktuellen Thematik aus afrikanischer, japanischer, US-amerikanischer, schweizerischer, lateinamerikanischer und deutscher Perspektive. Das Themenspektrum berührt alle drei Rechtsgebiete und reicht von grundlegenden Fragen der Verwaltungsautomatisierung, der Digitalisierung des Prozessrechts und der Regulierung künstlicher Intelligenz bis hin zu Spezialproblemen im Bereich des Ehevertragsrechts.

Unser besonderer Dank gilt den Referentinnen und Referenten, die ihre Beiträge im Rahmen des Symposions engagiert diskutiert und auf dieser Grundlage ihre Forschungsresultate dargestellt haben. Wertvolle Unterstützung bei der redaktionellen Betreuung der Manuskripte haben insbesondere die studentischen Hilfskräfte des Lehrstuhls für Öffentliches Recht und Europarecht in Würzburg geleistet. Eine besondere Hervorhebung verdienen Frau *Anna Blösch* und Frau *Charlotte Lorenz*. An der Tecnológico de Monterrey hat Frau *Marilupe Mirón Toruño* die formatierungstechnische Anpassung der Beiträge an die Formatvorlagen begleitet. Die Veröffentlichung des Bandes wurde dankenswerterweise durch einen Druckkostenzuschuss der Hanns-Seidel-Stiftung gefördert. Dem Verlag Würzburg University Press, namentlich Frau *Claudia Schober* und Herrn *Manuel Beck*, sei für die unkomplizierte Zusammenarbeit und vorzügliche Betreuung auch dieses Bandes herzlich gedankt.

Würzburg und Puebla, im Dezember 2022

Table of Contents

Ludwigs / Muriel Ciceri / Velling (eds.), Digitalization as a challenge for justice and administration, Abhandlungen zum Öffentlichen Recht 1, Würzburg, 2023, pp. 1-22.
DOI: 10.25972/978-3-95826-201-0-1

Digitalization, Fragmentation, and Justice in Nigeria

Olufunmilayo B. Arewa, Ayodeji O. Fakolade

A. Introduction: Digitalization and Fragmentation in African Legal Systems

Countries in Africa are experiencing a digital revolution that has expanded access to technological devices, including mobile phones, and a broad range of software applications and services. New and existing technologies are evident across a broad range of sectors, including in agriculture, healthcare, education, financial services, and entertainment, for example. It is likely that this digital revolution is being accelerated by Africa's large population of young people who are relatively quick learners and adopters of technology.[1] Digitalization in African contexts occurs in contexts shaped by a legacy of colonialism, exclusion, and societal divides.[2] Language is also a critical factor shaping both technology access and participation,[3] as well as effective participation in varied legal contexts.[4]

Since the last half of the twentieth century, a shift to the digital has occurred and shaped the business, economic, social, and cultural landscape in much of the world. For businesses, the digital economy has led to a paradigm shift in sources of value. During this digital era, intangibles such as intellectual property have become a core source of economic growth and business value on a global scale.

---

[1]   The United Nations has stated that Africa has the youngest population in the world and that 70 % of people in Sub-Saharan Africa are under 30 years old. *United Nations*, Young People's Potential, the Key to Africa's Sustainable Development, available at https://www.un.org/ohrlls/news/young-people%E2%80%99S-potential-key-africa%E2%80%99s-sustainable-development. The last access for all web addresses referenced in this chapter was on 27 October 2022. *Egboboh*, Why investment in tech, innovation should matter to Nigeria, available at https://businessday.ng/amp/business-economy/article/why-investment-in-tech-innovation-should-matter-to-nigeria/.

[2]   *Arewa*, Disrupting Africa: Technology, Law, and Development, 2021.

[3]   *Schelenz/Schopp*, IJDS 2018, Vol. 9 (4), 1412 (1417).

[4]   *Arewa* (Fn. 2).

Although the use of such resources in business contexts is certainly not new, their exploitation in the digital era is remarkable both in scope and intensity.

The shift to the digital in law has long been evident, with uneven movement in different areas. Digitalization has fundamentally impacted life, leading to new types of evidence and activities and new causes of action.[5] The advent of the digital has led at times to a mismatch between laws and regulations that must now apply to activities and technologies that were not contemplated or perhaps even conceivable at the time of adoption of such laws and regulations. This chapter will focus on the impact of digitalization of the law, particularly as digitalization relates to the administration of justice and access to justice in Nigeria and other countries in Africa.

Fragmentation has been a key feature of the digitalization of law and is evident in uneven implementation of legal digitalization initiatives. This fragmentation is apparent in varied areas of the law, legal practice, and legal administration that may be targets of digitalization efforts. Fragmentation has also had an impact on users of law and legal resources in an increasingly digitized legal universe. Fragmentation may also have a temporal element, which has meant that past design choices may have implications for future configurations. The reality of fragmentation may also have implications for users, particularly non-professional ones, who typically must confront a digitized legal world with potentially multiple interfaces and applications required for access. In many cases, these applications and interfaces may not have developed under an overarching plan but rather were developed sequentially and not always with significant attention to questions of interoperability and useability.

Fragmentation is a key issue in post-colonial legal contexts in Nigeria and other countries in Africa. Colonial legal frameworks were implemented in an uneven manner, often with inadequate conflict of law principles.[6] Patterns of cut-and-paste borrowing, which have been prominent during and after the formal end of colonialism, have contributed to fragmentation of African legal systems.[7] Existing patterns of fragmentation must be considered in digitalization design processes in African legal systems.

Digitalization of legal information (including legal cases, scholarship, laws and regulations, and secondary sources), court administration, court proceedings, legislation and legislative activities, advocacy and training, and access to legal resources has been varied and uneven. Digitalization came first in the legal information sphere, well before the widespread availability of the Internet. In the

---

[5]   *Hilgendorf*, in: Hilgendorf/Feldle (eds.), Digitization and the Law, 2018, p. 9.
[6]   *Arewa* (Fn. 2), pp. 28-35.
[7]   *Arewa* (Fn. 2), pp. 28-35.

United States, for example, Mead Data Central launched its Lexis service, the first broadly available full-text commercial legal information service, in 1973.[8] Commercial legal information services available through subscriptions based on the Lexis model became a norm in early digitalization efforts, at least in parts of the developed world. The expense of subscriptions makes the commercial model a less feasible option in developing countries,[9] as well as for some types of users in developed countries.

From the mid-1990s, the Internet has facilitated free access to legal information, which has been important in African contexts. Beginning in 1992, legal information institutes (LIIs) have provided free access to legal information from varied sources and have generally collaborated with one another through the free access to law movement (FALM).[10] LIIs have been developed in several areas of the world, including Australasia,[11] Britain and Ireland,[12] Canada,[13] Nigeria,[14] United States,[15] and several other countries in Africa.[16]

The digitalization of legal information in African contexts may offer lessons for future digitalization efforts. The Indigo Trust, a philanthropic foundation based in the United Kingdom, has been a financial supporter of a few African LIIs since 2013.[17] The LIIs and other early digitalization efforts in Africa and elsewhere have been targeted at legal professionals. Such digitalization efforts have had an impact beyond their intended audience. A 2019 study suggests that LIIs in Africa have been "well used resources for those interested in the law and acted as significant tools for social and legal change in sub-Saharan Africa, rather than as mere information repositories for professionals."[18] The broader impact of LIIs

---

[8]   Lexis, together with the Nexis news and information service, which was launched in 1979, now operates as LexisNexis, the global legal publishing arm of British multinational information and analytics company RELX (formerly Reed Elsevier). *Arewa*, Lewis & Clark L Rev 2006, 797 (816).

[9]   *Arewa,* Lewis & Clark L Rev 2006, 797 (829-832).

[10] *Greenleaf/Chung/Mowbray*, UPDATE: Legal Information Institutes and the Free Access to Law Movement, 2018, available at https://www.nyulawglobal.org/globalex/Legal_Information_Institutes1.html.

[11] *Australasian Legal Information Institute*, available at http://www.austlii.edu.au/.

[12] *British and Irish Legal Information Institute*, available at https://www.bailii.org/.

[13] *Canadian Legal Information Institute*, available at https://www.canlii.org/en/.

[14] *Nigeria Legal Information Institute*, available at https://nigerialii.org/home.

[15] *Legal Information Institute*, available at https://www.law.cornell.edu/.

[16] *African Legal Information Institute*, available at https://africanlii.org/; an explanatory video about the African Legal Information Institute is available at https://www.youtube.com/watch?v=og2YO8e_Dmc.

[17] *Rumbul/Moulder/Parsons*, The State of African Legal Information Institutes – How free access to law online is shaping justice in sub-Saharan African, 2019, available at https://research.mysociety.org/media/outputs/state-african-legal-information-institutes_OeQNyhG.pdf.

[18] *Rumbul/Moulder/Parsons* (Fn. 17), p. 8.

in Africa has meant that "LIIs were confirmed to be universally positive and progressive elements of developing and maturing legal systems in sub-Saharan Africa."[19]

The experience of the LIIs suggests that design choices in future digitalization efforts should be flexible and should periodically evaluate uses and outcomes of digitized legal resources. This is particularly true because digitalization efforts today may involve varied audiences and legal spheres. This moves digitalization efforts today beyond targeting professionals involved in the business and administration of law itself who were the primary intended beneficiaries of early legal information digitalization efforts. Notably, navigating legal systems has long been difficult for everyday people in pre-digitalization contexts, particularly when not represented by lawyers. Digitalization design choices must take account of this existing reality and the impact of digitalization for a broader range of intended users.

Outside events may also play an important role in accelerating digitalization in legal spheres. The COVID-19 pandemic has had a significant impact on digitalization in several legal spheres. In just a few short weeks beginning in 2020, varied public services were forced to rapidly migrate online. In the United States, courts had long been called upon to improve processes for those accessing court systems.[20] As a result of the coronavirus pandemic

> just months after the pandemic began, states throughout the country moved to adopt a range of technological tools to keep their court systems available to the public, quickly shifting from requiring people to submit paper documents and appear in person before judges to widespread use of electronic filing (e-filing) systems, virtual hearing platforms, and other tools.[21]

In many contexts, the pandemic has exacerbated existing inequalities and access to resources, particularly ones necessary for effective digital participation generally, including in the legal arena. The digital divide, which separates the information rich from the information poor,[22] has proven to be enduring and significant in the context of technology adoption in contexts of COVID-19. The COVID-19 pandemic underscores challenges of access and usability in contexts of technology deployed in law. These challenges raise continuing questions about

---

[19] *Rumbul/Moulder/Parsons* (Fn. 17), p. 8.
[20] *The Pew Charitable Trusts*, How Courts Embraced Technology, Met the Pandemic Challenge, and Revolutionized Their Operations, 2021, available at https://www.pewtrusts.org/-/media/assets/2021/12/how-courts-embraced-technology.pdf.
[21] *The Pew Charitable Trusts* (Fn. 20).
[22] *Leggon*, in: Fox/Johnson/Rosser (eds.), Women, Gender and Technology, 2006, p. 98.

technology and other design choices and the implications of such choices for legal participation and access to justice.

B. Administration of Justice in Nigeria

Nigeria and other African countries exemplify the opportunities that might be provided by digitalization. African contexts also highlight the continuing challenges evident in broader societal contexts that also shape access to and participation in legal systems. Technology initiatives in the administration of justice in Nigeria are best considered within a broader context of ongoing legal reform.

Nigeria is a federation that includes the federal government, 36 state governments, and the federal capital territory (FCT).[23] Nigeria also has 768 local government areas in the states,[24] and six area councils in the FCT.[25] Nigeria's justice system consequently comprises distinct, fragmented and, interrelated justice systems at the federal, state, and local government levels.[26]

This chapter, however, focuses on only some aspects of the federal government's justice system and Lagos State's justice system, as a representative of the justice system in the states. Our choice of both the federal government and Lagos State's justice systems is influenced by the fact that these systems are the most active justice systems in Nigeria. This is because of the scale of the federal government's responsibilities and Lagos State's large population and status as Nigeria's economic capital. Furthermore, both the federal government and Lagos State's justice systems are also likely the most fragmented and digitized justice systems in Nigeria.[27]

I. Federal Government's Administration of Justice System

The administration of justice is a crucial issue in every society. It is a major way for people and other legal persons to have access to justice for the enforcement of their rights, obligations, and the law. As Nigeria's Vice-President *Yemi*

---

[23]   Constitution of the Federal Republic of Nigeria (CFRN) (as amended), Sec. 2.
[24]   CFRN (as amended), Sec. 3 (6).
[25]   The area councils in the FCT are the equivalents of the local governments in the states.
[26]   CFRN (as amended), Sec. 3 (4), 297 and First Schedule, Part II.
[27]   For a discussion of legal fragmentation in Nigeria, see *Arewa* (Fn. 2), pp. 16-19 and 28-35.

Osinbajo, Senior Advocate of Nigeria (SAN),[28] said: "the administration of justice is the foundation of law and order."[29] The initial design and operation of Nigeria's current legal system, including the administration of justice, occurred during Nigeria's precolonial and colonial periods.[30] This template for administration of the justice system has also been retained in largely the same design since Nigeria's independence.[31] This system is a fragmented one comprising both superior courts of records and customary courts that administer received English law and statutory law and customary law and Islamic personal law, respectively.[32] The administration of justice in Nigeria can also be broadly divided into the criminal justice system and the civil justice system.[33]

The major participants in the administration of the justice system are law enforcement agencies,[34] defendants, litigants, lawyers, lawmakers, and courts. Although some efforts have been undertaken to reform the administration of justice in Nigeria,[35] the current system is ineffective and inefficient. Pervasive and severe delays in the administration of justice illustrate the justice system's ineffectiveness and inefficiency.[36] For instance, the former chief registrar of the

---

[28] SAN is a designation given to senior and distinguished lawyers in Nigeria: "Senior Advocate of Nigeria (SAN) is a privilege that is awarded as a mark of excellence to members of the legal profession who are in full time legal practice, who have distinguished themselves as advocates and have made significant contribution to the development of the legal profession in Nigeria." (*Ikimi*, NAUJILJ 2019, Vol. 10 (1), 69).

[29] *Osinbajo* made this statement during his keynote address at The Bankole Olumide Aluko, SAN, 20th Year Memorial Symposium with the theme "Administration of Justice: The Ideal Standard, The Nigerian Reality and Our Potential" on 18 February 2022, available at https://www.yemiosinbajo.ng/20th-year-memorial-symposium-in-honour-of-bankole-aluko-san/.

[30] *Arewa* (Fn. 2), p. 11.

[31] *Arewa* (Fn. 2), p. 11.

[32] *Arewa* (Fn. 2), pp. 28-35; CFRN (as amended), Sec. 6, Sec. 251, Sec. 272, Sec. 277, and Sec. 282.

[33] CFRN (as amended), Sec. 251 (1), Sec. 251 (3), Sec. 272 (1), Sec. 277, and Sec. 282.

[34] Major law enforcement agencies in Nigeria include the Police, the Ministry of Justice, and the Correctional Service.

[35] Reform efforts have included the enactment of new laws including the Evidence Act 2011, the Administration of Criminal Justice Act 2015, the Nigerian Correctional Service Act, 2019, and the Nigeria Police Act 2020. Reform efforts have also included modifications of practice directions and procedure rules by some courts.

[36] *Ilminska/Schoenteich*, Raising the Profile of Pretrial Detention in Africa, 2016, available at www.justiceinitiative.org/voices/raising-profile-pretrial-detention-africa; *Osigwe/Amali*, Enforcing Contracts and Business Survival in Nigeria: Calling Legislative Attention to World Bank 2018 Findings, NILDS Research Issue Brief 2019, Issue 4 (3), available at https://ir.nilds.gov.ng/bitstream/handle/123456789/368/Enforcing%20Contracts%20and%20 Business%20Survival%20in%20Nigeria%20Calling%20Legislative%20Attention%20to%20 World%20Bank%202018%20Findings%20Issue%204%20No%203%20April%202019.pdf;

Supreme Court of Nigeria, *Hadizatu Uwani Mustapaha*, noted in August 2021 that the Supreme Court had some 10,000 cases pending between 2017 to 2019.[37]

The federal government's current regulatory approach to digitalization of the administration of justice has been influenced by its general approach to the development of a digital economy. In 2022, President *Muhammadu Buhari* inaugurated the Presidential Council on Digital Economy and E-Government and said that "his administration will continue to take advantage of digital technologies to transform every sector of the economy."[38] The Nigerian National Information Technology Development Agency (NITDA) has engaged in capacity building as part of its execution of its mandate.[39] NITDA programs have included a training program on digital economy for justices of the court of appeal.[40] NITDA executed the program along with the court of appeal's committee on information communication technology. This training program seeks to ensure that justices of the court of appeal understand the relevant issues connected with different aspects of technology. The goal of the training program is for judges to apply knowledge from this technology training in the adjudication of cases in their courts.

II. Federal Legislation and Policy

Nigeria's constitution provides that a person is entitled to a fair hearing within a reasonable time by a court or tribunal.[41] This provision is aimed at ensuring that a person's rights or obligations are determined promptly in a fair manner. Per-

---

World Bank Group, Doing Business 2020 - Economy Profile Nigeria, available at https://www.doingbusiness.org/content/dam/doingBusiness/country/n/nigeria/NGA.pdf.

[37] *This Day,* With 10,000 Pending Appeals, The Supreme Court is Overworked, 2021, available at https://www.thisdaylive.com/index.php/2021/08/17/with-10000-pending-appeals-the-supreme-court-is-overworked/.

[38] *Adesina,* E-Government: President Buhari Inaugurates Presidential Council, Tasks Members on Improving Nigeria's Ranking in Ease of Doing Business, available at https://statehouse.gov.ng/news/e-government-president-buhari-inaugurates-presidential-council-tasks-members-on-improving-nigerias-ranking-on-ease-of-doing-business/.

[39] The NITDA was created in April 2001 to implement the Nigerian Information Technology Policy and co-ordinate general IT development in Nigeria, see *Nigerian Government,* NITDA - Background, accessible via https://nitda.gov.ng/background/.

[40] *Okeowo,* NITDA begins capacity building for court judges on digitization, 2022, available at https://techeconomy.ng/2022/01/nitda-begins-capacity-building-for-court-judges-on-digitization/.

[41] CFRN (as amended), Sec. 36 in Chapter IV "Fundamental Rights".

vasive delays in the administration of justice, however, mean that most people do not benefit from the right to a speedy trial.[42]

The federal government has enacted significant laws within the last decade aimed at improving the administration of justice. Some of these laws include provisions for the digitalization of some aspects of the administration of justice. The reform of the evidence law[43] for instance includes provisions for the admissibility of evidence from new technologies in the administration of justice.[44] The Nigerian Correctional Service Act also provides for the Nigerian Correctional Services' establishment of a centralised database management system for its operations.[45]

The Administration of Criminal Justice Act (ACJ Act) was also enacted as a major reform of the administration of criminal justice. The purpose of the ACJ Act is to

> ... ensure that the system of administration of criminal justice in Nigeria promotes efficient management of criminal justice institutions, speedy dispensation of justice, protection of the society from crime and protection of the rights and interest of the suspect, the defendant, and the victim.[46]

Provisions in the ACJ Act address a number of issues, including timelines for the commencement and determination of cases and the electronic recording of confessional statements.[47] The ACJ Act also established the Administration of Criminal Justice Monitoring Committee (Committee).[48] This Committee consists of the Chief Judge of the Federal Capital Territory who is the Chairman and the Attorney General of the Federation.[49] It also includes a judge of the Federal High Court, the Inspector-General of Police and the Comptroller General of the Nigerian Correctional Service. The Executive Secretary of the National Human Rights Commission and the chairman of a branch of the Nigerian Bar Association in the FCT are also members of the Committee. The Committee also includes the Director General of the Legal Aid Council of Nigeria and a representa-

---

[42]   *Ilminska/Schoenteich* (Fn. 36).
[43]   Nigeria Evidence Act 2011, Sec. 84.
[44]   *Arewa/Fakolade*, in: Ndulo/Emeziem (eds.), The Routledge Handbook of African Law, 2021, p. 297.
[45]   Nigerian Correctional Service Act 2019, Sec. 13 (2).
[46]   ACJ Act, Sec. 1.
[47]   ACJ Act, Sec. 110 and 396 (timelines) and Sec. 15(4) (electronic recording of confessions). Sec. 44 (4) of the Nigeria Police Act 2020 also has a similar provision.
[48]   ACJ Act, Sec. 469 (1).
[49]   ACJ Act, Sec. 469 (2).

tive of civil society working on human rights and access to justice or women's rights issues.

The Committee is responsible for the "efficient and effective application" of the ACJ Act by relevant law enforcement agencies.[50] The Committee's functions include ensuring the speedy trial of criminal cases and reduction of the backlog of criminal cases in courts.[51] Reducing congestion in prisons and facilitating maximum cooperation among the agencies responsible for administration of justice are part of the Committee's functions. The Committee is also responsible for the collation, analysis, and publication of information on the administration of criminal justice. The Committee is empowered to "carry out any such activities as are necessary for the effective and efficient administration of criminal justice."[52]

The Committee's composition is commendable and inclusive, including key stakeholders such as a member of civil society focused on access to justice. This inclusive approach could harmonize some of the fragmented approaches to administration of justice in Nigeria. Moreover, the effective implementation of the Committee's functions also has the potential to significantly improve the administration of criminal justice. The Committee can also use its omnibus function to advocate for the use of technology in all aspects of the administration of justice in Nigeria.[53]

The ACJ Act applies in federal courts in Nigeria and in cases where offences are stated in federal laws except for court martials.[54] The executive secretary of the Committee noted that 32 out of the 36 states in Nigeria had adopted the ACJ Act as the states' Administration of Criminal Justice Law as at December 2021.[55] The executive secretary, however, also stated that only some of the states that had adopted the ACJ Act have started implementing the provisions of the law.[56] The Body of Attorneys General of the 36 states in Nigeria has also recommended "inter-state collaboration on facilitating virtual hearings for police officers and

---

[50]   ACJ Act, Sec. 470 (1).

[51]   ACJ Act, Sec. 470 (2).

[52]   ACJ Act, Sec. 470 (2) (h).

[53]   ACJ Act, Sec. 470 (2) (h). The laws governing other aspects of law enforcement also contain similar omnibus function provisions that can also be used to promote the deployment of technology in the administration of justice. An example is Sec. 9 (1) (g) of the Nigeria Police Act 2020.

[54]   ACJ Act, Sec. 2.

[55]   *Ibunge*, FG Partners Rivers to Strengthen the Administration of Criminal Justice System, 2021, available at https://www.thisdaylive.com/index.php/2021/12/15/fg-partners-rivers-to-strengthen-the-administration-of-criminal-justice-system/.

[56]   *Ibunge* (Fn. 55).

witnesses outside the jurisdiction of the adjudication court."[57] Such inter-state collaboration for participants in virtual court hearings, who are outside a state and are in another state, can contribute to the success of such virtual hearings.

The Attorney General of the Federation (AGF) also established the Presidential Committee on Correctional Service Reforms and Decongestion in October 2017.[58] The Committee's functions include the development of a road map for the decongestion of prisons.[59] It also has the mandate to deploy technology and implement a virtual automated case management system for the decongestion of prisons. The committee submitted its report to the AGF in July 2020, and the chairman of the committee stated that it visited 39 prisons in 18 states. The chairman also stated that 7,813 inmates were released from the correctional centers because of the Committee's activities. The released inmates also included 3,789 persons who were released during the outbreak of COVID-19 in 2020. The AGF also subsequently said that over 10,000 inmates were freed as a result of the Committee's activities as at August 2021.[60]

Technology initiatives have been a notable aspect of the Committee's efforts. The Committee launched a pilot virtual court proceeding at the Kuje correctional center, FCT, in December 2021 as one of its efforts to decongest correctional centers.[61] The pilot program was launched in collaboration with the United Nations Development Program and the Japanese government. Virtual court proceedings have also been endorsed by others in Nigeria. The Nigerian Bar Association and the Justice Research Institute also organised a justice sector summit in January 2022. The summit was organised in collaboration with the National Judicial Council (NJC) and the Justice Reform Project. (JRP).[62] The summit's communique also recommended "… the enhanced use of virtual hearings …" as part of

---

[57]   *Igbintade*, State Govts Not Subservient to FG, Says Body of Attorneys-General, available at https://www.thisdaylive.com/index.php/2022/06/21/state-govts-not-subservient-to-fg-says-body-of-attorneys-general/.

[58]   *Malami*, Presidential Committee on Correctional Service Reform Submits Report, 2020, available   at   https://www.thisdaylive.com/index.php/2020/07/14/presidential-committee-on-correctional-service-reform-submits-report/.

[59]   *Malami* (Fn. 58).

[60]   *Nnochiri*, Prison decongestion: Over 10,000 inmates freed in 4 years, 2021, available at https://www.vanguardngr.com/2021/08/prison-decongestion-over-10-000-inmates-freed-in-4-years-malami/.

[61]   *Channels Television*, FG Launches Virtual Court Sitting at Correctional Centres, 2021, available at   https://www.channelstv.com/2021/12/07/fg-launches-virtual-court-sitting-at-correctional-centres/.

[62]   The Konrad Adenauer Foundation and the United Nations Office on Drugs and Crime also collaborated with the other organisations to organise the summit. The Justice Reform Project, available at https://www.facebook.com/TheJRPNG/ and https://twitter.com/jrp_ng.

actions to accelerate the speed of justice delivery.[63] The Police also recently launched a case management system for the digitalization of all criminal cases handled by the legal department of the Police from the commencement to the determination of the cases.[64]

Technology and legal reform initiatives have also been undertaken in the administration of civil justice in Nigeria. The JRP and the AGF have also advocated for the enactment of an administration of civil justice law as part of actions to also reform the administration of civil justice.[65] Ekiti State has enacted the Ekiti State Administration of Civil Justice Law in 2019 (ECJ Law).[66] The main objectives of the ECJ Law includes the reform of the law and procedure for the resolution of civil disputes in the high court of Ekiti State.[67] This law also aims to "... facilitate the just, efficient, timely and cost-effective resolution ..." of disputes.[68] The ECJ Law also provides for electronic filing, service, certification of court processes and recording of court proceedings.[69] Governor *Kayode Fayemi* of Ekiti State also recently stated that Ekiti State is likely the only state in Nigeria that has enacted an administration of civil justice law.[70]

The COVID-19 pandemic has also accelerated the use of technology in the justice sector, reflecting *Osinbajo's* view that "technology should be deployed at all phases of the administration of justice".[71] For example, because of the COVID-19 pandemic, the JRP asked the Chief Justice of Nigeria to "consider the urgent digitalization of court procedure".[72] As a result of the COVID-19 pandemic, the AGF also called for the extensive use of technology in the

---

[63] Communique issued by *Olumide Akpata*, president, Nigerian Bar Association, on behalf of all the organizers of the summit, available at https://barristerng.com/wp-content/uploads/2022/03/JSS-Communique_NBA-pres-sign1.pdf.

[64] *Punch*, Police Gets Digital System for Case File, Others Storage, available at https://punchng.com/police-get-digital-system-for-case-file-others-storage/.

[65] *Adekoya*, SAN, the chairman of the JRP's governing board advocated for this during the, Bankole Olumide Aluko, SAN, 20th Year Memorial Symposium; press statement issued by *Ogundoro*, Malami Rolls Out Plans for Post COVID-19 Justice System, 20 April 2020, available at https://fmic.gov.ng/malami-rolls-out-plans-for-post-covid-19-justice-system/.

[66] Ekiti State Administration of Civil Justice Law (ECJ Law), No. 9 of 2019, available at https://ekitistate.gov.ng/hoa/2020/No9of2019.pdf.

[67] ECJ Law, Sec. 1.

[68] ECJ Law, Sec. 5 (1).

[69] ECJ Law, Sec. 39 to 47 and 60.

[70] *This Day*, We Need an In-Depth Review of Judicial Salaries, 2022, available at https://www.thisdaylive.com/index.php/2022/05/09/we-need-an-in-depth-review-of-judicial-salaries/.

[71] *Osinbajo* (Fn. 29).

[72] *The Justice Reform Project*, Letter to the Chief Justice of Nigeria tilted "Remote Court Hearings: A Necessity in the Face of the Covid-19 Pandemic", 2022, available at https://twitter.com/JRP_ng/status/1250332562569846786/photo/1.

administration of justice as part of plans for the justice system after the COVID-19 pandemic.[73]

One of the objectives of the 2017 Nigerian National Policy on Justice (the Justice Policy) has been to encourage the holistic use of information communication technologies (ICTs) in the justice sector.[74] The Justice Policy also listed some challenges with the use of ICTs which include inadequate use of existing ICT facilities, shortage of trained persons, and inadequate infrastructure.[75] The Justice Policy has led to varied uses of ICTs in the administration of justice.

Implementation of technology initiatives in the justice sector has, however, largely been undertaken in a fragmented manner without sufficiently strategic and inclusive approaches. Technology challenges noted in the Justice Policy have also not been adequately addressed. Furthermore, a strategic and inclusive use of technology is only a part of the broader need for comprehensive reform of the law and administration of justice in Nigeria.[76]

III. Federal Judicial Policy, Procedure Rules, and Practice Directions

The federal judiciary has made policies, procedure rules, and practice directions that provide for digitalization of some aspects of the federal judiciary's operations. The National Judicial Council (NJC) made the National Judicial Policy in 2007 (Judicial Policy). The Judicial Policy's objective is to "… promote and ensure the highest possible standard of qualitative justice delivery".[77] The Judicial Policy includes a judicial education and training policy which states that "judicial education must be holistic, practical and supported by essential tools, … and use of the latest information technology".[78] The Judicial Policy also has an access to justice policy which provides that "all courts should promote the use of information communication technology".[79] The Judicial Policy also provides for the establishment of a working group for the study of the working of judicial sys-

---

[73] *Nnochiri* (Fn. 60).
[74] National Policy on Justice 2017, p. 4.
[75] National Policy on Justice 2017, pp. 29-31.
[76] *Arewa* (Fn. 2).
[77] *National Judicial Council*, The National Judicial Policy, Sec. 1.9, available at www.njc.gov.ng/national-judicial-policy.
[78] National Judicial Policy, Sec. 2.4.2.
[79] National Judicial Policy, Sec. 3.5.

tems.[80] The working group's functions include the study of methods of access to justice delivery and judicial decision making.

A former Chief Justice of Nigeria Justice *Dahiru Musdapher*, retired, inaugurated a judicial information technology policy formulation and implementation committee in January 2012.[81] The committee's role included the development of a "… comprehensive, pragmatic information technology policy".[82] The committee's work subsequently resulted in the enactment of the Nigerian Judiciary Information Technology Policy Document in July 2012 (Judiciary Tech Policy). The Judiciary Tech Policy's purpose is to effectively support the administration of justice by the optimal use of ICT by the Nigerian judiciary.[83] The Judiciary Tech Policy established the Judiciary Technology Policy Committee (JITPCO) as the regulatory authority for the implementation of the Judiciary Tech Policy.[84] The Judiciary Tech Policy also provides that every judicial authority should establish an ICT committee or department with the responsibility for implementation of the Judiciary Tech Policy within that judicial authority.[85]

The Judiciary Tech Policy deals with the use of ICT in several parts of the court system. These parts are the central administration, the litigation department, the courtrooms, and the offices of judicial and non-judicial officers.[86] The Judiciary Tech Policy also provides that judicial institutions need to conduct an adequate feasibility study and network planning before acquiring ICT systems.[87] The Judiciary Tech Policy also has guidelines on network infrastructure, communication infrastructure, customised software including enterprise resource planning and case management software, hardware, capacity building and security.[88] The JITPCO has used the Supreme Court of Nigeria as one of its pilot sites for the implementation of the Judiciary Tech Policy.[89] JITPCO has established a data center with ICTs in the Supreme Court and retrofitted one of the court rooms with ICTs as part of its digitalization of the Supreme Court.[90] The Nigerian

---

[80]   *National Judicial Policy* (Fn. 77), Summary of Some Institutions of the Policy.
[81]   *Musdapher*, Foreword to the Judicial Information Technology Policy of the Nigerian Judiciary, 2012, p. 5, available at https://nji.gov.ng/images/PDF/JITPO_Policy_Document.pdf.
[82]   *Musdapher* (Fn. 81), p. 5.
[83]   National Policy on Justice 2017, p. 5.
[84]   National Policy on Justice 2017, p. 33.
[85]   National Policy on Justice 2017, pp. 33-34.
[86]   National Policy on Justice 2017, pp. 8-9.
[87]   National Policy on Justice 2017, pp. 11-15.
[88]   National Policy on Justice 2017, pp. 14-29.
[89]   *Idaeho*, Digitalisation of the Supreme Court: Way Forward for the Nigerian Legal Profession, 2018, available at https://www.pressreader.com/nigeria/thisday/20180227/282046212589817; *This Day* (Fn. 37).
[90]   *Idaeho* (Fn. 89); *This Day* (Fn. 37).

Case Management System (NCMS) was also developed under the Judiciary Tech Policy.[91]

The Judiciary Tech Policy is a relatively good basis for the comprehensive use of technology in all aspects of the courts' operations. There has been some implementation of the Judiciary Tech Policy, and this implementation was also accelerated because of the COVID-19 pandemic. The implementation, however, has been fragmented and the judiciary and its users have therefore not realized the entire benefits of the Judiciary Tech Policy. Moreover, there needs to be a comprehensive review of both the impact of and the provisions of the Judiciary Tech Policy as it is now about ten years since it was made.

The NJC also made the Guidelines for Court Sittings and Related Matters in the COVID-19 Period (the NJC Guidelines) which became effective in May 2020.[92] The NJC Guidelines are a complement to the existing rules of court, the electronic filing system, and case management system that had been adopted by some courts.[93] The NJC Guidelines provides for electronic filing and service of process, electronic payment of court fees, and virtual court proceedings. The NJC Guidelines apply to all courts in Nigeria, and the JITPCO has the mandate to work with all courts to implement the ICT tools proposed in the NJC Guidelines.[94] The need for continuous training in virtual court sittings for judicial officers is also emphasised in the NJC Guidelines. The NJC Guidelines also states that courts should consider "… the poor state of our power and communications infrastructure … particularly in … underserved or unserved locations …".[95]

Courts in Nigeria began to conduct proceedings virtually in increasing numbers after the publication of the NJC Guidelines. For instance, the President of the Court of Appeal disclosed that the Court of Appeal delivered 528 judgments virtually using the Zoom video conference application during the 2020 to 2021 legal year.[96] The Court of Appeal's virtual judgments were 16.97 % of the total number of judgments delivered during the 2020 to 2021 legal year.[97]

Digitalization efforts in Nigeria also illustrate potential legal impediments such efforts may face. For example, in two cases filed by Lagos State and Ekiti

---

[91] *Idaeho* (Fn. 89); *This Day* (Fn. 37).
[92] *National Judicial Council*, Guidelines for Court Sittings and Related Matters in the Covid-19 Period, available at https://www.njc.gov.ng/30/news-details/.
[93] *National Judicial Council* (Fn. 92).
[94] *National Judicial Council* (Fn. 92).
[95] *National Judicial Council* (Fn. 92).
[96] *Abuja*, Appeal Court promises improved performance in new legal year, 2022, available at https://thenationonlineng.net/appeal-court-promises-improved-performance-in-new-legal-year.
[97] *Abuja* (Fn. 96).

State about the constitutionality of virtual court sittings, the Supreme Court of Nigeria held that virtual court sittings are not unconstitutional.[98] These states had filed the cases at the Supreme Court because of the lack of an express constitutional provision for virtual court sittings. The Supreme Court also stated virtual court proceedings should be conducted within practice directives for virtual proceedings issued by the head of courts.[99] To clarify the constitutionality of virtual court proceedings, the chairman of the senate committee on judiciary, Senator *Opeyemi Bamidele*, introduced a bill to amend the constitution to support virtual court proceedings.[100]

The NJC Guidelines, developed because of the COVID-19 pandemic, accelerated the use of technology and particularly virtual court proceedings in Nigeria's judicial system. The consistent and enhanced use of virtual court proceedings has the potential to both improve access to justice and accelerate the administration of justice. The challenges of ICT infrastructure, accessibility, language, value creation, flexibility, training, legal reform, and finance, however, have the potential to limit the potential gains from use of technology to improve the administration of justice and access to justice. Further, digitalization initiatives in Nigeria highlight the potential for digitalization to further contribute to fragmentation.

IV. Lagos State Government's Administration of Justice System

Since Nigeria's return to democracy in 1999, Lagos State government (LASG) has developed and implemented several significant measures aimed at improving the administration of justice and access to justice in Lagos State.[101] These measures include the expansion of the judiciary by the appointment of new judges and the creation of several new courts in different areas of Lagos State.[102] The judiciary has also reviewed its civil procedure rules of court three times.[103] An electronic

---

[98] *Adebusoye*, LegalTech: Nigerian Supreme Court Says Virtual Court Judgments are Binding, 2020 available at https://technext.ng/2020/07/16/virtual-court-sittings-and-the-evolution-of-virtual-legal-system-in-nigeria/.

[99] *Adebusoye* (Fn. 98).

[100] *Iroanusi*, Nigerian Senate introduces bill to legalise virtual court proceedings, 2020, https://www.premiumtimesng.com/news/headlines/392429-nigeria-senate-introduces-bill-to-legalise-virtual-court-proceedings.html.

[101] *Centre for Public Impact*, Reforming the civil justice system in the state of Lagos, 2016, available at https://www.centreforpublicimpact.org/case-study/judicial-reform-lagos.

[102] *Centre for Public Impact* (Fn. 101); the Lagos Judicial Services Commission appointed 26 judges to the High Court on 22 May 2001.

[103] High Court new civil procedure rules were made in 2004, 2012 and 2019.

case management system called the Court Automation Information System (CAIS) was also developed and implemented to some extent.[104]

A new magistrate court law and magistrate court civil procedure rules were also enacted in 2009 to reform the law and practice in the magistrate courts as magistrate courts deal with a significant number of disputes.[105] LASG also established the Office of the Public Defender in 2000 to provide legal aid to residents in Lagos State.[106] The Lagos State Office of the Public Defender Law was also enacted in 2003 and subsequently amended in 2008. LASG established five citizen mediation centers for alternative dispute resolution, as part of its access to justice program, in 2000.[107] The Centre for Public Impact also reported that 17,000 cases had reached a mediated settlement at the citizen mediation centers by 2007.[108] Some of these mediated settlements involved disputes that might have been instituted in the courts and could therefore had contributed to the congestion of cases in the courts.

V. Legislation, Policy, and Digitalization in Lagos State

The Ministry of Justice (MOJ) is a lead agency for the administration of justice in Lagos State.[109] The MOJ has utilised ICTs in the execution of both its internal and external duties. For instance, the MOJ has implemented an internal case management system across all departments in the MOJ which includes the digitalization of documents and approvals.[110] This system enables officials in the MOJ to upload and retrieve documents and approvals remotely. The dashboard aspect of the case management system also empowers the Attorney General of Lagos State (AGL) and other relevant officials to track productivity and the status of work items remotely. The success of Lagos State and similar case management

---

[104] *Centre for Public Impact* (Fn. 101); It appears that the CAIS has been replaced by the Judicial Information System (JIS). The electronic filing system is a major part of the case management system that is being used regularly in the High Court of Lagos State. The other features of the case management system have not yet been used. An official in the MOJ, who prefers to remain anonymous, provided this information on the JIS to the writers of this chapter during an interview in March 2022.

[105] The Magistrate Court Law No. 16 of 2009 and The Magistrate (Civil Procedure) Rules 2009. The jurisdiction of the Magistrate Courts was increased by the Magistrate Court Law.

[106] *Lagos State,* Office of the Public Defender, available at https://opd.lagosstate.gov.ng.

[107] *Centre for Public Impact,* (Fn. 101); *Wheeler,* Directorate for Citizens' Rights, 2022, available at http://lagosministryofjustice.org/directorate-for-citizens-rights/.

[108] *Centre for Public Impact,* (Fn. 101); *Wheeler* (Fn. 107).

[109] *Lagos Ministry of Justice,* available at http://lagosministryofjustice.org/.

[110] Interview with MOJ official (Fn. 104).

systems in Nigeria would, however, depend on several factors. These factors include the quality of software and hardware, training, resources, and overcoming officials' resistance to the use of ICTs.[111]

The Directorate of Advisory Services and Judicial Liaison, which is part of the MOJ, also provides legal advice, in response to civil petitions received by members of the public or government agencies by electronic mail.[112] A legal advice is an opinion by the Directorate on a civil petition submitted to the MOJ by members of the public or government agencies. This approach dispenses with the use of intermediaries for the issuance of a legal advice, and it has the potential to improve both the ease and pace of administration of justice. Furthermore, a person can track the status of a legal advice on the MOJ's website, and such person therefore does not necessarily have to physically go to the MOJ's office for the status of a legal advice.[113]

LASG also enacted the Lagos State Administration of Criminal Justice Law (ACJ Law) in 2007. The ACJ Law, which was enacted before the federal ACJ Act of 2015, was subsequently amended in 2011 and 2021.[114] Provisions in the ACJ Law address several issues, including the video or electronic recording of confessional statements.[115] The ACJ Law provides for the conduct of court proceedings by audio, virtual, video conference or another technological platform.[116] The ACLJ Law also provides for the establishment of an electronic crime data management system for suspects and criminals called the Lagos State Criminal Information System (LCIS).[117] The LCIS includes the relevant details of all persons in the criminal justice system and tracks all related activities from the arrest of such persons until the adjudication of their cases.[118] The ACJ Law also has a measure for the protection of victims or witnesses by providing that such persons may be masked and give their evidence by video link.[119] There are, however, inadequate or no facilities in some police stations for video recording of confessional

---

[111] Interview with MOJ official (Fn. 104).

[112] *Wheeler*, Directorate of Advisory Services and Judicial Liason, 2022, available at http://lagosministryofjustice.org/directorate-of-advisory-services-and-judicial-liason/; Interview with MOJ official (Fn. 104).

[113] *Wheeler* (Fn. 112); Interview with MOJ official (Fn. 104).

[114] *British Council*, Implementation of the Administration of Justice Law in Lagos, 2016, available at https://www.britishcouncil.org.ng/about/press/implementation-administration-justice-law-lagos: The Lagos State Administration of Criminal Justice (Amendment) Law No. 14 of 2021's commencement date is September 30, 2011.

[115] ACJ Law, Sec. 9 (3).

[116] ACJ Law, Sec. 200 (2) and (3).

[117] ACJ Law, Sec. 370.

[118] *Lagos Criminal Information System*, About US, available at https://lcis.com.ng/about.

[119] ACJ Law, Sec. 371 (3) and 373.

statements.[120] There has also been inadequate training of magistrates and police officers who are some of the key persons responsible for the implementation of the ACJ Law.[121]

The MOJ also collaborates with other statutory agencies responsible for administration of justice on the use of ICTs. For instance, although the MOJ is responsible for maintaining the LCIS,[122] the database provides an interface for the Police, the Correctional Service, the Judiciary and the MOJ.[123] The MOJ has also collaborated with the High Court of Lagos State on the digitalization of the courts' operations.[124] The digitalization includes the installation and operation of software, hardware including speech to text transcription and full recording capacity in the courts. The digitalization of the courts' activities is being undertaken in phases. Phase One, of the digitalization of the courts' activities, which involves ten courts, started in 2022.[125]

VI. Lagos State Judicial Policy, Procedure Rules, and Practice Directions

The Lagos State judiciary has also made some policies, procedure rules and practice directions which provide for digitalization of some aspects of the judiciary's operations. The Judicial Information System (JIS) is an electronic filing and payment system which was introduced in December 2010.[126] A practice direction was also subsequently issued in 2013 which made it mandatory for all cases filed in the High Court to be filed through the JIS.[127] The JIS, which was developed as a comprehensive case management system, is currently being underutilized. This is because it is currently primarily used for just electronic filings and tracking the status of cases in Court on the Lagos State judiciary website and not as a compre-

---

[120] *Access to Justice*, A Report - On the implementation of the Administration of Criminal Justice Law 2011 of Lagos State, 2011, available at https://www.accesstojustice-ng.org/Research%20Report%20-%20Implementation%20of%20the%20ACJ%20Law.docx.
[121] *Access to Justice* (Fn. 120).
[122] ACJ Law, Sec. 370 (7).
[123] About LCIS *supra* note 118.
[124] Interview with MOJ official, (Fn. 104).
[125] Interview with MOJ official, (Fn. 104).
[126] *Lagos State Judiciary*, About the High Court of Lagos, available at https://lagosjudiciary.gov.ng/aboutus.html; *Centre for Public Impact* (Fn. 101).
[127] *Lagos State Judiciary* (Fn. 126); *Centre for Public Impact* (Fn. 101).

hensive case management system.[128] The JIS was nevertheless crucial for the recovery of filings that were filed through the JIS after the High Court was severely vandalized in October 2020.[129] The High Court's officials were able to retrieve the filings from the JIS database, which helped to recreate copies of the physical filings that were lost as a result of the vandalization of the High Court.[130] The use of the JIS to retrieve the filings is a great example of the benefits of digitalization of the judiciary's operations.

The Chief Judge of Lagos State, Justice *Kazeem Alaogba* also issued the Lagos State Judiciary, Remote Hearing of Cases (COVID-19 Pandemic Period) Practice Direction (Remote Direction), which became effective on May 4, 2020.[131] One of the objectives of the Remote Direction is to ensure "the use of suitable technology".[132] The Remote Direction has guidelines for the electronic filing and service of process, electronic payment of court fees, and virtual court proceedings.[133] The Remote Direction, however, only applies to urgent and new cases in the High Court of Lagos State (Lagos Court).[134] It was also reported that the Lagos Court held the first virtual court hearing in Nigeria on May 4, 2020.[135] The proceeding was conducted on the Zoom video conference application (Zoom), with Justice *Mojisola Dada* in court in Ikeja, Lagos, while the defendant was in the Apapa, Lagos correctional center.[136] The witnesses and lawyers in the cases were in different locations and also participated on Zoom.[137]

---

[128] Interview with MOJ official, (Fn. 104); Online Search/Case Status Information, available at https://lagosjudiciary.gov.ng/onlinesearch.html#onlinesearch.

[129] Interview with MOJ official, (Fn. 104).

[130] Interview with MOJ official, (Fn. 104).

[131] *Lagos State Judiciary*, Remote Hearing of Cases (COVID-19 Pandemic Period) - Practice Direction, 2020, available at https://www.aelex.com/wp-content/uploads/2020/05/LAGOS-STATE-JUDICIARY-COVID-19-PRACTICE-DIRECTION.pdf.

[132] *Lagos State Judiciary* (Fn. 131), Sec. 3 of the Remote Direction.

[133] *Lagos State Judiciary* (Fn. 131), Sec. 5 to 20 of the Remote Direction.

[134] *Lagos State Judiciary* (Fn. 131), Introductory Paragraph of the Remote Direction.

[135] *Sahara Reporters*, Nigeria Holds First Online Court Sitting in Lagos, Man Sentenced to Death for Murder, 2020, available at https://saharareporters.com/2020/05/04/nigeria-holds-first-online-court-sitting-lagos-man-sentenced-death-murder.

[136] *Sahara Reporters* (Fn. 135).

[137] *Sahara Reporters* (Fn. 135).

C. Implications of Digitalization for Consumers and Court Administration

Questions about digitalization, law, and access to justice, digitalization mandated by government and other authorities are noteworthy in many contexts in Africa. In addition to questions of access, the digitalization of personally identifiable information (PII) has become prevalent throughout the African continent. The collection of biometric and other PII, as well as data emanating from participation in legal processes, raises continuing questions about privacy, security, and data protection. Privacy, security, and data protection issues represent a continuing challenge in many African contexts where effective privacy, security, and data protection frameworks may be elusive. As is currently the case with biometric and other PII, further digitalization of the Nigerian legal system will require that privacy, security, and protection of PII and other data arising from legal cases and interactions be considered when design choices are made.

Digitalization offers important potential opportunities to increase access to justice and provide for faster administration of justice. The speed of administration of justice is a problem in Nigeria, where pretrial detention levels are among the highest in the world. Nigeria's levels of pretrial detention are high: "[o]f the world's ten prison system[s] with the highest proportion of pretrial detainees, half are in Africa. In places such as … Benin, DRC, Liberia, Libya and Nigeria, 70 percent or more of all prisoners have not been convicted".[138] In the commercial law sphere, enforcement of contracts in Nigeria may take an extended period and is often costly.[139]

Digitalization may promote the rule of law by providing a potential opportunity for greater transparency in the administration of justice. New technologies may also "enable the provision of more and better legal assistance".[140] Digitalization will require significant investment in legal and court administration systems in Nigeria that have been persistently underfunded.[141] An investment in digitalization may, however, reduce aggregate costs of access to justice. If implemented with care, digitalization may offer the opportunity to increase peoples' familiarity with the administration of justice. Improvements in the administration of justice may also increase confidence in the integrity of courts and legal systems more generally. Participation in digitized legal systems is, however, likely to be costly

---

[138]   *Ilminska/Schoenteich*, (Fn. 36).
[139]   *Osigwe/Amali*, (Fn. 36).
[140]   *Cabral et. al.*, Harv. J. Law Technol. 2012, Vol. 26 (1), 241 (243).
[141]   *Doma*, J Marshall J Info Tech & Privacy L, 2016, Vol. 32 (2), 89 (104).

to users, who will need devices that permit them to access the digital systems, and Internet access, the latter of which can be costly in African contexts.

Digitalization may pose significant challenges. Digital approaches to law and legal systems will require making choices about the design of technologies and legal systems after digitalization that will require greater flexibility than is present in legal systems in Nigeria and elsewhere in Africa. These choices will determine what type of value creation is to accompany digitalization. Such choices will also mandate decisions about processes and procedures within digitized justice systems.

Development of robust technologies to enable electronic justice systems and facilitate digitalization of court processes in Nigeria and other contexts in Africa may also present challenges related to information technology infrastructure and language and literacy issues,[142] some of which emerge from existing gaps and issues in contexts of digitalization. For example, effective digitalization in Africa will require addressing existing gender divides already evident in access to justice, as well as technology.[143] Digitalization will also require significant continuing training for lawyers, judges, court administrators, and users, among others. In Nigeria and other countries in Africa, the dominance of languages of former colonising powers in court systems may limit effective access to justice in non-digitized contexts. In Nigeria, for example, English is the language of courts even though most Nigerians do not speak sufficient English to navigate in contexts of legal English.[144] Given the global prominence of English in technology contexts, digitalization is likely to intensify the effects of English language dominance in the Nigerian legal system. As a result, digitalization design in Nigeria and elsewhere in Africa must also be attentive to facilitating ease of use in countries with many different languages spoken that also have varied levels of literacy and language capacity in languages used by courts and in other legal contexts.

Digitalization will require reorienting existing and future legal reform efforts to address existing shortcomings and issues that arise in the transition to digital systems. Legal reform efforts connected to digitalization must also deal with potential regulatory overreach, which is an existing problem with Nigeria. Regulatory overreach has potential to be significantly increased in digitized contexts.

---

[142]   *Drabo*, The Digitization of Court Processes in African Regional and Subregional Judicial Institutions, 2021, p. 21.

[143]   *United Nations Women,* Justice for women amidst COVID-19, 2020, available at https://www.unwomen.org/en/digital-library/publications/2020/05/justice-for-women-amidst-covid-19; *Organisation for Economic Co-operation and Development*, Bridging the Digital Gender Divide - Include, Upskill, Innovate, 2018, available at https://www.oecd.org/digital/bridging-the-digital-gender-divide.pdf.

[144]   *Arewa* (Fn. 2).

Access to tools to enable participation in digitalization in legal systems will likely present a continuing challenge, particularly given the high levels of poverty in Nigeria and many other countries in Africa. Digitalization has the potential to ameliorate existing shortcomings in legal systems in Nigeria and other contexts in Africa. Technology initiatives must address existing challenges related to the administration of justice and access to justice to maximize their potential success.

Ludwigs / Muriel Ciceri / Velling (eds.), Digitalization as a challenge for justice and administration, Abhandlungen zum Öffentlichen Recht 1, Würzburg, 2023, pp. 23-34.
DOI: 10.25972/978-3-95826-201-0-23

Stand der Digitalisierung und rechtliche Herausforderungen in der Schweiz

Nadja Braun Binder

A. Einleitung

Die Digitalisierung in den öffentlichen Verwaltungen und den Gerichten in der Schweiz ist stark durch den föderalen Staatsaufbau und die damit verbundene Kompetenzverteilung zwischen dem Bund und den 26 Kantonen geprägt. Dies führt zu heterogenen Entwicklungen im Bereich der E-Government-Leistungen.[1] Diese Vielfalt kann auf der einen Seite als nützlich eingestuft werden, weil daraus ein Wettbewerb der Ideen entsteht und gute E-Government-Dienste zu einem Standortfaktor für einzelne Kantone werden können. Sie birgt andererseits die Gefahr der Entwicklung von Einzellösungen, die nicht mit anderen Systemen kommunizieren können. Den Nachteil tragen die Nutzerinnen und Nutzer, wenn sie die mangelnde Interoperabilität durch Verwendung unterschiedlicher Systeme kompensieren müssen.

Über Kooperations- und Koordinationsgremien wird deshalb versucht, die digitale Transformation der öffentlichen Verwaltungen und der Gerichte in der Schweiz harmonisiert voranzutreiben, wobei den gegebenen Kompetenzverteilungen stets Rechnung getragen werden soll. So kommt der Zusammenarbeit zwischen den föderalen Ebenen im Bereich des E-Government, die erstmals 2007 in einer öffentlich-rechtlichen Rahmenvereinbarung zwischen Bund und Kantonen geregelt wurde, eine wichtige Rolle zu.[2] Die Vereinbarung wurde in der Folge mehrmals angepasst und weitergeführt.[3] Gestützt auf die Rahmenvereinbarung entstand die Organisation *E-Government Schweiz*, die sich als Integrationsinstanz für die verschiedenen Staatsebenen in der Schweiz versteht.[4] Per

---

[1] Siehe *Brugger/Faoro*, in: Stember et al. (Hrsg.), Handbuch E-Government, 2019, S. 53, 57 f.

[2] Öffentlich-rechtliche Rahmenvereinbarung über die E-Government-Zusammenarbeit in der Schweiz (2007-2011) vom 22.6.2007 bzw. 29.8.2007, BBl 2008 3391.

[3] Änderung v. 16.11./16.12.2011, BBl 2011 9345.

[4] Öffentlich-rechtliche Rahmenvereinbarung über die E-Government-Zusammenarbeit in der Schweiz 2016-2019 vom 18.11.2015 bzw. 18.12.2012, BBl 2015 9637, sowie Öffentlich-rechtliche

1. Januar 2022 wurde *E-Government Schweiz* in die neue Zusammenarbeitsorganisation *Digitale Verwaltung Schweiz* überführt.[5] Gemäss Art. 1 Abs. 1 ÖRR-DVS regelt die Rahmenvereinbarung die Zusammenarbeit zwischen Bund und Kantonen im Bereich der digitalen Transformation ihrer Verwaltungen. Art. 1 Abs. 2 ÖRR-DVS präzisiert sodann, dass die Rahmenvereinbarung nicht in die Zuständigkeiten des Bundes, der Kantone und der Gemeinden eingreift. Die *Digitale Verwaltung Schweiz* gibt Empfehlungen ab, entwickelt Standards und versteht sich als politische Plattform.[6] Sie erlässt hingegen keine verbindlichen Regelungen.

Während die Organisation *Digitale Verwaltung Schweiz* die digitale Transformation der Verwaltungen fördert, existieren für den Bereich der Justiz zwei erwähnenswerte Organisationen. Dazu zählt der Verein *eJustice.CH*, der den Einsatz von Informationstechnologie zur Steigerung der Leistungsfähigkeit und Bürgernähe in der Rechtspflege von Bund, Kantonen und Gemeinden, unter anderem im Bereich der Gerichte und der Justiz bzw. im Bereich des elektronischen Rechtsverkehrs, fördern will.[7] Über regelmässig stattfindende Veranstaltungen[8] und die Erarbeitung von gemeinsamen Papieren[9] trägt der Verein zur schweizweiten Vernetzung und zum Austausch von Know-how zwischen einer Vielzahl von Akteuren aus öffentlichen Verwaltungen aller Staatsebenen, Privatwirtschaft, zivilgesellschaftlichen Organisationen und der Wissenschaft bei.[10] 2019 wurde mit *Justitia 4.0* ausserdem eine Projektorganisation ins Leben gerufen, die sich die Einführung der elektronischen Aktenführung (eJustizakte) und des elektronischen Rechtsverkehrs zum Ziel gesetzt hat. In die Projektorganisation *Justitia 4.0* sind Vertreterinnen und Vertreter der Kantonalen Konferenz der Justiz- und Polizeidirektorinnen und -direktoren (KKJPD) sowie Fachexpertinnen und Fachexperten aus den Gerichten, Staatsanwaltschaften, Vollzugsbehörden-

---

Rahmenvereinbarung über die E-Government-Zusammenarbeit in der Schweiz 2020 vom 20.11.2019 bzw. 20.12.2019, BBl 2019 8729.

[5]   Öffentlich-rechtliche Rahmenvereinbarung über die Digitale Verwaltung Schweiz vom 27.9.2021 bzw. 17.12.2021 (ÖRR-DVS), BBl 2021 3030.

[6]   *Digitale Verwaltung Schweiz*, abrufbar unter https://www.digitale-verwaltung-schweiz.ch. Der letzte Abruf aller in diesem Kapitel referenzierten Web-Adressen ist der 27.10.2022.

[7]   *Leupold/Holenstein*, Statuten des Vereins eJustice.CH vom 28.3.2011, Stand 13.5.2019, abrufbar unter https://www.ejustice.ch/de/statuten.html.

[8]   Etwa das jährlich stattfindende Magglinger Rechtsinformatikseminar, dem im Jahr 2022 das erste Mal ein Open Legal Lab voranging; siehe *eJustice.CH*, Magglinger Rechtsinformatikseminar, 2022, abrufbar unter https://www.ejustice.ch/de/m_rechtsinformatikseminar.html.

[9]   Siehe etwa *eJustice.CH*, Eine Vision für eJustice in der Schweiz, 2016, abrufbar unter https://www.ejustice.ch/de/pdf/Vision%20eJustice_de.pdf.

[10] Siehe die Mitgliederliste unter *eJustice.CH*, Mitglieder, Stand 1.1.2022, abrufbar unter https://www.ejustice.ch/de/mitglieder.html.

und Anwaltschaften eingebunden.[11] *Justitia 4.0* hat u. a. ein Konzept erarbeitet, mit welchem der Rahmen für die professionelle Begleitung aller Betroffenen im Umgang mit der digitalen Transformation in der Justiz vorgegeben wird.[12] In technischer Hinsicht soll die Digitalisierung der Justiz über eine zentrale Plattform (justitia.swiss) abgewickelt werden. *Justitia 4.0* hat in der Konzeptphase zentrale Vorarbeiten für die Entwicklung der Plattform geleistet.[13]

Parallel zu den strategischen und operativen Tätigkeiten der eben skizzierten Organisationen, laufen in der Schweiz verschiedene Rechtsetzungsprojekte, die der Schaffung von weiteren Grundlagen für die digitale Transformation in den Verwaltungen und in den Gerichten dienen und über das hinausgehen, was nach dem Status Quo (siehe B.) bereits zulässig ist. Dazu zählen auf Bundesebene der Entwurf für ein Bundesgesetz über den Einsatz elektronischer Mittel zur Erfüllung von Behördenaufgaben (EMBAG)[14], die Rechtsetzungsarbeiten zur Schaffung von Grundlagen für einen staatlich anerkannten elektronischen Identifikationsnachweis (E-ID)[15] sowie der Vernehmlassungsentwurf für ein Bundesgesetz über die Plattform für die elektronische Kommunikation in der Justiz (BEKJ)[16]. Diese drei Vorhaben werden im Folgenden näher erörtert (C.). Dabei ist darauf hinzuweisen, dass damit kein vollständiges Bild der künftigen Rechtslage für digitale Behördenleistungen auf allen Staatsebenen gezeichnet werden kann. Ergänzend wäre insbesondere ein Blick auf die bestehenden oder geplanten Regelungen in den Kantonen zu werfen.[17] Dies würde den Umfang des vorliegenden Beitrages allerdings sprengen.[18]

---

[11] *Projekt Justitia 4.0*, Projektorganisation, abrufbar unter https://www.justitia40.ch/de/projektorganisation.

[12] *Projekt Justitia 4.0*, Transformation im Projekt Justitia 4.0, abrufbar unter https://www.justitia40.ch/de/teilprojekte/transformation.

[13] *Projekt Justitia 4.0*, Basis des Projekts Justitia 4.0, abrufbar unter https://www.justitia40.ch/de/justitia40/basisinformationen.

[14] BBl 2022 805.

[15] *Bundesamt für Justiz*, Staatliche E-ID, 2022, abrufbar unter https://www.bj.admin.ch/bj/de/home/staat/gesetzgebung/staatliche-e-id.html.

[16] BBl 2020 8915 bzw. *Bundesamt für Justiz*, Elektronische Kommunikation mit Gerichten und Behörden, 2022, abrufbar unter https://www.bj.admin.ch/bj/de/home/staat/gesetzgebung/e-kommunikation.html.

[17] Exemplarisch sei auf das Rechtsetzungsvorhaben DiGiLex des Kantons Zürich hingewiesen, mit welchem Rechtsgrundlagen für den elektronischen Geschäftsverkehr mit den Behörden im Kanton Zürich geschaffen werden sollen; *Staatskanzlei*, Eröffnung Vernehmlassung DigiLex: Der elektronische Geschäftsverkehr mit den Behörden im Kanton Zürich soll ermöglicht werden, 2021, abrufbar unter https://www.zh.ch/de/news-uebersicht/medienmitteilungen/2021/07/mitteilung-eroeffnung-vernehmlassung-digilex-der-elektronische-geschaeftsverkehr-mit-den-behoerden-im-kanton-zuerich-soll-ermoeglicht-werden.html.

[18] Siehe aber etwa *Glaser/Ehrat*, LeGes 2019, Heft 3, abrufbar unter https://leges.weblaw.ch/dam/

B. Bestehende Rechtsgrundlagen für (teilweise) digitale Verfahren

In der Schweiz wurden im Zuge der Neuordnung der Bundesrechtspflege[19] Rechtsgrundlagen für den elektronischen Schriftverkehr zwischen Parteien und Behörden erlassen. In verschiedenen Bestimmungen des Bundesgerichtsgesetzes[20] werden die Voraussetzungen für die Gleichstellung des elektronischen Rechtsverkehrs mit dem bisherigen Schriftverkehr vor dem Bundesgericht verankert.[21] Die entsprechenden Bestimmungen sind seit dem 1. Januar 2007 in Kraft.[22] Mit der Schaffung des Bundesverwaltungsgerichts bzw. der grundsätzlichen Anwendbarkeit des Verwaltungsverfahrensgesetzes[23] auf das Beschwerdeverfahren vor dem Bundesverwaltungsgericht (Art. 37 VGG[24]) wurde eine Anpassung des VwVG notwendig.[25] Im Rahmen der Justizreform wurden deshalb auch im VwVG Regelungen über die elektronische Zustellung (Art. 11*b* Abs. 2, Art. 34 Abs. 1bis VwVG), über elektronische Eingaben (Art. 21*a* VwVG) und zur elektronischen Akteneinsicht (Art. 26 Abs. 1bis VwVG) geschaffen.[26] Einzelheiten zur Übermittlung von Verfügungen im Sinne von Art. 5 VwVG sowie Eingaben im Hinblick auf Verfügungen sind in der Verordnung über die elektronische Übermittlung im Rahmen eines Verwaltungsverfahrens (VeÜ-VwV)[27] verankert.[28]

Die erwähnten Regelungen beziehen sich lediglich auf den elektronischen Schriftverkehr zwischen Parteien und Behörden. Grundsätzlich sollte damit in Fällen, in denen das Bundesrecht die Schriftform verlangt, die elektronische

---

publicationsystem_leges/2019/3/e-government-gesetzg_57af12d3ff/LeGes_e-government-gesetzg_57af12d3ff_de.pdf.
[19] Vgl. die Botschaft des Bundesrates zur Totalrevision der Bundesrechtspflege v. 28.2.2001, BBl 2001 4202 ff. sowie die entsprechenden Erlassentwürfe in BBl 2001 4480 ff.
[20] Bundesgesetz v. 17.6.2005 über das Bundesgericht (BGG), SR 173.110. Zu den erwähnten Bestimmungen zählen namentlich Art. 39 Abs. 2 (Zustellungsdomizil), Art. 42 Abs. 2 (Rechtsschriften), Art. 48 Abs. 2 (Einhaltung der Frist) und Art. 60 Abs. 3 (Eröffnung des Entscheids).
[21] Siehe *Dolge*, AJP 2007, 299 (299 f.).
[22] AS 2006 1205.
[23] Bundesgesetz v. 20.12.1968 über das Verwaltungsverfahren (VwVG), SR 172.021.
[24] Bundesgesetz v. 17.6.2005 über das Bundesverwaltungsgericht (VGG), SR 173.32.
[25] Siehe BBl 2001 4403.
[26] Siehe *Kneubühler/Pedretti*, in: Auer/Müller/Schindler (Hrsg.), VwVG, Bundesgesetz über das Verwaltungsverfahren, 2. Aufl. 2019, Art. 34 Rn. 12.
[27] Art. 1 Abs. 2 lit. a und b Verordnung über die elektronische Übermittlung im Rahmen eines Verwaltungsverfahrens vom 18.6.2010, SR 172.021.2.
[28] Siehe zu den aktuellen Regelungen etwa auch *Braun Binder*, ZSR 2020, 253; *Meyer*, SJZ 2021, 836.

Form ermöglicht werden.[29] Insofern waren die für das analoge Verwaltungshandeln geltenden Vorschriften nur leicht zu modifizieren.[30] So haben zum Beispiel Verfügungen nach wie vor schriftlich zu ergehen (Art. 34 Abs. 1 VwVG), aber mit Einverständnis der Parteien dürfen sie elektronisch eröffnet werden (Art. 34 Abs. 1bis VwVG). Damit sind elektronische Verfügungen zwar grundsätzlich zulässig. Ein eigentlicher Systemwechsel, etwa der konsequente Übergang vom schriftlichen zum elektronischen Rechtsverkehr, fand jedoch nicht statt. Dies liegt zum einen an der mangelnden Attraktivität des elektronischen Rechtsverkehrs, zum anderen an dessen Freiwilligkeit.[31] So sind Art. 11b Abs. 2 und Art. 21a VwVG als „kann-Vorschriften" formuliert. Gleiches gilt für die Möglichkeit, elektronische Akteneinsicht zu gewähren (Art. 26 Abs. 1bis VwVG). Entsprechend konstatiert auch der Bundesrat in einem Bericht aus dem Jahr 2015, dass sich der elektronische Rechtsverkehr in der Praxis noch nicht durchsetzen konnte und die elektronische Akteneinsicht bei Verwaltungsverfahren nach Bundesrecht soweit bekannt nicht praktiziert werde.[32]

Neben den soeben skizzierten, bereits seit Längerem bestehenden Rechtsgrundlagen ist auf die Totalrevision des Datenschutzgesetzes hinzuweisen. Das neue Datenschutzgesetz (nDSG) wurde im September 2020 von der Bundesversammlung beschlossen[33], tritt allerdings erst am 1. September 2023 in Kraft.[34] Mit Blick auf die Digitalisierung von Verwaltungsverfahren ist Art. 21 Abs. 4 nDSG zu erwähnen, wonach für Bundesorgane eine Kennzeichnungspflicht für automatisierte Einzelentscheidungen verankert wird. In der Botschaft hat der Bundesrat präzisiert, dass es dabei um den Erlass von Verfügungen gehen soll.[35] Obwohl mit Art. 21 Abs. 4 nDSG keine hinreichende Rechtsgrundlage für den Erlass vollautomatisierter Verfügungen geschaffen wurde, impliziert die Bestimmung doch, dass der Bundesgesetzgeber davon ausgeht, dass es inskünftig

---

[29]   BBl 2001 4405 (mit Blick auf Art. 21a VwVG).
[30]   *Glaser*, SJZ 2018, 181 (187).
[31]   Siehe nur etwa *Häner*, in: Schweizerische Vereinigung für Verwaltungsorganisationsrecht (SVVOR) (Hrsg.), Verwaltungsorganisationsrecht – Staatshaftungsrecht – öffentliches Dienstrecht, Jahrbuch 2017/2018, 2018, S. 23, 26 ff.
[32]   *Schweizerische Eidgenossenschaft*, Bericht des Bundesrates vom 4.12.2015 zur Einführung des elektronischen Rechtsverkehrs in Erfüllung der Motion 12.4139, Pirmin Bischof, SR, 12. Dezember 2012, S. 8, 11, abrufbar unter https://www.bj.admin.ch/dam/data/bj/staat/rechtsinformatik/e-akteneinsicht/ber-motion-d.pdf.
[33]   BBl 2020 7639.
[34]   Siehe *Bundesamt für Justiz*, Stärkung des Datenschutzes, 2022, abrufbar unter https://www.bj.admin.ch/bj/de/home/staat/gesetzgebung/datenschutzstaerkung.html.
[35]   BBl 2017 6941, 7059.

auf Bundesebene möglich sein könnte, dass Verfügungen ohne menschliches Zu-
tun ergehen könnten.[36]

C. Ausgewählte Rechtsetzungsvorhaben

Im Folgenden werden drei Rechtsetzungsvorhaben näher erörtert, welche auf der
einen Seite wichtige Grundlagen für die Digitalisierung in den Verwaltungen
oder in den Gerichten schaffen, auf der anderen Seite aber auch paradigmatisch
für die unterschiedlichen Herausforderungen in der Rechtsetzung in diesen Be-
reichen stehen.

I. Elektronische Mittel zur Erfüllung von Behördenaufgaben

Am 4. März 2022 hat der Bundesrat den Entwurf für das EMBAG (E-EMBAG)
verabschiedet. Ziel des neuen Gesetzes ist es, Rechtsgrundlagen für eine wir-
kungsvolle digitale Transformation in der Bundesverwaltung sowie für die Zusammenarbeit zwischen Behörden verschiedener Gemeinwesen und Dritten auf
dem Gebiet des E-Government zu schaffen.[37] In den Anwendungsbereich des
Gesetzes soll lediglich die zentrale Bundesverwaltung fallen; der Bundesrat kann
allerdings vorsehen, dass das Gesetz auch für Einheiten der dezentralen Verwaltung gilt (Art. 1 Abs. 1 und 2 E-EMBAG). Dieser Anwendungsbereich ist im Ver-
gleich zur Vernehmlassungsvorlage enger gefasst. In der ursprünglichen Fassung
hätten auch kantonale Stellen für den Vollzug von Bundesrecht zur Nutzung von
elektronischen Behördendiensten und von technischen, organisatorischen und
prozeduralen Standards verpflichtet werden können.[38] Dieser Aspekt wurde allerdings aufgrund entsprechender Vorbehalte in der Vernehmlassung fallen ge-
lassen.[39]
    Gemäss Art. 3 Abs. 1 E-EMBAG sollen Bundesbehörden, soweit sinnvoll,
elektronische Mittel für die Interaktion mit anderen Behörden, mit

---

[36]   Ausführlich *Braun Binder*, ZSR 2020, 253 (257 ff.); *dies.*, SZW 2020, 27; *Rechsteiner*, Der Algo-
       rithmus verfügt, Jusletter 26.11.2018.
[37]   Botschaft v. 4.3.2022 zum Bundesgesetz über den Einsatz elektronischer Mittel zur Erfüllung von
       Behördenaufgaben (Botschaft E-EMBAG), BBl 2022 804, S. 2.
[38]   Siehe Art. 12 und 13 der Vernehmlassungsvorlage zum EMBAG; *Bundesrat*, Bundesrat eröffnet
       Vernehmlassung zum Bundesgesetz über den Einsatz elektronischer Mittel zur Erfüllung von
       Behördenaufgaben, 2020, abrufbar unter https://www.admin.ch/gov/de/start/dokumentation/
       medienmitteilungen.msg-id-81580.html.
[39]   Botschaft E-EMBAG (Fn. 37), S. 17.

Unternehmen und mit natürlichen Personen verwenden. Mit dieser Vorgabe soll für Bundesbehörden der Grundsatz „digital first" eingeführt werden.[40] Weitere Grundsätze verpflichten die Bundesbehörden zur Abstimmung ihrer Tätigkeiten mit den Kantonen und zur Wahrung von deren Autonomie; zur Berücksichtigung des Prinzips der Nachhaltigkeit sowie zur Sicherstellung der Zugänglichkeit ihrer Leistungen für die gesamte Bevölkerung (Art. 3 Abs. 2–4 E-EMBAG). Neben verschiedenen organisatorischen und finanzrechtlichen Normen, Vorgaben zu Standards und Schnittstellen, zur Bereitstellung von IKT-Mitteln von Bundesbehörden, zur Schaffung einer Interoperabilitätsplattform und zur Durchführung von Pilotversuchen, enthält der E-EMBAG Bestimmungen zu Open Source Software und Open Government Data.

Bundesbehörden sollen verpflichtet werden, „wenn es möglich und sinnvoll ist und die Rechte Dritter gewahrt werden", den Quellcode von Software, die sie zur Erfüllung ihrer Aufgaben entwickeln oder entwickeln lassen, offenzulegen (Art. 9 E-EMBAG). Die Verpflichtung zur Freigabe von Open Source Software soll dabei nicht schrankenlos gelten. So ist Software Dritter, die unverändert erworben wird, von der Bestimmung nicht erfasst.[41] Ferner ist nach dem Wortlaut die Pflicht zur Freigabe nur vorgesehen, wo dies möglich und sinnvoll erscheint. In der Botschaft wird dies wie folgt erläutert:

> „Eine Freigabe kann beispielsweise ausscheiden, wenn dafür nötige Rechte Dritter nicht zu angemessenen Bedingungen erworben werden können, Geheimhaltungsgründe dagegensprechen oder wenn die Freigabe mit einem hohen technischen oder finanziellen Aufwand verbunden wäre."[42]

Ein weiterer zentraler Aspekt des E-EMBAG ist die Bestimmung zu Open Government Data. Gemäss Art. 10 Abs. 1 E-EMBAG sollen die dem Gesetz unterstehenden Verwaltungseinheiten ihre Daten, die sie zur Erfüllung ihrer gesetzlichen Aufgaben beschaffen oder generieren und die elektronisch gespeichert und in Sammlungen strukturiert vorliegen, öffentlich zugänglich machen. Personendaten und Daten juristischer Personen sind von dieser Verpflichtung explizit ausgenommen (Art. 10 Abs. 2 lit. a E-EMBAG). Mit dieser Bestimmung soll dem Leitgedanken „open data by default" Rechnung getragen werden.[43] Die unter diese Bestimmung fallenden Daten sollen auf der Plattform opendata.swiss referenziert werden.[44] Damit soll eine einfache Nutzung sowohl durch Dritte als

---

[40]   Botschaft E-EMBAG (Fn. 37), S. 54.
[41]   Botschaft E-EMBAG (Fn. 37), S. 64.
[42]   Botschaft E-EMBAG (Fn. 37), S. 64.
[43]   Botschaft E-EMBAG (Fn. 37), S. 67 f.
[44]   Botschaft E-EMBAG (Fn. 37), S. 68 f.

auch durch Behörden, die nicht nur Datenlieferanten, sondern auch Datennut-zende sind, ermöglicht werden. Da die Zurverfügungstellung von Open Govern-ment Data keine eigenständige Verwaltungsaufgabe sein soll, sollen die Verwal-tungseinheiten keine neuen zusätzlichen Daten beschaffen oder generieren und aufbereiten müssen. Vielmehr sollen ohnehin beschaffte und generierte Daten, die einen Mehrwert für die Gesellschaft, die Umwelt und die Wirtschaft darstel-len, zur freien Weiterverwendung zur Verfügung gestellt werden.[45] Mit der For-mulierung „Daten, die sie zur Erfüllung ihrer gesetzlichen Aufgabe beschaffen oder generieren" in Art. 10 Abs. 1 E-EMBAG wird klargestellt, dass nur ohnehin und systematisch anfallende Daten bekannt gemacht werden müssen.[46]

II. Elektronischer Identitätsnachweis

Der elektronische Identitätsnachweis (E-ID) einer Person stellt eine wesentliche Voraussetzung für die Entwicklung von E-Government-Anwendungen dar. Aus diesem Grund sollen in der Schweiz Rechtsgrundlagen für einen staatlich aner-kannten Identifizierungsnachweis geschaffen werden. Die entsprechenden Be-mühungen können inzwischen als bewegte Geschichte mit für die Schweiz und ihre direktdemokratischen Verfahren prägenden Meilensteinen umrissen wer-den. Im Jahr 2015 wurden erste Konsultationen durchgeführt, im Februar 2017 ein erster Entwurf in die Vernehmlassung geschickt und am 1. Juni 2018 verab-schiedete der Bundesrat den Entwurf für ein Bundesgesetz über elektronische Identifizierungsdienste (E-ID-Gesetz).[47] Der Entwurf wurde sodann in National- und Ständerat beraten[48] und am 27. September 2019 schließlich vom Parlament verabschiedet.[49]

Bundesgesetze unterliegen in der Schweiz dem fakultativen Referendum (Art. 141 Abs. 1 lit. a BV[50]). Das bedeutet, dass eine Volksabstimmung stattfin-det, wenn 50'000 Stimmberechtigte dies innerhalb von 100 Tagen seit der amtli-chen Veröffentlichung des Erlasses verlangen. Im Falle des E-ID-Gesetzes wurde das Referendum erfolgreich ergriffen und die Volksabstimmung am 7. März

---

[45] Botschaft E-EMBAG (Fn. 37), S. 69.
[46] Botschaft E-EMBAG (Fn. 37), S. 69.
[47] BBl 2018 3989. Siehe auch Botschaft vom 1.6.2018 zum Bundesgesetz über elektronische Identi-fizierungsdienste, BBl 2018 3915.
[48] *Die Bundesversammlung – Das Schweizer Parlament*, Bundesgesetz über elektronische Identifi-zierungsdienste, 2018, abrufbar unter https://www.parlament.ch/de/ratsbetrieb/suche-curia-vista/geschaeft?AffairId=20180049.
[49] BBl 2019 6567.
[50] Bundesverfassung der Schweizerischen Eidgenossenschaft vom 18.4.1999, SR 101.

2021 durchgeführt. Die Stimmberechtigten lehnten das E-ID-Gesetz ab.[51] Ausschlaggebend für das Nein an der Urne dürfte der Kritikpunkt gewesen sein, dass mit dem neuen Gesetz ein amtlicher Ausweis kommerzialisiert und durch private Anbieterinnen herausgegeben werde. Unternehmen wie Banken und Versicherungen würden die sensiblen Daten der Bürgerinnen und Bürger verwalten, so die Kritik des Referendumskomitees.[52] Die Herausgabe von Identitätsnachweisen müsse aber in staatlicher Verantwortung bleiben. Demgegenüber führte der Bundesrat aus, dass die E-ID freiwillig sei und der Bund die Anbieterinnen laufend kontrollieren werde.[53] Das der Abstimmung unterbreitete E-ID-Gesetz sah vor, dass eine Person, die eine E-ID wollte, den Antrag bei einer vom Bund anerkannten Anbieterin stellen sollte. Als Anbieterin wären Unternehmen, Kantone oder Gemeinden in Frage gekommen. Die Anbieterin hätte den Antrag an den Bund übermittelt, der die Identität der antragstellenden Personen überprüft und der Anbieterin sodann grünes Licht für die Ausstellung der E-ID gegeben hätte.[54] Mit der Ablehnung des E-ID-Gesetzes war das entsprechende Rechtsetzungsvorhaben vorerst gescheitert.[55]

Im Mai 2021 nahm der Bundesrat das Vorhaben E-ID erneut in Angriff. Auf Basis verschiedener öffentlicher Konsultationsrunden wurde ein Grobkonzept erarbeitet.[56] Im Dezember 2021 fällte der Bundesrat einen Grundsatzentscheid und legte insbesondere fest, dass die staatliche E-ID den Nutzerinnen und Nutzern die größtmögliche Kontrolle über ihre Daten ermöglichen solle.[57] Der Staat soll als Herausgeber der E-ID auftreten und für den Betrieb der nötigen Vertrauensinfrastruktur sorgen. Der Entwurf zum neuen Gesetz zur E-ID ging Mitte 2022 in die Vernehmlassung.

---

[51] BBl 2021 1185.

[52] Kritik abrufbar unter E.ID.Gesetz Nein, https://www.e-id-referendum.ch/.

[53] Siehe *Bundeskanzlei*, Erläuterungen des Bundesrates zur Volksabstimmung vom 7.3.2021, 2021, S. 6 f., 20 ff. abrufbar unter https://www.admin.ch/dam/gov/de/Dokumentation/Abstimmungen/Marz2021/DE_volksabstimmung.pdf.download.pdf/DE_volksabstimmung.pdf.

[54] Siehe *Bundeskanzlei* (Fn. 53), S. 6.

[55] Siehe zum abgeschlossenen E-ID-Rechtsetzungsprojekt auch *Bundesamt für Justiz*, Bundesgesetz über elektronische Identifizierungsdienste, 2020, abrufbar unter https://www.bj.admin.ch/bj/de/home/staat/gesetzgebung/archiv/e-id.html.

[56] Siehe zum neuen E-ID-Rechtsetzungsprojekt *Bundesamt für Justiz*, Staatliche E-ID, 2022, abrufbar unter https://www.bj.admin.ch/bj/de/home/staat/gesetzgebung/staatliche-e-id.html.

[57] Siehe *Der Bundesrat*, Bundesrat trifft Richtungsentscheid zur E-ID, 2021, abrufbar unter https://www.bj.admin.ch/bj/de/home/aktuell/mm.msg-id-86465.html.

III. Elektronischer Rechtsverkehr

Die Einführung des elektronischen Rechtsverkehrs (auch: E-Justice) ist keine ganz neue Entwicklung. Die Prozessgesetze sehen bereits seit 2011 vor, dass die Übermittlung von Eingaben und Verfügungen auf elektronischem Weg erfolgen kann.[58] Trotzdem wird der Verkehr zwischen Gerichten und den Verfahrensbeteiligten bisher nur in wenigen Fällen elektronisch abgewickelt.[59]

Die KKJPD ist an ihrer Herbstversammlung vom 17./18. November 2016 einstimmig zum Schluss gekommen, dass rechtliche Grundlagen für die obligatorische Einführung von E-Justice im Bereich der Zivil-, Straf- und Verwaltungsgerichte sowie der Strafverfolgungsbehörden geschaffen werden sollen.[60] Die entsprechende gesetzliche Grundlage soll mit dem BEKJ geschaffen werden. Bis Ende Februar 2021 lief die Vernehmlassung zu diesem Gesetzesentwurf.[61] Zu der Vorlage gingen zahlreiche Stellungnahmen ein.[62] Es ist zu erwarten, dass der Gesetzentwurf in Folge der verschiedenen Stellungnahmen Anpassungen erfahren wird. Die folgenden Ausführungen konzentrieren sich deshalb auf grundlegende Eckpunkte der vorgeschlagenen Regelung, wobei noch nicht absehbar ist, inwieweit diese in den Gesetzesentwurf einfließen werden, der dem Parlament dereinst unterbreitet werden wird.

Ein zentrales Anliegen des geplanten Gesetzes ist, die rechtlichen Voraussetzungen für eine zentrale Plattform zu schaffen, über welche Behörden[63], Gerichte, Anwaltschaft, Verfahrensparteien sowie weitere Verfahrensbeteiligte Dokumente zustellen und empfangen können.[64] Auch die elektronische Akten-

---

[58]   Siehe Kapitel B. hiervor.

[59]   Zur Frage der Digitalisierung des Bundesverwaltungsverfahrens parallel zum Vorhaben *Justitia 4.0* siehe ausführlich *Meyer*, SJZ 2021, 855.

[60]   *Bundesamt für Justiz*, Erläuternder Bericht zum Vorentwurf des Bundesgesetzes über die Plattform für die elektronische Kommunikation in der Justiz, 2020, S. 3, abrufbar unter https://www.bj.admin.ch/dam/bj/de/data/staat/gesetzgebung/e-kommunikation/vn-ber.pdf.download.pdf/vn-ber-d.pdf.

[61]   Siehe Fn. 16.

[62]   *Bundesamt für Justiz*, Bericht über die Ergebnisse des Vernehmlassungsverfahrens, abrufbar unter https://www.bj.admin.ch/dam/bj/de/data/staat/gesetzgebung/e-kommunikation/ve-ber.pdf.download.pdf/ve-ber-d.pdf.

[63]   Der Behördenbegriff definiert sich im Rahmen der E-Justiz-Plattform eigenständig und umfasst die Strafbehörden von Bund und Kantonen sowie die Verwaltungsbehörden des Bundes – sofern diese am Verfahren beteiligt sind – sowie die Gerichte (ohne kantonale Verwaltungsgerichte). Siehe *Bühler/Widmer*, Anwaltsrevue 2021, 169 (171).

[64]   Art. 1 Vorentwurf des Bundesgesetzes über die Plattform für die elektronische Kommunikation in der Justiz BEKJ (VE-BEKJ).

einsicht soll über diese Plattform stattfinden.[65] Die Plattform soll von Bund und Kantonen gemeinsam betrieben werden – das wäre jedenfalls nach dem Vernehmlassungsentwurf die prioritäre Lösung.[66] Zu diesem Zweck soll eine Körperschaft gegründet werden, an der Bund und Kantone beteiligt sind.

Die Pflicht zur Benutzung der Plattform, also das eigentliche Obligatorium, wird in den jeweiligen Prozessgesetzen geregelt.[67] Das Obligatorium trifft Behörden und berufsmässig handelnde Personen, nicht aber Private. Private sollen weiterhin auch physische Eingaben machen und in die bei den Gerichten vorhandenen Akten Einsicht erhalten können. Den Gerichten und Behörden wird eine Pflicht zur elektronischen Aktenführung auferlegt.[68] Heute bestehende Unterschriftserfordernisse werden bei der Nutzung der elektronischen Kommunikation aufgehoben. An Stelle der Unterschriften tritt die Authentifizierung an der Plattform sowie das automatisierte Anbringen von geregelten elektronischen Siegeln.[69]

Mit der geplanten Regelung sind einige Herausforderungen verbunden. So ist hinsichtlich der Verwaltungsgerichtsbarkeit die Kompetenzverteilung im föderalistischen Staatsgefüge zu berücksichtigen. Während die Zivil- und Strafprozesskompetenz in der Schweiz beim Bund liegt (Art. 122 Abs. 1 bzw. Art. 123 Abs. 1 BV), ist die Verwaltungsprozesskompetenz nach Sachzuständigkeit zwischen Bund und Kantonen aufgeteilt und die Gerichtsorganisation ist grundsätzlich Sache der Kantone.[70] Der Bund verfügt mithin nicht über die Kompetenz der Rechtsetzung im Bereich des kantonalen Verwaltungsgerichtsverfahrens. Das Obligatorium zur Führung einer digitalisierten Akte und zur Nutzung der Plattform trifft die kantonalen Verwaltungsgerichte folglich nur im Anwendungsbereich des Bundesgerichtsgesetzes, d. h. wenn ein Entscheid mit Beschwerde ans Bundesgericht weitergezogen werden kann. Nicht zulässig wäre es hingegen, die kantonalen Gerichte zu zwingen, die Gerichtsdossiers elektronisch zu führen. Im Verwaltungsprozess gelangt das Vorhaben damit an föderalistische Grenzen bzw. erstaunt es nicht, dass verschiedene Stellungnahmen im Vernehmlassungsverfahren die Einbindung der kantonalen Verwaltungsgerichte als Vorinstanzen des Bundesgerichts kritisierten. Befürchtet wird insbesondere, dass die Umstellung auf den elektronischen Rechtsverkehr sich auch auf die Vorinstanzen der kantonalen Verwaltungsgerichte – z. B. verwaltungsinterne Rechtsmittelbehörden – auswirkt.

---

[65] Erläuternder Bericht zum VE-BEKJ (Fn. 60), S. 6.
[66] Art. 3 ff. VE-BEKJ; erläuternder Bericht zum VE-BEKJ (Fn. 60), S. 10 f.
[67] Erläuternder Bericht zum VE-BEKJ (Fn. 60), S. 6.
[68] Erläuternder Bericht zum VE-BEKJ (Fn. 60), S. 6.
[69] Erläuternder Bericht zum VE-BEKJ (Fn. 60), S. 6.
[70] *Kiener/Rütsche/Kuhn*, Öffentliches Verfahrensrecht, 3. Aufl. 2021, S. 33 ff.

Eine weitere Herausforderung kann in der Ausbalancierung zwischen Exekutive und Judikative gesehen werden. Das Spannungsverhältnis zwischen den beiden Gewalten kommt in zwei Punkten besonders zum Ausdruck. Einerseits sollen die Exekutiven sowohl der Kantone als auch des Bundes stark in den Aufbau und den Betrieb der Justiz-Plattform involviert werden.[71] Andererseits ist bislang unklar, wer für den Erlass der Ausführungsvorschriften zum BEKJ zuständig sein soll, der Bundesrat oder das Bundesgericht. Dies ist zwischen den beiden Behörden umstritten; der Punkt wurde in der Vernehmlassung denn auch zu einer gesonderten Frage gemacht.[72] Für den Bundesrat spricht, dass er institutionell besser geeignet ist als das Bundesgericht, um Rechtsetzungsaufgaben zu übernehmen. Allerdings geht es um Ausführungsregelungen, die unmittelbar die Verwaltungsautonomie der Gerichte betreffen, was für eine Regelung durch das Bundesgericht spricht.

D. Fazit

Die Digitalisierung in öffentlichen Verwaltungen und Gerichten der Schweiz soll voranschreiten; dahingehend besteht wohl bei allen Akteuren grundsätzlich Einigkeit. Die föderalistische Struktur und die damit verbundene Aufteilung der Kompetenzen zwischen Bund und Kantonen führt allerdings dazu, dass hinsichtlich der konkreten Ausgestaltung unterschiedliche Vorstellungen aufeinandertreffen, die es in Einklang zu bringen gilt. Hinzu kommt, dass in direktdemokratischen Verfahren Lösungen gefunden werden müssen, die auch den Bedenken der Bürgerinnen und Bürger Rechnung tragen. Die skizzierten Rechtsetzungsprojekte illustrieren diese Herausforderungen, zeigen aber auch auf, dass Wege gefunden werden können, um Rechtsgrundlagen zu schaffen, die eine digitale Transformation unter Berücksichtigung heterogener Interessenlagen erlauben.

---

[71]   Erläuternder Bericht zum VE-BEKJ (Fn. 60), S. 10 ff.

[72]   Siehe *Eidgenössisches Justiz- und Polizeidepartment*, Frage betreffend Delegation von Rechtssetzungsbefugnissen im Vorentwurf zum Bundesgesetz über die Plattform für die elektronische Kommunikation in der Justiz, 2020, abrufbar unter https://fedlex.data.admin.ch/filestore/fedlex.data.admin.ch/eli/dl/proj/6020/67/cons_1/doc_5/de/pdf-a/fedlex-data-admin-ch-eli-dl-proj-6020-67-cons_1-doc_5-de-pdf-a.pdf.

Ludwigs / Muriel Ciceri / Velling (eds.), Digitalization as a challenge for justice and administration, Abhandlungen zum Öffentlichen Recht 1, Würzburg, 2023, pp. 35-54.
DOI: 10.25972/978-3-95826-201-0-35

Vollautomatisierte Verwaltungsakte im deutschen Recht

Markus Ludwigs, Annika Velling*

A. Einführung

Die Handlungsformenlehre im deutschen Verwaltungsrecht ist durch ein hohes Maß an Ausdifferenzierung geprägt und kennt keinen festgefügten *numerus clausus*.[1] Instrumente zur Regelung von Einzelfällen (Verwaltungsakt und öffentlich-rechtlicher Vertrag) stehen Handlungsformen gegenüber, die der abstrakt-generellen Regelung von Sachverhalten (Rechtsverordnung, Satzung und Verwaltungsvorschriften) dienen. Hinzu tritt das auf die Herbeiführung eines tatsächlichen Erfolgs gerichtete schlichthoheitliche Handeln, auch Verwaltungsrealakt genannt. Überragende Bedeutung kommt in diesem System vor allem dem Verwaltungsakt als „typische[r] Handlungsform der Verwaltung gegenüber dem Bürger"[2] zu. Seine Herausbildung ist untrennbar mit dem Namen von *Otto Mayer*, dem Wegbereiter der deutschen Verwaltungsrechtswissenschaft, verbunden.[3] *Mayer* konzipierte den Verwaltungsakt als „Zentralbegriff"[4] und definierte ihn bereits in der Erstauflage seines Deutschen Verwaltungsrechts als „ein der Verwaltung zugehöriger obrigkeitlicher Ausspruch, der dem Unterthanen gegenüber im Einzelfall bestimmt, was für ihn Rechtens sein soll".[5] Bis heute wird verbreitet davon ausgegangen, dass diese klassische Definition in der gesetzli-

---

* Eine ausführliche Fassung des Beitrags mit Fokus auf den europa- und verfassungsrechtlichen Grenzen vollständig automatisierter Verwaltungsakte erscheint demnächst in der Zeitschrift *Verwaltungsarchiv (VerwArch).*

1 Umfassend *Kahl*, in: ders./Ludwigs (Hrsg.), Handbuch des Verwaltungsrechts, Bd. V, 2023, § 140 Rn. 24 ff. (im Erscheinen).

2 BVerwGE 158, 364 Rn. 15.

3 Näher zur Entstehung des Verwaltungsakts im 19. Jahrhundert *Engert*, Die historische Entwicklung des Rechtsinstituts Verwaltungsakt, 2002, S. 47 ff.

4 Zu dieser Einordnung *Bachof*, in: Külz/Naumann (Hrsg.), Staatsbürger und Staatsgewalt, Bd. 2, 1963, S. 3 (5); hierauf rekurrierend *Mangold*, in: Kahl/Ludwigs (Hrsg.), Handbuch des Verwaltungsrechts, Bd. V, 2023, § 141 Rn. 8 (im Erscheinen).

5 *Mayer*, Deutsches Verwaltungsrecht, Bd. I, 1895, S. 95.

chen Begriffsbestimmung des § 35 S. 1 VwVfG fortwirkt.[6] Im Übrigen speichert
die Dogmatik des Verwaltungsakts ein regelrechtes „Reservoir unterschiedlicher
Rechtswirkungen und Funktionen",[7] das im Verwaltungsverfahrensgesetz als
„Grundgesetz der Verwaltung"[8] seine legislative Basis findet.

Der vorliegende Beitrag legt sein Augenmerk auf den automatisierten Erlass
des Verwaltungsakts nach § 35a VwVfG als Bestandteil der Verwaltungsdigitalisierung.[9] Die normative Grundlage für eine elektronische Interaktion der Verwaltung mit Bürgerinnen und Bürgern wurde bereits im VwVfG vom 25. Mai
1976[10] gelegt. Schon hier war in den §§ 28 Abs. 2 Nr. 4, 37 Abs. 4 (heute Abs. 5)
und § 39 Abs. 2 Nr. 3 die Möglichkeit angelegt, Verwaltungsakte „mit Hilfe automatischer Einrichtungen" zu erlassen. In diesen Fällen sind Ausnahmen von
der Pflicht zur Anhörung, dem Formerfordernis und der Begründungspflicht
vorgesehen. Spätere Novellen führten neben der allgemeinen Eröffnung des
elektronischen Kommunikationswegs mit der Verwaltung (§ 3a VwVfG bzw.
§ 71e VwVfG) auch zur Implementierung expliziter Vorgaben für den „elektronischen Verwaltungsakt" (§§ 37 Abs. 2, 3 und 6, 39 Abs. 1, 41 Abs. 2 und 4, 44
Abs. 2 Nr. 1 und 69 Abs. 2 VwVfG).[11] Der jüngste Entwicklungsschritt wurde mit
dem Gesetz zur Modernisierung des Besteuerungsverfahrens (StModG)[12] vollzogen. Nach Maßgabe des zum 1. Januar 2017 eingeführten § 35a VwVfG verfügen
die Behörden über die Möglichkeit, Verwaltungsakte auch vollautomatisiert zu
erlassen.[13]

Nachfolgend gilt es zunächst, den vollständig automatisierten Verwaltungsakt in die unterschiedlichen Stufen der Digitalisierung des Verwaltungshandelns
einzuordnen (B.). Im Anschluss rückt eine nähere Analyse der Zentralnorm des

---

[6]   Vgl. z. B. *Ruffert*, in: Ehlers/Pünder (Hrsg.), Allgemeines Verwaltungsrecht, 15. Aufl. 2016, § 21
      Rn. 2; kritisch *Schmidt-De Caluwe*, Der Verwaltungsakt in der Lehre Otto Mayers, 1999, S. 265.
[7]   *Ruffert* (Fn. 6), § 21 Rn. 5.
[8]   *Schmitz*, in: Stelkens/Bonk/Sachs (Hrsg.), VwVfG, 10. Aufl. 2022, § 1 Rn. 1; siehe auch schon
      Häberle, FS Boorberg Verlag, 1977, S. 47 (49).
[9]   Zum Verwaltungsverfahrensgesetz als „Grundgesetz der Verwaltung" *Schmitz*, (Fn. 8), § 1 Rn. 1;
      siehe auch schon *Häberle*, FS Boorberg Verlag, 1977, S. 47 (49).
[10] BGBl. 1976, I S. 1253.
[11] Für einen Überblick zur Vielzahl weiterer Regelwerke wie dem Onlinezugangsgesetz (BGBl.
      2017, I S. 3122, 3138, zgd. BGBl. 2021, I S. 2250), den E-Government-Gesetzen auf Bundes- und
      Landesebene oder der Single Digital Gateway-Verordnung (EU) 2018/1724 (ABl. 2018 L 295/1,
      zgd. ABl. 2022 L 152/1) auf Unionsebene vgl. instruktiv *Martini*, in: Kahl/Ludwigs (Hrsg.),
      Handbuch des Verwaltungsrechts, Bd. I, 2021, § 28 Rn. 16 ff.
[12] BGBl. 2016, I S. 1679.
[13] Vgl. noch den ebenfalls mit dem StModG eingefügten § 41 Abs. 2a VwVfG zur Bekanntgabe
      durch Abruf eines elektronischen Verwaltungsakts über öffentlich zugängliche Netze sowie die
      klarstellend aufgenommene Regelung zur Geltung der Amtsermittlung auch für automatisierte
      Verwaltungsverfahren in § 24 Abs. 1 S. 3 VwVfG.

§ 35a VwVfG in den Fokus (C.), bevor die Rechtsfolgen der Vollautomation und etwaige Konsequenzen für den Rechtsschutz in den Blick zu nehmen sind (D.). Ein abschließendes Fazit bringt die gewonnenen Erkenntnisse nochmals auf den Punkt (E.).

B. Stufen der Verwaltungsdigitalisierung

Das Ausmaß der Verwaltungsdigitalisierung kann holzschnittartig in vier, sich zeitlich zum Teil überschneidende Stufen gegliedert werden, die von der bloßen Elektronifizierung bis hin zum Einsatz selbstlernender Algorithmen reichen. Die Elektronifizierung des Verwaltungshandelns als Ausgangspunkt zeichnet sich dadurch aus, dass elektronische Hilfsmittel für Berechnungen oder zur Erstellung von Schriftstücken genutzt werden. Zu denken ist etwa an die Ausrüstung von Arbeitsplätzen mit elektrischen Schreibmaschinen oder in heutigen Zeiten mit Computern und Internetanbindung sowie die hiermit ermöglichte elektronische Erfassung relevanter Daten bzw. die elektronische Übermittlung von Verwaltungsakten. Die Debatten um eine Teilautomatisierung von Verwaltungsentscheidungen als zweite funktionale Stufe der Verwaltungsdigitalisierung lassen sich bis in die 1950er-Jahre zurückverfolgen.[14] Den Auslöser bildete der zunehmende Einsatz von Großrechenanlagen in Massenverfahren.[15] Folgerichtig sah bereits die Ursprungsfassung des VwVfG vom 25. Mai 1976 die Möglichkeit vor, Verwaltungsakte „mit Hilfe automatischer Einrichtungen" zu erlassen. Das Fehlen einer klaren Definition dieses *modus operandi* erschwert freilich eine Abgrenzung der Teilautomatisierung von den ihr vor- und nachgelagerten Stufen der Digitalisierung.[16] Im Schrifttum wird als Leitbild die Ermittlung des Sachverhalts durch Sachbearbeiterinnen und Sachbearbeiter mit hieran anknüpfender (vorstrukturierter) Subsumtion durch eine Maschine ausgemacht.[17] Somit sind bei der Teilautomatisierung weiterhin stets menschliche Amtswalterinnen und

---

[14] Für einen Überblick zu den historischen Entwicklungslinien vgl. *Britz*, in: Hoffmann-Riem/Schmidt-Aßmann/Voßkuhle (Hrsg.), Grundlagen des Verwaltungsrechts, Bd. II, 2. Aufl. 2012, § 26 Rn. 15 ff.; *Hornung*, in: Schoch/Schneider (Hrsg.), Verwaltungsrecht – VwVfG, Bd. III, 3. EL 2022, § 35a Rn. 25 ff.; komprimiert *Britz/Eifert*, in: Voßkuhle/Eifert/Möllers (Hrsg.), Grundlagen des Verwaltungsrechts, Bd. I, 3. Aufl. 2022, § 26 Rn. 5.

[15] Kompakt *Guckelberger*, VVDStRL 78 (2019), S. 235 (237 f.); eingehend zur Debatte über die Verwaltungsautomation in den 1950er und 1960er Jahren *Kaiser*, in: Collin/Lutterbeck (Hrsg.), Eine intelligente Maschine?, 2009, S. 233 (234 ff.).

[16] Zur Unterscheidung zwischen Teilautomatisierung und Vollautomatisierung als nächster Stufe der Verwaltungsdigitalisierung *Guckelberger*, DÖV 2021, 566 (568).

[17] *Britz/Eifert* (Fn. 14), § 26 Rn. 86; *Guckelberger*, DÖV 2021, 566 (568); *Harbou*, JZ 2020, 340 (341).

Amtswalter involviert.[18] Zugleich geht die Teilautomatisierung über eine bloße Elektronifizierung insoweit hinaus, als die Automationstechnologie eigenständig (Zwischen-)Ergebnisse erzeugt und damit deutlich stärker zur inhaltlichen Ebene des Entscheidungsprozesses beiträgt.

In Abgrenzung zur Teilautomatisierung ist für die – gleichfalls nicht legaldefinierte, aber durch § 35a explizit ins VwVfG aufgenommene – Vollautomatisierung des Verwaltungshandelns als dritter Stufe der Digitalisierung charakteristisch, dass zusätzlich die „Sammlung, Auswertung und Verifizierung der Sachverhaltsdaten" in den Aufgabenbereich des eingesetzten Algorithmus fallen.[19] Dergestalt bedarf eine maschinelle Entscheidung nicht mehr der Aufbereitung des Tatbestands durch menschliche Amtswalterinnen und Amtswalter,[20] sondern wird auch insoweit autonom getroffen. Daraus folgt allerdings nicht, dass menschliche Eingriffe der Vollautomatisierung von vornherein entgegenstehen. Ungeachtet des zunächst ganzheitlich anmutenden Begriffs sind solche Einwirkungen unschädlich, sofern der Entscheidungsgehalt des Verwaltungsakts unverändert bleibt.[21] Darüber hinaus kann selbst bei einer programmseitig angelegten Aussteuerungsoption noch von einer Vollautomatisierung des zugrundeliegenden Verfahrens auszugehen sein. Tatsächlich findet die Aussteuerung aus einzelfallspezifischen Gründen in § 24 Abs. 1 S. 3 VwVfG für voll- und teilautomatisierte Verfahren einen expliziten Anknüpfungspunkt.[22] Mit Überführung in die menschliche Bearbeitung verliert der Vorgang seinen Vollautomationscharakter nur dann, wenn er im Anschluss an die Prüfung aufgrund der Bedeutsamkeit der Änderung für das Ergebnis nicht wieder in die Automatisierung zurückgeführt werden kann.[23] Im Übrigen ist die Annahme einer Vollautomatisierung für diejenigen Sachverhalte ausgeschlossen, welche kategorisch (in der Praxis z. B. bei Ablehnung begünstigender Verwaltungsakte) oder spezifisch (aufgrund

---

[18]   *Guckelberger*, DÖV 2021, 566 (569); *Herold*, Demokratische Legitimation automatisiert erlassener Verwaltungsakte, 2020, S. 31 f.; ferner *Braun Binder*, in: Seckelmann (Hrsg.), Digitalisierte Verwaltung – Vernetztes E-Government, 2. Aufl. 2019, S. 311 Rn. 5 m. w. N.

[19]   *Stelkens*, in: Hill/Kugelmann/Martini (Hrsg.), Digitalisierung in Recht, Politik und Verwaltung, 2018, S. 81 (96).

[20]   So bei der Teilautomatisierung der Fall; vgl. *Guckelberger*, DÖV 2021, 566 (569); *Herold*, Demokratische Legitimation automatisiert erlassener Verwaltungsakte, 2020, S. 31 f.; ferner *Braun Binder*, in: Seckelmann (Hrsg.), Digitalisierte Verwaltung – Vernetztes E-Government, 2. Aufl. 2019, S. 311 Rn. 5 m. w. N.

[21]   *Stelkens* (Fn. 19), S. 81 (99).

[22]   *Martini/Nink*, DVBl. 2018, 1128 (1130).

[23]   BT-Drs. 18/8434, S. 122 (Beschlussempfehlung und Bericht des Finanzausschusses); auch sollten formelle Änderungen z. B. der Anschrift oder des Datums den Automatisierungscharakter des Verwaltungshandelns nicht ändern und einer Rückführung daher nicht entgegenstehen; ähnlich *Stelkens* (Fn. 19), S. 81 (Fn. 31).

besonderer Tatsachen oder Umstände des Einzelfalls) zur abschließenden Bearbeitung durch eine Amtswalterin oder einen Amtswalter ausgesteuert werden.[24] Irrelevant für die Einordnung als vollautomatisierter Verwaltungsakt ist dagegen seine zeitlich nachgelagerte Bekanntgabe, die ebenso gut in nicht-automatisierter Weise erfolgen kann.[25]

Eine vierte, noch nicht verwirklichte Stufe der Digitalisierung des Verwaltungshandelns bildet der Einsatz selbstlernender Algorithmen.[26] Im Unterschied zur bisherigen Vollautomation werden die Kompetenzen des Systems in dieser Stufe so weit ausgebaut, dass die Algorithmen in der Lage sind, ihre Effizienz und Effektivität bei der Verfahrensbearbeitung selbstständig – z. B. mithilfe von Trainingsdatensets oder der kontinuierlichen Verarbeitung neuer Input-Daten – zu steigern.[27] Dadurch können sich im Kontrast zu deterministischen Systemen[28] – d. h. Programmen ohne selbstständige Weiterentwicklung – auch andere als die erwarteten Lösungen einstellen.[29] Allerdings ist die digitale Entscheidungsfindung unter diesen Bedingungen im Nachhinein noch weitaus schwieriger nachzuvollziehen, als bei den aktuellen Vollautomatisierungsprogrammen.[30] Sowohl deterministische als auch selbstlernende Algorithmen sind Ausprägungen schwacher künstlicher Intelligenz (KI).[31] Abzugrenzen hiervon sind Erscheinungsformen starker KI.[32] Dabei handelt es sich um Programme, die dem heutzutage noch nicht technisch realisierbaren Anspruch unterliegen, menschlicher Intelligenz in allen Aspekten wenigstens gleichgestellt zu sein.[33] Kennzeichnend ist hier vor allem die Fähigkeit, sich Fragestellungen kreativ zu nähern, während

---

[24]   *Stelkens* (Fn. 19), S. 81 (98).
[25]   *Siegel*, DVBl. 2017, 24 (25).
[26]   Grundsätzlich optimistisch *Adrian*, Rechtstheorie 48 (2017), 77 (118 ff.).
[27]   Allgemein zur Effizienz als Maßstab der Verwaltung zuletzt *Ellerbrok*, in: Kahl/Ludwigs (Hrsg.), Handbuch des Verwaltungsrechts, Bd. III, 2022, § 76 Rn. 47; vgl. auch *Ludwigs*, Unternehmensbezogene Effizienzanforderungen im Öffentlichen Recht, 2013, S. 96 ff.
[28]   Für die determinationsbezogene Terminologie vgl. *Stelkens* (Fn. 19), S. 81 (101).
[29]   *Siegel*, DVBl. 2020, 552 (557 f.); zu den sich daraus ergebenden Implikationen für die demokratische Legitimation der Verwaltungshandlung siehe *Ludwigs/Velling*, VerwArch 114 (2023), Heft 1 (im Erscheinen).
[30]   *Tischbirek*, in: Kahl/Ludwigs (Hrsg.), Handbuch des Verwaltungsrechts, Bd. V, 2023, § 126 Rn. 14 ff. (im Erscheinen). Oftmals ist daher im Zusammenhang mit selbstlernenden Systemen auch von einer *black box* die Rede, siehe etwa *Martini/Nink*, NVwZ-Extra 10/2017, 1 (10); *Harbou*, JZ 2020, 340 (345).
[31]   *Tischbirek* (Fn. 30) § 126 Rn. 7 (im Erscheinen).
[32]   Zum Begriffsverständnis vgl. *Lorse*, NVwZ 2021, 1657 (1658); *Siegel*, DVBl. 2020, 552 (557 f.); instruktiv auch *Tischbirek* (Fn. 30), § 126 Rn. 5 ff. (im Erscheinen).
[33]   *Siegel*, DVBl. 2020, 552 (557).

schwache KI sich allenfalls in der spezifischen Ausgestaltung der Lösungsfindung von dem ansonsten fest vorgeschriebenen Anwendungsfeld lösen kann.[34]

C. Vollautomatisierung von Verwaltungsentscheidungen nach § 35a VwVfG

Während das VwVfG von Beginn an einen rechtlichen Rahmen für den Erlass von Verwaltungsakten unter Zuhilfenahme elektronischer Einrichtungen bereitstellte, wurde die Möglichkeit vollautomatisierter Verwaltungsakte lange Zeit kontrovers diskutiert.[35] Kritiker bezweifelten das in § 35 S. 1 VwVfG vorausgesetzte Vorliegen einer „hoheitlichen Maßnahme", da es hierfür einer menschlichen Willensbetätigung bedürfte.[36] Dem ist überzeugend entgegengehalten worden, dass auch vollautomatisiert getroffene Entscheidungen auf eine behördliche Willensbildung zurückgehen, da der grundlegende, zurechnungsbegründende Entschluss zur Übergabe des Verfahrens in die Automatisierung durch die zuständigen Amtswalterinnen und Amtswalter gefasst wird.[37] Die Debatte aufgreifend, plädierte der Finanzausschuss des Deutschen Bundestages in seiner Beschlussempfehlung zum Entwurf eines Gesetzes zur Modernisierung des Besteuerungsverfahrens vom 11. Mai 2016 für die Einfügung sowohl des neuen § 35a VwVfG als auch einer Parallelnorm für die Sozialverwaltung in § 31a SGB X.[38] Hiermit sollte ein Gleichlauf mit der bereits im Gesetzentwurf der Bundesregierung vom 18. Dezember 2015[39] enthaltenen Regelung über vollautomatisierte Verwaltungsentscheidungen der Finanzverwaltung in § 155 Abs. 4 AO hergestellt werden.[40] Die inhaltlich weitgehend übereinstimmenden Vorschriften traten nach Verabschiedung des Gesetzes am 1. Januar 2017 in Kraft und zielen auf eine Verfahrensbeschleunigung und Kostenreduzierung.[41]

---

[34]   *Lorse*, NVwZ 2021, 1657 (1661).
[35]   *Harbou*, JZ 2020, 340 (341 f.).
[36]   Grundlegend *Zeidler*, Über die Technisierung der Verwaltung, 1959, S. 14 ff.; aus jüngerer Zeit zweifelnd etwa *Ziekow*, NVwZ 2018, 1169 (1170 f.).
[37]   So bereits *Bull*, Verwaltung durch Maschinen. Rechtsprobleme der Technisierung der Verwaltung, 1964, S. 64 ff.; zuletzt etwa *Stelkens* (Fn. 19), S. 81 (104 f.); ausführlich *Eifert*, Electronic Government, 2006, S. 127 ff.; *Stegmüller*, NVwZ 2018, 353 (354 ff.); im Ergebnis auch OVG NRW, Beschl. V. 10.12.2021 – 2 A 51/21, Rn. 9, 12.
[38]   BT-Drs. 18/8434, S. 122; eingehend zu § 31a SGB X insb. *Luthe*, SGb 2017, 250 ff.
[39]   BR-Drs. 631/15.
[40]   Deutlich BT-Drs. 18/8434, S. 121 (zu § 31a SGB X); auf die Konzentration der personellen Ressourcen rekurrierend BT-Drs. 18/7457, S. 48 (zu § 155 Abs. 4 AO).
[41]   *Hornung* (Fn. 14), § 35a Rn. 25 sowie BT-Drs. 18/8434 S. 122.

Im Folgenden gilt es, nach einem kurzen Blick auf die Funktionen des § 35a VwVfG (I.) zunächst den Anwendungsbereich der Norm zu bestimmen (II.), bevor die darin formulierten Schranken einer Vollautomation näher betrachtet werden (III.).

I. Funktionen

Mit der Aufnahme von § 35a VwVfG in das Verwaltungsverfahrensgesetz sind im Wesentlichen vier Funktionen verbunden. Im Gesetzgebungsverfahren wurde vom Finanzausschuss insbesondere die *Klarstellungsfunktion* betont, da durch die Neuregelung eine ausdrückliche Anerkennung der Existenz vollständig automatisierter Verwaltungsakte erfolgt.[42] An zweiter Stelle zu nennen ist die *Begrenzungs- und Warnfunktion* des § 35a VwVfG. Sie kommt in der Konzentration vollautomatisierter Verwaltungsakte auf Fälle zum Ausdruck, in denen „weder ein Ermessen noch ein Beurteilungsspielraum besteht". Der Finanzausschuss hat insoweit treffend darauf hingewiesen, dass „[d]ie Ausübung von Ermessen […] ebenso eine menschliche Willensbetätigung voraus[setzt] wie die individuelle Beurteilung eines Sachverhalts". Eine Vollautomatisierung ist deshalb von vornherein nur bei Vorliegen einer gebundenen Entscheidung der Verwaltung denkbar.[43] Drittens resultiert aus dem Normvorbehalt in § 35a VwVfG („sofern dies durch Rechtsvorschrift zugelassen ist") eine *Kompetenzzuweisungsfunktion*. Allein dem (Fach-)Gesetzgeber – und nicht etwa der Behörde selbst[44] – wird die Beurteilung anvertraut, geeignete Verwaltungsverfahren für den Erlass vollautomatisierter Verwaltungsakte zu identifizieren. Hierin kommt als Viertes zugleich eine *Schutzfunktion* zugunsten der Gestaltungsfreiheit des Normgebers zum Ausdruck.[45] Sobald ein Verfahren automatisiert vollzogen wird, müssen jegliche normative Anpassungen der zugrundeliegenden Vorschriften in den algorithmischen Unterbau der Automation integriert werden. Aufgrund der anzunehmenden Komplexität des Programms kann die notwendige Modifikation

---

42 BT-Drs. 18/8434, S. 122; siehe auch *Berger*, NVwZ 2018, 1260 (1262); kritisch *Stegmüller*, NVwZ 2018, 353 (354 f.), wonach eine Anpassung des § 35 VwVfG („… jede – auch vollautomatisch ausgeführte – Verfügung, Entscheidung …") dieselbe Funktion erfüllt hätte; die Klarstellung in § 35a VwVfG begrüßend dagegen *Ziekow*, NVwZ 2018, 1169 (1170 f.).

43 BT-Drs. 18/8434, S. 122 (dort auch das wörtliche Zitat aus dem vorherigen Satz); *Stelkens* (Fn. 19), S. 81 (83) für eine Verortung der Warnfunktion im Kontext des Gesetzesvorbehalts vgl. *Martini/Nink*, DVBl. 2018, 1128 (1130) sowie *Harbou*, JZ 2020, 340 (342).

44 BT-Drs. 18/8434, S. 122; *Stelkens* (Fn. 19), S. 81 (83); *Berger*, NVwZ 2018, 1260 (1262).

45 *Schmitz/Prell*, NVwZ 2016, 1273 (1276).

erhebliche Zeit beanspruchen.[46] Vor diesem Hintergrund überlässt § 35a VwVfG ausschließlich dem Normgeber die Wahl, bei welchen Verfahren er dazu bereit ist, den potenziellen Implementierungsverzug einer geänderten Rechtslage in Kauf zu nehmen. Im Übrigen spricht auch das programmierungsbedingt gesteigerte Haftungsrisiko dafür, grundsätzliche Fragen der Vollautomatisierung einer einheitlichen Klärung auf dieser Ebene zuzuführen.[47]

II. Anwendungsbereich

Was den Anwendungsbereich vollautomatisierter Verwaltungsakte im deutschen Recht betrifft, so ist im föderalen System des deutschen Grundgesetzes zunächst zwischen den Ebenen des Bundes und der Länder zu unterscheiden. Die Inhalte der bundesrechtlichen Vorschrift des § 35a VwVfG werden daher nicht gleichförmig umgesetzt. Derzeit lassen sich mit Blick auf das allgemeine Verwaltungsverfahrensrecht drei Herangehensweisen identifizieren. So haben die Länder Baden-Württemberg, Hamburg, Hessen, Mecklenburg-Vorpommern, Nordrhein-Westfalen, das Saarland und Schleswig-Holstein (§ 106a LVwG) eine explizite Parallelvorschrift zu § 35a VwVfG in ihr jeweiliges Landesrecht eingefügt. Daneben gilt § 35a VwVfG auch in den Ländern mit dynamischen Verweisungen auf das VwVfG des Bundes. Dies betrifft namentlich Berlin, Brandenburg, Niedersachsen, Rheinland-Pfalz, Sachsen und Sachsen-Anhalt. In Bremen und Thüringen hängt die Zulässigkeit einer vollständigen Automatisierung *prima facie* von der Antwort auf die überkommene Streitfrage ab, ob man im Rahmen von § 35 (L)VwVfG eine menschliche Willensbetätigung als begriffsnotwendig für das Vorliegen eines Verwaltungsakts erachtet.[48] Der vollständig automatisierte Erlass von Verwaltungsakten ist nach Maßgabe von Art. 22 der

---

[46] *Prell*, in: Bader/Ronellenfitsch (Hrsg.), BeckOK VwVfG, 57. Ed. 2022, § 35a Rn. 12; *Schmitz/Prell*, NVwZ 2016, 1273 (1277).
[47] *Stelkens* (Fn. 19), S. 81 (108). Zur Haftungsproblematik bei selbstlernenden Algorithmen *Martini* (Fn. 11), § 28 Rn. 94.
[48] Hierzu schon unter C. Zum jüngst im bayerischen Digitalgesetz (BayDiG) v. 22.7.2022 (GVBl. S. 374, BayRS 206-1-D, zgd GVBl. S. 374) beschrittenen »Sonderweg« vgl. *Hornung* (Fn. 14), § 35a Rn. 12. Nach Art. 5 Abs. 2 S. 1 BayDiG sind bei Verwaltungsverfahren, die vollständig durch automatische Einrichtungen durchgeführt werden, die eingesetzten Einrichtungen regelmäßig auf ihre Zweckmäßigkeit, Objektivität und Wirtschaftlichkeit hin zu überprüfen. Zudem ist der Einsatz von Künstlicher Intelligenz in der Verwaltung gem. Art. 5 Abs. 2 S. 2 BayDiG durch geeignete Kontroll- und Rechtsschutzmaßnahmen abzusichern. Der sofortige Vollzug vollständig automatisiert erlassener Verwaltungsakte ist nach Art. 12 Abs. 3 BayDiG nur aufgrund gesetzlicher Ermächtigung zulässig.

Datenschutz-Grundverordnung (DSGVO)[49] allerdings ohnehin regelungsbedürftig.[50] Bis zur Etablierung entsprechender Zulässigkeitstatbestände (im LVwVfG bzw. im einschlägigen Fachrecht[51]) dürften vollautomatisierte Verwaltungsentscheidungen daher in den Ländern ohne explizite Regelung unzulässig sein.[52] Etwas anderes wird man allein für solche Erscheinungsformen der Vollautomation annehmen können, die schon lange vor Einführung des § 35a VwVfG etabliert waren. Dazu zählen etwa Ampelanlagen im Straßenverkehr oder die Bewertung von Multiple Choice-Prüfungen. Seit Inkrafttreten von § 35a VwVfG (bzw. der Gegenstücke auf Länderebene) bedarf es für die fortwährende Zulässigkeit dieser Vorgänge einer teleologischen Reduktion des Normvorbehalts.[53] Für die Zulässigkeit spricht, dass sich in diesen Fällen aus der automatischen Bearbeitung keine Gefahren ergeben, vor denen der Zulassungsvorbehalt schützen soll.[54] Andere Stimmen wollen dagegen für Ampeln aus den einschlägigen StVO-Normen zu Lichtzeichenanlagen (wie § 37 StVO) die entsprechende Zulassung ableiten und mahnen im Hinblick auf Multiple Choice-Bewertungen eine sorgfältige Prüfung an, ob diese bereits den endgültigen Verwaltungsakt beinhalten oder nur als Vorbereitungsmaßnahme zu qualifizieren sind.[55]

Einheitliche Anwendung in Bund und Ländern finden die Parallelregelungen für die Finanz- und Sozialverwaltung nach § 155 Abs. 4 AO und § 31a SGB X. Von herausragender praktischer Bedeutung ist als Pionierprojekt staatlicher Vollautomatisierung insbesondere die „ausschließlich automationsgestützte" Infrastruktur rund um den Steuerbescheid.[56]

---

[49] Verordnung (EU) 2016/679 des Europäischen Parlaments und des Rates v. 27.04.2016 zum Schutz natürlicher Personen bei der Verarbeitung personenbezogener Daten, zum freien Datenverkehr und zur Aufhebung der Richtlinie 95/46/EG (Datenschutz-Grundverordnung), ABl. 2016 L 119/1.

[50] Hierzu auch noch unter C. III. 1.

[51] Zur auch im Hinblick auf § 35a VwVfG geltenden Subsidiarität des (L)VwVfG gegenüber dem Fachrecht statt vieler *Ziekow*, VwVfG, 4. Aufl. 2020, § 35a Rn. 1; siehe auch noch unter C. III. 2.

[52] Überzeugend *Hornung* (Fn. 14), § 35a Rn. 11 ff.

[53] Eingehend *Stelkens*, (Fn. 19), S. 81 (99 ff.); siehe auch *Guckelberger*, DÖV 2021, 566 (570).

[54] *Ziekow*, VwVfG, 4. Aufl. 2020, § 35a Rn. 10.

[55] *Guckelberger*, DÖV 2021, 566 (570).

[56] Vgl. *Mund*, in: Greve et al. (Hrsg.), Der digitalisierte Staat, 2020, S. 177 (179 f.), *Hornung* (Fn. 14), § 35a Rn. 96 ff. sowie *Stelkens* (Fn. 19), S. 81 (91 f.); zu den verfassungsrechtlichen Aspekten im Zusammenhang mit § 155 Abs. 4 AO siehe *Maier*, JZ 2017, 614.

Fragt man nach Anwendungsfällen von § 35a (L)VwVfG, rücken vor allem standardisierte Verfahren (sog. unechte Massenverfahren[57]) ins Visier.[58] Exemplarisch hierfür steht zum einen die internetbasierte Kfz-Zulassung, welche in § 6g StVG ermöglicht wird.[59] Durch Konkretisierung des § 6g Abs. 2 StVG in §§ 15a ff. Fahrzeug-Zulassungsverordnung[60] wurde der bereits im Jahr 2015 angestoßene Prozess einer sukzessiven Vollautomatisierung aller Vorgänge im Zusammenhang mit der standardmäßigen Fahrzeugzulassung für natürliche Personen abgeschlossen.[61] Zum anderen ist auf die Erhebung des Rundfunkbeitrags hinzuweisen.[62] Seit dem 1. Juni 2020 legitimiert § 10a des Rundfunkbeitragsstaatsvertrags (RBeitrStV)[63] den vollautomatisierten Erlass rundfunkbeitragsrechtlicher Bescheide.[64]

III. Zulässigkeitsvoraussetzungen

In Anbetracht der vielfältigen Möglichkeiten einer Vollautomation des Verwaltungshandelns dienen die restriktiven Zulässigkeitsvoraussetzungen in § 35a VwVfG der Beschränkung auf geeignete Verfahren.[65] Im Einzelnen handelt es sich um den bereits hervorgehobenen Normvorbehalt (a.) sowie das Fehlen eines Ermessens- oder Beurteilungsspielraums (b.).

---

[57]   Zur Differenzierung zwischen echten und unechten Massenverfahren vgl. *Geis*, in: Schoch/Schneider (Hrsg.), Verwaltungsrecht – VwVfG, Bd. III, 2. EL 2022, § 17 Rn. 3 ff.

[58]   Statt vieler *Siegel*, DVBl. 2017, 24 (26); vgl. für einen detaillierten Überblick zu den bisherigen Anwendungsfällen jüngst *Hornung* (Fn. 14), § 35a Rn. 82 ff.

[59]   BT-Drs. 18/9084, S. 15.

[60]   Fahrzeug-Zulassungsverordnung v. 3.2.2011, BGBl. I S. 139, zgd. BGBl. 2022, I S. 986.

[61]   Eingehend *Albrecht et al.*, DAR 2019, 555 (558); *Guckelberger*, DÖV 2021, 566 (571); *Hornung* (Fn. 14), § 35a Rn. 82.

[62]   Ausführlich hierzu *Guckelberger*, DÖV 2021, 566 (571 ff.).

[63]   Rundfunkbeitragsstaatsvertrag v. 15.12.2010, GVBl. 2011 S. 258, 404; 2012 S. 18, BayRS 02-28-S, zgd. GVBl. 2018 S. 210, 2020 S. 203.

[64]   Vgl. insoweit auch OVG NRW, Beschl. v. 9.9.2021 – 2 BV 1276/21, Rn. 49, wonach sich die Neuregelung des § 10a RBeitrStV „aus der Ergänzung der Verwaltungsverfahrensgesetze des Bundes und der Länder um § 35a VwVfG [begründet]"; näher *Lent*, in: Gersdorf/Paal (Hrsg.), BeckOK Informations- und Medienrecht, 38. Ed. 2022, § 2 RBeitrStV Rn. 12 ff. und § 10a RBeitrStV Rn. 2, auch zur Anwendbarkeit der Landes-VwVfG auf das Rundfunkbeitragsverfahren.

[65]   Vgl. für die Zulassung durch Rechtsvorschrift explizit BT-Drs. 18/8434, S. 122.

1. Zulassung durch Rechtsvorschrift

Die Vollautomatisierung eines Verwaltungsverfahrens bedarf zunächst der Zulassung durch Rechtsvorschrift.[66] Diese Notwendigkeit wurzelt nicht nur in § 35a VwVfG selbst, sondern entspricht auch den unionsrechtlichen Vorgaben des Art. 22 DSGVO[67].[68] Das grundsätzliche Verbot des Art. 22 Abs. 1 DSGVO, Entscheidungen ausschließlich auf der automatisierten Verarbeitung personenbezogener Daten beruhen zu lassen, gilt gem. Art. 22 Abs. 2 lit. b) DSGVO nicht, sofern hierfür eine nationale oder unionale Zulassungsvorschrift besteht.[69] Im nationalen Recht können entsprechende Regelungen sowohl in formellen Gesetzen als auch in Rechtsverordnungen oder Satzungen enthalten sein.[70] Welcher normhierarchische Rang im Einzelfall gefordert ist, bestimmt sich nach verfassungsrechtlichen Maßstäben – insbesondere der Wesentlichkeitstheorie.[71] Auf dieser Grundlage ist die Zulassungsvorschrift im Zusammenhang mit der Verwaltungsautomatisierung danach insbesondere dann als formelles Gesetz zu erlassen, wenn die Verwaltungsentscheidungen für die „Verwirklichung der Grundrechte" wesentlich sind.[72] Ausgeschlossen ist dagegen die eigenmächtige Zulassung durch eine Verwaltungsvorschrift der Behörde.[73] Für die spezifische Umsetzung des Normvorbehalts enthält § 35a VwVfG im Übrigen keine weiteren Vorgaben. So wird zum Beispiel auch kein ausdrücklicher Rückverweis in der Zulassungsvorschrift vorausgesetzt.[74] Ein Seitenblick auf die Parallelregelungen in § 155 Abs. 4 AO und § 31a SGB X[75] zeigt schließlich, dass diesen ein gänzlich anderer Ansatz zugrunde liegt. Beide Vorschriften verzichten auf einen

---

[66] Zum Schutzgedanken bereits C. I.; dezidiert kritisch *Stegmüller*, NVwZ 2018, 353 (356): „technikverzögernd, formalistisch und letztlich eGovernment-feindlich".

[67] Nachweis in Fn. 49.

[68] Näher *Ludwigs/Velling*, VerwArch 114 (2023), Heft 1 (im Erscheinen).

[69] Instruktiv im Kontext der Verwaltungsautomatisierung siehe *Hornung* (Fn. 80), § 35a Rn. 14 ff.; näher zu der Anforderung, die automatisierte Verarbeitung mit „angemessene[n] Maßnahmen" zu flankieren *Martini*, in: Paal/Pauly (Hrsg.), DS-GVO BDSG, 3. Aufl. 2021, Art. 22 DS-GVO Rn. 35 ff.

[70] *Siegel*, DVBl. 2017, 24 (26).

[71] *Guckelberger*, DÖV 2021, 566 (570); *Hornung* (Fn. 14), § 35a Rn. 42; *Ludwigs/Velling*, VerwArch 114 (2023), Heft 1 (im Erscheinen).

[72] BVerfGE 47, 46 (79); BVerfGE 49, 89 (126 f.); vgl. *Schmidt-Aßmann*, in: Isensee/Kirchhof (Hrsg.), HStR, Bd. II, 3. Aufl. 2004, § 26 Rn. 64 f. m. w. N.

[73] *Guckelberger*, DÖV 2021, 566 (571); *Siegel*, DVBl 2017, 24 (26); zur grundsätzlichen Einordnung von Verwaltungsvorschriften als bloßes Innenrecht vgl. statt vieler *Groh*, in: Kahl/Ludwigs (Hrsg.), Handbuch des Verwaltungsrechts, Bd. V, 2023, § 155 Rn. 3, 21 ff. (im Erscheinen).

[74] *Martini/Nink*, DVBl. 2018, 1128 (1130).

[75] Die Unanwendbarkeit von § 35a VwVfG auf Verfahren nach der Abgabenordnung und dem Sozialgesetzbuch folgt aus § 2 Abs. 2 Nr. 1 und Nr. 4 VwVfG.

Normvorbehalt und ermächtigen die Finanz- bzw. Sozialverwaltung direkt zum vollständig automatisierten Erlass eines Verwaltungsakts. Die Einsatzfelder erstrecken sich auf den Erlass von Steuerbescheiden (AO) sowie – sehr allgemein – den Anwendungsbereich des SGB X[76].

2. Kein Ermessen oder Beurteilungsspielraum

Als weitere (negative) Zulässigkeitsvoraussetzung erlaubt § 35a VwVfG den vollautomatisierten Erlass von Verwaltungsakten nur, „sofern […] weder ein Ermessen noch ein Beurteilungsspielraum besteht".[77] Zur Begründung dieser Schranke wurde im Gesetzgebungsverfahren auf die Notwendigkeit einer „menschliche[n] Willensbetätigung" bei der Ausübung von Ermessen bzw. der Wahrnehmung eines Beurteilungsspielraums verwiesen.[78] Dahinter steht die Erkenntnis, dass vollautomatisierte Einrichtungen – zumindest bislang[79] – nicht zur Herstellung von Einzelfallgerechtigkeit geeignet sind.[80] Mit Blick auf die in § 1 Abs. 1 zum Ausdruck kommende Subsidiarität des VwVfG ist allerdings zu betonen, dass sich der jeweilige Fachgesetzgeber – vorbehaltlich verfassungsrechtlicher Restrik-

---

[76] *Stelkens* (Fn. 19), S. 81 (92 f.), mit dem Bsp. einer „„maschinelle[n] Anpassung laufender Sozialleistungen der Höhe nach in einer Vielzahl von gleichgelagerten Einzelfällen'".

[77] Hiermit korrespondierend § 2 Abs. 2 S. 1 Nr. 4 des schleswig-holsteinischen IT-Einsatz-Gesetzes (ITEG) v. 16.3.2022 (GVOBl. Schl.-H. S. 285, 296); dazu *Hornung* (Fn. 14), § 35a Rn. 42. In rechtspolitischer Perspektive kritisch (zu § 35a VwVfG) *Stegmüller*, NVwZ 2018, 353 (357): „massive Bremse für eGovernment". Zur Erfassung auch des Regulierungs- und des Planungsermessens *Ziekow* (Fn. 54), § 35a Rn. 13; ausführlich zur Typologie behördlicher Entscheidungsspielräume zuletzt *Ludwigs*, in: Kahl/Ludwigs (Hrsg.), Handbuch des Verwaltungsrechts, Bd. V, 2023, § 124 Rn. 48 ff. (im Erscheinen), mit Plädoyer für eine einheitliche Systemkategorie des Verwaltungsermessens; zur umstrittenen Zulässigkeit vollautomatisierter Verwaltungsakte im Falle administrativer Letztentscheidungsbefugnisse vor Etablierung von § 35a VwVfG vgl. *Siegel*, DVBl. 2017, 24 (26) m. w. N.

[78] BT-Drs. 18/8434, S. 122; vgl. auch *Hornung* (Fn. 14), § 35a Rn. 69 m. w. N.; zu den Besonderheiten beim verwaltungsrechtlichen Widerspruchsverfahren *Martini/Nink*, DVBl. 2018, 1128 (1129 ff.), die u. a. darauf hinweisen, dass die Zweckmäßigkeitsprüfung des Widerspruchsverfahrens nach dem Sinn des § 35a i. V. m. § 79 Abs. 2 VwVfG „a maiore ad minus" einer Automatisierung verschlossen [bleibt]" (Hervorhebung im Original).

[79] *Siegel*, DVBl. 2020, 552 (556); vgl. *Hornung* (Fn. 14), § 35a Rn. 71 mit Blick auf selbstlernende Algorithmen.

[80] *Braun Binder* DÖV 2016, 891 (894); *Guckelberger*, DÖV 2021, 566 (569); *Windoffer*, in: Mann/Sennekamp/Uechtritz (Hrsg.), VwVfG, 2. Aufl. 2019, § 35a Rn. 28; *Siegel*, DVBl. 2020, 552 (556). Vgl. aber auch Art. 5 Abs. 2 S. 1 BayDiG (hierzu bereits Fn. 48), wo der vollständig automatisierte Erlass eines Verwaltungsakts in Fällen von Ermessen oder Beurteilungsspielraum weder durch den Wortlaut der Norm noch durch die Begründung zum Gesetzentwurf (Bay. LT-Drs. 18/19572, S. 49) ausgeschlossen wird (darauf hinweisend auch *Hornung* [Fn. 14], § 35a Rn. 12).

tionen[81] – über die Beschränkung des § 35a VwVfG auf gebundene Entscheidungen hinwegsetzen kann.[82] Insoweit entfaltet die Vorgabe mithin „nur" eine Warnfunktion.[83]

Wie eng oder weit die Beschränkung auf Verfahren ohne Ermessen oder Beurteilungsspielraum auszulegen ist, um der beabsichtigten Einzelfallgerechtigkeit Genüge zu tun, gilt es bei einer näheren Normanalyse kritisch zu hinterfragen. Kontrovers diskutiert wird zum einen, ob der Ausschluss vollautomatisierter Verfahren auch bei einer Reduzierung des Ermessens- oder Beurteilungsspielraums auf Null zum Tragen kommt.[84] Maßgeblich erscheint insoweit, dass hier nur eine Entscheidung rechtmäßig ist, so dass es sich materiell betrachtet um eine gebundene Entscheidung handelt.[85] Die Anwendbarkeit von § 35a VwVfG ist daher grundsätzlich zu bejahen und resultiert aus einer teleologischen Reduktion der Norm. Zutreffend wird allerdings darauf hingewiesen, dass eine vollständige Automatisierung nur bei einer Reduzierung auf Null in Betracht kommt, die aus Verwaltungsvorschriften oder sonstigen generalisierbaren Gründen resultiert.[86] Für eine mit den Besonderheiten des Einzelfalls begründete Reduzierung erscheint die Bewertung und Feststellung durch einen Algorithmus dagegen zumindest technisch bis auf Weiteres ausgeschlossen.[87]

In gegenläufiger Richtung wird zum anderen die Frage erörtert, ob über den Wortlaut des § 35a VwVfG hinaus auch solche Entscheidungen von der Vollautomatisierung auszunehmen sind, die zwar nicht in Ausübung eines Beurteilungsspielraums ergehen, aber hohe Anforderungen an die Auslegung und Anwendung unbestimmter Rechtsbegriffe stellen.[88] Die Befürworter eines solchen

---

[81]   *Ludwigs/Velling*, VerwArch 114 (2023), Heft 1 (im Erscheinen).
[82]   *Stelkens* (Fn. 19), S. 81 (111); *Ziekow* (Fn. 54), § 35a Rn. 12. Dem Vorbild des § 35a VwVfG folgend dagegen § 10a RBeitrStV; hierzu näher *Guckelberger*, DÖV 2021, 566 (571 ff.).
[83]   *Schmitz/Prell*, NVwZ 2016, 1273 (1276); *Ziekow* (Fn. 54), § 35a Rn. 12.
[84]   Bejahend *Windoffer* (Fn. 80), § 35a Rn.30; in kritischer Perspektive aus *Stegmüller*, NVwZ 2018, 353 (357); verneinend *Braun-Binder*, DÖV 2016, 891 (894); *Djeffal*, DVBl. 2017, 808 (814); *Guckelberger*, DÖV 2021, 566 (569 f.); *Hornung* (Fn. 14), § 35a Rn. 72 ff.; *Siegel*, DVBl. 2017, 24 (26); *Ziekow* (Fn. 54), § 35a Rn. 13; zur mangelnden Erfassung der Fälle eines intendierten Ermessens überzeugend *Martini/Nink*, NVwZ-Extra 10/2017, 1 (2), unter Verweis auf die geforderte „individuelle Prüfung auf eine Atypik, die zur Abweichung von der Regelfolge zwingt".
[85]   Ähnlich *Siegel*, Allgemeines Verwaltungsrecht, 14. Aufl. 2022, Rn. 218, 583.
[86]   *Hornung* (Fn. 14), § 35a Rn. 74; vgl. auch *Siegel*, DVBl. 2017, 24 (26).
[87]   *Hornung* (Fn. 14), § 35a Rn. 74; weitergehende rechtliche Bedenken äußern *Braun-Binder*, DÖV 2016, 891 (894 f.); *Siegel*, DVBl. 2017, 24 (26); *Ziekow*, VwVfG, 4. Aufl. 2020, § 35a Rn. 13; anders *Eifert* (Fn. 37), S. 140 sowie *Ritgen*, in: Bauer et al. (Hrsg.), Verwaltungsverfahrensgesetz und E-Government, 2. Aufl. 2014, § 35 VwVfG Rn. 57.
[88]   In diese Richtung *Harbou*, JZ 2020, 340 (342); *Siegel*, DVBl. 2017, 24 (26); *Stelkens*, in: Stelkens/Bonk/Sachs (Hrsg.), VwVfG, 10. Aufl. 2022, § 35a Rn. 45; *Windoffer* (Fn. 80), § 35a Rn. 29; zurückhaltender *Berger*, NVwZ 2018, 1260 (1263); *Schmitz/Prell*, NVwZ 2016, 1273 (1276).

Verständnisses machen geltend, dass der Ausschluss bei behördlichen Beurteilungsspielräumen weniger durch die Reduktion der gerichtlichen Kontrolldichte motiviert sei, als durch die Komplexität unbestimmter Rechtsbegriffe.[89] Die hiermit verbundene Problematik entstehe aber nicht nur bei Vorschriften mit Beurteilungsspielräumen, sondern ebenso bei zahlreichen Normen, deren Tatbestand durch unbestimmte Rechtsbegriffe ohne Beurteilungsspielräume geprägt wird.[90] Hierzu ist allerdings kritisch anzumerken, dass eine erweiternde Auslegung von § 35a VwVfG mit dem Wortlaut schwerlich in Einklang zu bringen ist und zudem in der Entstehungsgeschichte keinen Anhalt findet. Sprachlich offener gefasst sind dagegen die Parallelregelungen in § 155 Abs. 4 AO und § 31a SGB X. Dort werden Vollautomatisierungen zugelassen, „soweit kein Anlass dazu besteht, den Einzelfall durch Amtsträger zu bearbeiten".[91] Einen solchen Anlass wird man gerade dann anzunehmen haben, wenn die Auslegung und Anwendung unbestimmter Rechtsbegriffe hohe Anforderungen an die Behörde stellt.[92] Entschärft wird die Problematik freilich dadurch, dass eine Vollautomation in komplexen Entscheidungssituationen ohnehin regelmäßig an § 24 Abs. 1 S. 3 VwVfG scheitern dürfte.[93] Die zeitgleich zu § 35a VwVfG etablierte Norm stellt klar, dass der Untersuchungsgrundsatz auch beim Einsatz automatisierter Einrichtungen gilt.[94] Von der Behörde sind tatsächliche Angaben des Beteiligten zu berücksichtigen, die für den Einzelfall bedeutsam sind und im automatischen Verfahren nicht ermittelt würden.[95] In der Konsequenz wird der Vorgang

---

[89]   *Stelkens* (Fn. 88), § 35a Rn. 45 (auch zum Folgenden).
[90]   *Harbou*, JZ 2020, 340 (343); siehe auch (mit Beispielen) *Guckelberger*, DÖV 2021, 566 (569) sowie *Martini/Nink*, DVBl. 2018, 1128 (1130); das mit unbestimmten Rechtsbegriffen einhergehende Hindernis für die weitergehende Umsetzung der Vollautomatisierung relativierend *Schröder*, VerwArch 110 (2019), 328 (334 f.), mit Verweis auf *Bull*, DVBl. 2017, 409 (412).
[91]   So die Formulierung in § 155 Abs. 4 S. 1 AO (der Wortlaut des § 31a S. 1 Hs. 1 SGB X weicht nur geringfügig hiervon ab); diese Variante der Eingrenzung befürwortend *Schröder*, VerwArch 110 (2019), 328 (333); a. A. *Bull*, DVBl. 2017, 409 (412 f.); vgl. zum ähnlich offen formulierten Art. 5 Abs. 2 S. 1 BayDiG bereits die Hinweise in Fn. 48 und Fn. 80.
[92]   *Martini* (Fn. 11), § 28 Rn. 47; vgl. auch die Einzelbegründung des Finanzausschusses zu § 31a SGB X in BT-Drs. 18/8434, wonach die Bearbeitung durch einen Amtsträger nicht nur im Falle einer Ermessensentscheidung oder eines Beurteilungsspielraums zwingend ist, sondern auch dann gefordert wird, „wenn die Subsumtion unter einen konkreten Tatbestand nicht durch automatische Einrichtungen erfolgen kann."
[93]   Überzeugend *Windoffer* (Fn. 80), § 35a Rn. 29.
[94]   BT-Drs. 18/8434, S. 122; kritisch zur Formulierung und Erforderlichkeit von § 24 Abs. 1 S. 3 VwVfG *Stegmüller*, NVwZ 2018, 353 (358); zur Erfassung voll- und teilautomatisierter Verwaltungsakte *Siegel*, DVBl. 2020, 552 (554).
[95]   Vgl. auch den wortlautidentischen § 31a S. 2 SGB X sowie die Parallelregelung in § 155 Abs. 4 S. 3 i. V. m. § 150 Abs. 7 AO. Letztere sieht eine Aussteuerung aus einem ausschließlich automationsgestützten Steuerverfahren vor, soweit die bzw. der Steuerpflichtige in einem dafür

ausgesteuert und abhängig von der Relevanz des Einzelvortrags aus dem automatisierten Verfahren in die menschliche Bearbeitung überführt.[96]

D. Rechtsfolgen und Konsequenzen für den Rechtsschutz

I. Anwendbare Vorschriften

Lenkt man den Blick auf die Rechtsfolgen der Qualifizierung einer behördlichen
Maßnahme als vollautomatisierter Verwaltungsakt im Sinne des § 35a VwVfG,
so ist im Ausgangspunkt festzuhalten, dass auf diesen grundsätzlich alle anderen
Vorschriften des VwVfG über Verwaltungsakte anwendbar sind.[97] Richtiger-
weise gilt dies auch mit Blick auf die bereits seit der Ursprungsfassung existie-
renden Sonderregelungen zu teilautomatisierten Verwaltungsakten in § 28
Abs. 2 Nr. 4 VwVfG, § 39 Abs. 2 Nr. 3 VwVfG und § 37 Abs. 5 (früher Abs. 4)
VwVfG.[98] Die in den Bestimmungen verwendete Präposition „mit Hilfe" ist im
Sinne von „unter Zuhilfenahme" bzw. „unter Verwendung" zu begreifen. Da
Verwaltungsakte bei der Vollautomation ebenfalls unter (umfassender) Zuhilfenahme automatisierter Einrichtungen erlassen werden, ist § 35a VwVfG richtig-
erweise als Unterfall der Automation zu qualifizieren.[99] Es bedarf allerdings einer
kritischen Reflexion, inwiefern die Sonderregelungen zur Anhörung, Begründung und Form mit Blick auf den heutigen Stand der Technik überhaupt noch
verfassungsrechtlich gerechtfertigt sind.[100] Als Grund für den ermessensbeding-
ten Verzicht auf Verfahrensrechte der Betroffenen durch die Behörden wurden
zu Beginn der Verwaltungsdigitalisierung vornehmlich die begrenzten Speicher-
kapazitäten der eingesetzten Rechner angeführt.[101] Dieses Argument erscheint

---

vorgesehenen Abschnitt oder Datenfeld der Steuererklärung Angaben gemacht hat, die nach ihrer bzw. seiner Auffassung Anlass für eine Bearbeitung durch Amtsträger geben. Zur Diskussion
weiterer Mechanismen zum Schutz rechtsstaatlich fundierter Verfahrensrechte der Betroffenen
im Lichte vollständig automatisierter Verwaltungsakte siehe *Ludwigs/Velling*, VerwArch 114
(2023), Heft 1 (im Erscheinen).

[96]   BT-Drs. 18/8434, S. 122.
[97]   BT-Drs. 18/8434, S. 122; siehe auch *Braun-Binder*, DÖV 2016, 891 (892).
[98]   Ebenso *Siegel*, DVBl. 2017, 24 (28); siehe bereits unter A.
[99]   *Guckelberger*, DÖV 2021, 566 (573 f.); *v. Harbou*, JZ 2020, 340 (345); *Stelkens* (Fn. 19), S. 81 (117);
       a. A. *Braun Binder* DÖV 2016, 891 (895).
[100] *Ludwigs/Velling*, VerwArch 114 (2023), Heft 1 (im Erscheinen).
[101] *Stelkens* (Fn. 19), S. 81 (118); in der BT-Drs. 7/910, S. 58 f. wird die Sonderregelung (dort noch
       in § 33 Abs. 4 VwVfG-E) mit der „Rücksicht auf die technische Entwicklung" und dem Verzicht

angesichts des fortgeschrittenen Stands der Technik heute nicht mehr tragfähig. Daraus kann allerdings nicht ohne Weiteres abgeleitet werden, dass die Anwendung der Sonderregelungen grundsätzlich ermessensfehlerhaft ist.[102] Hierzu können in Bezug auf die Verfahrensrechte in § 28 Abs. 2 Nr. 4 VwVfG, § 39 Abs. 2 Nr. 3 VwVfG und § 37 Abs. 5 VwVfG die folgenden Argumente angeführt werden: Erstens wird den rechtsstaatlichen Bedenken gegenüber dem Anhörungsverzicht in § 28 Abs. 2 Nr. 4 VwVfG mit der Förderung von Einzelfallgerechtigkeit durch § 24 Abs. 1 S. 3 VwVfG begegnet.[103] Zweitens ist die in § 37 Abs. 5 VwVfG gewährte Entbehrlichkeit von Unterschrift und Namenswiedergabe angesichts der rein maschinellen Erstellung der Verwaltungsakte weiterhin sinnvoll,[104] weshalb hier ein Hinweis auf den automatisierten Erlass hinreichend (und geboten) erscheint, um auf das Rechtssicherheitsbedürfnis der Empfängerinnen und Empfänger zu reagieren.[105] Drittens kommt der in § 39 Abs. 2 Nr. 3 VwVfG formulierten Ausnahme von der verfassungsrechtlich fundierten Begründungspflicht keine eigenständige Bedeutung mehr zu, da automatisiert erlassene Verwaltungsakte regelmäßig auch unter die Ausnahmetatbestände des § 39 Abs. 2 Nr. 1 und Nr. 2 VwVfG fallen.[106] Die vorstehend nur angerissene Diskussion um Verfahrenserleichterungen im Rahmen der Verwaltungsautomatisierung lässt im Übrigen auch die mit einer fortschreitenden Digitalisierung einhergehenden Implikationen auf verfassungsrechtlicher Ebene erkennen.[107]

---

des Gesetzgebers auf „inhaltlosen Formalismus" begründet.

[102] Hierzu *Stelkens* (Fn. 19), S. 81 (117 f.), nach dessen Ansicht z. B. die Anwendung des § 37 Abs. 5 VwVfG in Anbetracht des Fortschritts der Technik „zwingend ermessensfehlerhaft" ist; bezüglich der Regelung des § 39 Abs. 2 Nr. 3 VwVfG geht *ders.* (Fn. 88), § 39 Rn. 97 vor diesem Hintergrund so weit, die Vorschrift als „totes Recht" zu bezeichnen.

[103] *Stelkens* (Fn. 19), S. 81 (118); die Anwendbarkeit von § 24 Abs. 1 S. 3 VwVfG auch für teilautomatisierte Verfahren bejahend *Schneider*, in: Schoch/Schneider (Hrsg.), Verwaltungsrecht – VwVfG, Bd. III, 3. EL 2022, § 24 Rn. 133, mit überzeugendem Hinweis auf den offenen Wortlaut und den rein klarstellenden Charakter der Regelung.

[104] *Schröder*, in: Schoch/Schneider (Hrsg.), Verwaltungsrecht – VwVfG, Bd. III, 3. EL 2022, § 37 Rn. 88 ff; auf rechtspolitisch begründete Kritik dieser Argumentation hinweisend *Schönenbroicher*, in: Mann/Sennekamp/Uechtritz (Hrsg.), VwVfG, 2. Aufl. 2019, § 37 Rn. 170 m. w. N.

[105] Zurückhaltender *Tiedemann* in: Bader/Ronellenfitsch (Hrsg.), BeckOK VwVfG, 57. Ed. 2022, § 37 Rn. 51: „zweckmäßig und wünschenswert"; vgl. auch BVerwG, NJW 1993, 1667 (1668), mit Hinweis auf den in der Verwaltungspraxis üblichen Hinweis, wonach der Bescheid mit Hilfe einer elektronischen Datenverarbeitungsanlage gefertigt worden und ohne Unterschrift gültig ist.

[106] In diese Richtung auch *Tiedemann*, in: Bader/Ronellenfitsch (Hrsg.), BeckOK VwVfG, 57. Ed. 2022, § 39 Rn. 80 ff.; *Stelkens* (Fn. 88), § 39 Rn. 95 ff.; rechtspolitisch für die Verzichtbarkeit der Variante in Nr. 3 argumentierend *Schuler-Harms*, in: Schoch/Schneider (Hrsg.), Verwaltungsrecht – VwVfG, Bd. III, 3. EL 2022, § 39 Rn. 90.

[107] Ausführlich *Ludwigs/Velling*, VerwArch 114 (2023), Heft 1 (im Erscheinen).

II. Fehlerfolgen

Wird ein vollautomatisierter Verwaltungsakt ohne die in § 35a VwVfG vorausgesetzte normative Ermächtigung erlassen, folgt daraus nicht, dass es sich um einen bloßen Scheinverwaltungsakt handelt.[108] Vielmehr sollte durch die Etablierung des § 35a VwVfG allgemein klargestellt werden, dass der vollständig durch automatische Einrichtungen erlassene Verwaltungsakt in jeder Hinsicht als Verwaltungsakt im Sinne des § 35 VwVfG zu qualifizieren ist.[109] Im Übrigen dürften die Schwierigkeiten einer trennscharfen Abgrenzung zwischen einer Teilautomatisierung und einer allein den Schranken des § 35a VwVfG unterfallenden Vollautomatisierung dem Verdikt der Nichtigkeit (§ 44 Abs. 1 VwVfG) eines unter Verstoß gegen den Normvorbehalt erlassenen Verwaltungsakts regelmäßig entgegenstehen.[110] Typischerweise hat die Nichtbeachtung daher „nur" die Rechtswidrigkeit des so erlassenen Verwaltungsakts zur Folge.[111] Da § 35a VwVfG keine inhaltlichen Vorgaben zur Verwaltungsentscheidung trifft, handelt es sich um eine Verfahrensvorschrift,[112] bei deren Verletzung von einem formellen Fehler auszugehen ist. Hieraus folgt zugleich die Möglichkeit einer Heilung nach § 45 VwVfG analog[113] oder einer Unbeachtlichkeit etwaiger Verstöße gemäß § 46 VwVfG.[114] Folgerichtig hat etwa das Oberverwaltungsgericht für das Land Nordrhein-Westfalen mit Blick auf einen Rundfunkbeitragsbescheid

---

[108] OVG NRW, Beschl. v. 10.12.2021 – 2 A 51/21, Rn. 9 mit Verweis auf *Stelkens* (Fn. 88), § 35a Rn. 56; anders *Stegmüller*, NVwZ 2018, 353 (356), der aufgrund des nach außen entstehenden Rechtsscheins aber eine analoge Anwendung der Verwaltungsaktnormen „überall dort" erwägt, „wo das zugunsten des Bürgers wirkt".

[109] Überzeugend *Stelkens* (Fn. 88), § 35a Rn. 55, wonach das „kann" in § 35a VwVfG als „darf" zu lesen ist.

[110] OVG NRW, Beschl. v. 10.12.2021 – 2 A 51/21, Rn. 9 (juris); OVG NRW, Beschl. v. 9.9.2021 – 2 B 1276/21, Rn. 49 (juris); *Stelkens* (Fn. 88), § 35a Rn. 56; siehe auch *Hornung* (Fn. 14), § 35a Rn. 106, der von einer Nichtigkeit nach § 44 Abs. 1 nur bei „besonders groben Verstößen" ausgeht, die dann vorliegen sollen, „wenn beispielsweise ein evident für die Automatisierung ungeeigneter Verwaltungsablauf automatisiert wird und in der Folge grob fehlerhafte (z. B. offensichtlich diskriminierende) Entscheidungen getroffen werden".

[111] *Siegel*, DVBl. 2017, 24 (26); kritisch *Stegmüller*, NVwZ 2018, 353 (356), wonach § 35a VwVfG der Verwaltung einen „Bärendienst" erwiesen hätte, wenn entsprechende Verwaltungsakte dann allein aufgrund formeller Rechtswidrigkeit stets anfechtbar und aufhebbar wären.

[112] *Martini/Nink*, DVBl. 2018, 1128 (1130 f.); siehe auch *Guckelberger*, DÖV 2021, 566 (572).

[113] Zum Vorliegen der Analogievoraussetzungen näher *Guckelberger*, DÖV 2021, 566 (572) in Auseinandersetzung mit *Martini/Nink*, DVBl. 2018, 1128 (1131); allgemein zur analogen Anwendbarkeit von § 45 VwVfG auf andere als die in Abs. 1 genannten Verfahrenserfordernisse *Emmenegger*, in: Mann/Sennekamp/Uechtritz (Hrsg.), VwVfG, 2. Aufl. 2019, § 35a Rn. 58 ff.

[114] Deutlich OVG NRW, Beschl. v. 10.12.2021 – 2 A 51/21, Rn. 7, 13 f.; *Hornung* (Fn. 14), § 35a Rn. 106; a. A. *Stelkens* (Fn. 88), § 35a Rn. 56.

festgestellt, dass „keine ernstlichen Zweifel an der Richtigkeit der Annahme [bestehen], dass ein möglicher Verstoß gegen den Rechtsvorschriftenvorbehalt aus § 35a VwVfG NRW jedenfalls durch den Widerspruchsbescheid geheilt worden sei".[115] Ein Sonderfall liegt schließlich vor, wenn der Erlass eines nicht durch Rechtsvorschrift zugelassenen vollständig automatisierten Verwaltungsakts weitergehend die Ausübung von Ermessen bzw. die Wahrnehmung eines Beurteilungsspielraums erfordert. In diesem Fall ist der Verwaltungsakt nicht nur wegen eines Verstoßes gegen § 35a VwVfG formell rechtswidrig, sondern leidet aufgrund eines (nicht heilbaren) Ermessens-/Beurteilungsausfalls zusätzlich an einem materiellen Mangel.[116]

III. Primär- und Sekundärrechtsschutz

Keine Besonderheiten gelten schließlich mit Blick auf den Rechtsschutz. Dieser bestimmt sich nach allgemeinen Regeln. Wenn auf den vollständig automatisierten Verwaltungsakt alle Vorschriften des VwVfG über Verwaltungsakte anwendbar sind, muss Gleiches auch für die entsprechenden Vorschriften der VwGO gelten.[117] Mit Blick auf den Sekundärrechtsschutz kommt es nicht schon dann zu Ansprüchen aus Amtshaftung, wenn die Vollautomation in rechtswidriger Weise auf das Verfahren angewendet wird. Gefordert ist vielmehr die präzise Herleitung der Verletzung einer drittschützenden Amtspflicht. Hieran ist etwa dann zu denken, wenn ein Sachverhalt fälschlicherweise nicht ausgesteuert wird, wodurch sich das Verfahren rechtswidrig verzögert und dem Adressaten des Verwaltungsakts ein kausaler Schaden entsteht.[118] Mit Blick auf das im Rahmen des Anspruchs aus § 839 BGB i. V. m. Art. 34 GG geforderte Verschulden kommt es auf die Vorwerfbarkeit der behördlichen Entscheidung zur vollautomatisier-

---

[115] OVG NRW, Beschl. v. 10.12.2021 – 2 A 51/21, Rn. 14; siehe auch VGH Baden-Württemberg, Beschl. v. 13.11.2020 – 2 S 2134/20, LS 1 und Rn. 15 f. (juris); VGH Bayern, Beschl. v. 26.1.2021 – 7 ZB 20.2029, Rn. 11 (juris); VG Frankfurt (Oder), Urt. v. 9.9.2020 – 3 K 616/17, Rn. 33 (juris). Für eine rechtspolitische Argumentation zugunsten einer Stärkung des Widerspruchsverfahrens bei vollständig automatisierten Verwaltungsakten siehe *Stelkens* (Fn. 88), § 35a Rn. 64.

[116] *Hornung* (Fn. 14), § 35a Rn. 107.

[117] *Hornung* (Fn. 14), § 35a Rn. 105, mit dem ergänzenden Hinweis, dass dies sowohl für die gerichtlichen Rechtsschutzmöglichkeiten als auch (im Rahmen der Statthaftigkeit) für das Vorverfahren gilt (vgl. auch Rn. 105, zur Anwendbarkeit der FGO bzw. des SGG in den Fällen von § 155 Abs. 4 AO bzw. § 31a SGB X). Vgl. zu § 5 BayDiG noch die Hinweise in Fn. 48.

[118] *Stelkens* (Fn. 88), § 35a Rn. 57; ausführlich zu Haftungsfragen im Kontext teilautomatisierter Verwaltungsakte *Lazaratos*, Rechtliche Auswirkungen der Verwaltungsautomation auf das Verwaltungsverfahren, 1990, S. 379 ff.

ten Durchführung eines hierfür ungeeigneten Verwaltungsverfahrens, respektive der Verweigerung einer „Aussteuerung", an.[119]

E. Fazit und Ausblick

Resümierend bleibt festzuhalten, dass der vollständig automatisierte Erlass von Verwaltungsakten nach § 35a VwVfG eine fortgeschrittene Stufe der Digitalisierung des Verwaltungshandelns darstellt. Durch die Nutzbarmachung informationstechnologischer Entwicklungen sollen verfahrensökonomische Potentiale gehoben werden. Besondere Relevanz hat diese Veränderung für sog. unechte Massenverfahren, die durch ein hohes Maß an Standardisierung aufgrund gleichgelagerter Fallkonstellationen gekennzeichnet sind. Aus Gründen der Einzelfallgerechtigkeit (und der demokratischen Legitimation)[120] wird die Umsetzung der (Voll-)Automation an das Fehlen von Ermessens- oder Beurteilungsspielräumen sowie an die Zulassung durch eine Rechtsvorschrift (sog. Normvorbehalt) geknüpft. Dabei zeigt eine nähere Betrachtung, dass noch zahlreiche offene Fragen bestehen, die insbesondere den Umgang mit Fällen einer Ermessensreduzierung auf Null und mit unbestimmten Rechtsbegriffen ohne Beurteilungsspielraum sowie die Ausfüllung des Normvorbehalts nach Maßgabe der Wesentlichkeitstheorie betreffen. Im Übrigen muss sich der vollständig automatisierte Erlass von Verwaltungsakten *in concreto* an den Maßstäben der EU-DSGVO messen lassen, sofern persönliche Daten verarbeitet werden. Die Einhaltung der unionsrechtlichen Anforderungen betrifft § 35a VwVfG freilich nicht isoliert, sondern bestimmt sich auch nach den jeweiligen Zulassungsvorschriften bzw. ergänzenden fachgesetzlichen Bestimmungen.

Neben der vorliegend ins Zentrum gerückten Untersuchung von § 35a VwVfG wirft der vollautomatisierte Verwaltungsakt auch komplexe verfassungsrechtliche Fragen auf, die hier nur angerissen werden und andernorts zu vertiefen sind.[121] Die Implikationen werden insbesondere mit Blick auf das Rechtsstaats- und Demokratieprinzip deutlich. Obwohl § 35a VwVfG im Rahmen seiner Klarstellungsfunktion die überkommene Diskussion über das Erfordernis einer menschlichen Willensbetätigung bei automatisierten Verwaltungshandlungen beendet hat, besteht die Problematik der demokratischen Legitimation

---

[119] *Stelkens* (Fn. 88), § 35a Rn. 57, mit Hinweis auf die drittschützende „Pflicht des Unterlassens rechtswidriger Verfahrensverzögerungen".

[120] Hierzu näher *Ludwigs/Velling*, VerwArch 114 (2023), Heft 1 (im Erscheinen).

[121] Für eine ausführliche Betrachtung der nachfolgend skizzierten Fragestellungen siehe *Ludwigs/Velling*, VerwArch 114 (2023), Heft 1 (im Erscheinen).

angesichts der vielfach geforderten lückenlosen Legitimationskette beim maschinellen Erlass fort. Aus rechtsstaatlicher Perspektive verdienen nicht nur die bereits erwähnten Auswirkungen des vollständig automatisierten Erlasses auf die
Verfahrensrechte der Betroffenen verstärkte Aufmerksamkeit. Auch die Kontrolle und Nachvollziehbarkeit entsprechender Verwaltungsakte bedarf näherer
Analyse. Schwierigkeiten bereitet insoweit vor allem die algorithmische Daten-
verarbeitung, die den Zugang zum Regelungsinhalt des Verwaltungsakts sowohl
für Kontrollinstanzen als auch für Betroffene (im Rahmen ihres Akteneinsichts-
rechts) signifikant erschwert. Angesichts dieser automatisierungsbedingten
Komplikationen gilt es in besonderer Weise, die Gewährleistung effektiven
Rechtsschutzes in die Erwägungen einzubeziehen. Noch weiter verschärft werden die rechtsstaatlichen und demokratietheoretischen Herausforderungen im
Übrigen durch den sich abzeichnenden technischen Fortschritt hin zu selbstlernenden Algorithmen und starker KI. Vor diesem Hintergrund erweist sich die
Ankernorm des § 35a VwVfG nur als erster Schritt, der auf eine an den Vorgaben
der Verfassung ausgerichtete Konkretisierung durch die jeweiligen Zulassungsvorschriften und ergänzenden fachgesetzlichen Bestimmungen angewiesen ist.
Dergestalt ließe sich gewährleisten, dass die verfahrensökonomischen Vorteile
einer Vollautomation nicht auf Kosten der Verkürzung verfassungsrechtlicher
Garantien gehen, sondern diese angemessen berücksichtigen.

Ludwigs / Muriel Ciceri / Velling (eds.), Digitalization as a challenge for justice and administration, Abhandlungen zum Öffentlichen Recht 1, Würzburg, 2023, pp. 55-69.
DOI: 10.25972/978-3-95826-201-0-55

Auf dem Weg zur Regelung der künstlichen Intelligenz in Lateinamerika

José Hernán Muriel Ciceri[*]

A. Einleitung

Hoffmann-Riem bezeichnet die Digitalisierung als einen „Transformationsprozess", der sich auf alle Bereiche menschlicher Interaktion erstreckt.[1] Es sei eine Ära der technologischen und gesellschaftlichen Entwicklung mit „Chancen und Risiken" und entsprechenden Herausforderungen für das Recht.[2] Die Anwendungen der Digitalisierung erstrecken sich auf alle Bereiche menschlichen Handelns. Sie reichen von der menschlichen Interaktion mit dem Internet der Dinge, der Ausübung von Rechten und der staatlichen Aufgabenerfüllung[3] bis hin zur Erforschung des Weltraums[4]. Dies kann es durch technologische Innovationen ermöglichen,[5] den Anforderungen des Kampfes gegen den Klimawandel und neue Epidemien zu begegnen sowie die Nachhaltigkeit[6], die Energieversor-

---

[*] Der Autor drückt seine Dankbarkeit gegenüber seinem Kollegen Markus Ludwigs und seinem Lehrstuhl für ihre freundliche stetige Unterstützung aus. Ein ganz besonderer Dank gilt auch den Kollegen, die freundlicherweise wesentliche Materialien für die Erstellung dieses Beitrags teilten: Annette Guckelberger, Martin Eifert, Wolfgang Hoffmann-Riem, Frank Peter Schuster und Thomas Wischmeyer.

[1] *Hoffmann-Riem*, Recht im Sog der digitalen Transformation, 2022, S. 294, S. 303.

[2] *Hoffmann-Riem* (Fn. 1), S. 4; *Ertel*, Grundkurs Künstliche Intelligenz, 2021, S. 344.

[3] *Hoffmann-Riem* (Fn. 1), S. 37.

[4] Vgl. *Chien/Morris*, AI Magazine 2014, 3.

[5] *Hoffmann-Riem* (Fn. 1), S. 6.

[6] Vgl. Entschließung des Europäischen Parlaments vom 3.5.2022 zur künstlichen Intelligenz im digitalen Zeitalter (2020/2266(INI)), lit b), Nr. 37, 46, 82, 137; Vereinte Nationen, Resolution der Generalversammlung, verabschiedet am 25. September 2015 Transformation unserer Welt: die Agenda 2030 für nachhaltige Entwicklung, Ziele 2a, 5b, 7a, 7.b, 8.2., 9.4, 9.5, 9 a-c, 12a, 17.6-9, 17.16, abrufbar unter https://www.un.org/Depts/german/gv-70/band1/ar70001.pdf (der letzte Abruf aller in diesem Kapitel referenzierten Web-Adressen ist der 27.10.2022); Vereinte Nationen, Report of the World Commission on Environment and Development: Our Common Future, Our Common Future, Chapter 2: Towards Sustainable Development, 4.8.1987, S. 41, abrufbar unter https://sustainabledevelopment.un.org/content/documents/5987our-common-

gungs-[7] und Ernährungssicherheit[8] zu gewährleisten. Wie *Wischmeyer* feststellt, ermöglicht es uns die Technik, zur Verwirklichung des Rechts beizutragen. Demnach können die in einem demokratischen Rechtsstaat entstehenden Spannungen durch entsprechende rechtliche Gestaltungen bewältigt werden.[9] Die künstliche Intelligenz (KI) stellt daher einen Baustein des dynamischen Prozesses der digitalen Transformation dar.[10]

Die künstliche Intelligenz lässt sich als ein materialisiertes oder in der Cloud dematerialisiertes System[11] verstehen. Eher könnte man von Anwendungen der künstlichen Intelligenz sprechen. Solche Anwendungen finden sich in vielen der technischen Geräte, die uns heute weltweit umgeben. In diesem Zusammenhang werden die sich aus der Interaktion dieser Anwendungen mit dem Menschen und seiner Umwelt ergebenden Haftungsfragen sowie die Regulierung solcher Anwendungen u. a. relevant werden.

B. Begriff und Anwendungen der künstlichen Intelligenz

I. Begriff

Zur Begriffsbestimmung verweisen *Ertel*[12] und *Schael*[13] übereinstimmend auf das Konzept von *Rich* aus dem Jahr 1950. Demnach ist künstliche Intelligenz die Untersuchung der Frage „wie man Computer dazu bringen kann, Dinge zu tun, die Menschen einstweilen noch besser erledigen".[14]

---

future.pdf; vgl. auch z. B. *Djeffal*, VEREINTE NATIONEN, 2019, 207 ff.; *Zech*, ZfDR 2022, 123 (129-131); *Ludwigs*, in: Ludwigs (Hrsg.), Berliner Kommentar zum Energierecht, Bd. 3, 5. Aufl., 2022, Einl. A Rn. 11, 12.

[7]   Vgl. *Ludwigs* (Fn. 6), Einl. A S. 1 ff.; *Ludwigs*, NVwZ 2022, 1086 ff.
[8]   *Zech*, ZfDR 2022, 123 (124).
[9]   *Wischmeyer*, DGRI-Jahrbuch 2019/2020, 2021, Rn. 33.
[10] *Hoffmann-Riem* (Fn. 1), S. 39.
[11] Vgl. Vorschlag für eine Verordnung des Europäischen Parlaments und des Rates zur Festlegung harmonisierter Vorschriften für künstliche Intelligenz (Gesetz über künstliche Intelligenz) und zur Änderung bestimmter Rechtsakte der Union, COM(2021) 206 final, (KI-VO-Entwurf), Art. 3.1.
[12] *Ertel* (Fn. 2), S. 3.
[13] *Schael*, DuD 2018, 547 (548).
[14] *Ertel* (Fn. 2), S. 3; *Schael*, DuD 2018, 547 (548).

Die künstliche Intelligenz lässt sich von natürlicher Intelligenz unterscheiden. Wie *Evers* in seiner Erläuterung zu *Gödel* ausführt:

> „Es zeigt sich nämlich, daß bei einem systematischen Aufstellen der Axiome der Mathematik immer wieder neue und neue[(re)] Axiome evident werden, die nicht formallogisch aus den bisher aufgestellten folgen [...]. [Eben] dieses Evidentwerden immer neuerer Axiome auf Grund des Sinnes der Grundbegriffe ist etwas, was eine Maschine nicht nachahmen kann."[15]

Jenseits dessen ist nach *Schaels* Auffassung unter Bezugnahme auf *Sternberg* die menschliche Intelligenz als ein dynamisches Konzept zu verstehen.[16] *Ertel* verweist auch auf die Stärke der menschlichen Intelligenz bei der Anpassung an die verschiedensten Umweltbedingungen und der Änderung unseres Verhaltens durch Lernen. Diesbezüglich sei die Lernfähigkeit der Computer einer der Hauptbereiche der künstlichen Intelligenz.[17]

Bestandteil der künstlichen Intelligenz ist das maschinelle Lernen (*Machine learning*). Dies wird hier nach der Auffassung von *Ganapathy, Abdul und Nursetyo* verstanden als „ein Bereich der Informatik, der Computern die Fähigkeit verleiht, zu lernen, ohne ausdrücklich programmiert zu werden". Aus der „Theorie der Mustererkennung und des computergestützten Lernens" geht hervor, dass „Algorithmen lernen und Vorhersagen über Daten treffen können".[18] Das „Deep Learning"[19] ist seinerseits eine Lernmethode der künstlichen Intelligenz[20].[21]

Überdies basiert die künstliche Intelligenz zum Teil auf Algorithmen, die laut *Hoeren und Niehoff* der systematischen Lösung eines Problems dienen und es erlauben, menschliches Verhalten durch neuronale Netze zu simulieren.[22] Der Einsatz von maschinellem Lernen[23] könnte auch den Brückenschlag zum Wohl der Menschheit und ihrer Umwelt[24] ermöglichen.

---

[15] *Evers*, NZSTh 2005, 101 (108); *Gödel*, in: Feferman et al. (Hrsg.), Kurt Gödel - Collected Works, Vol. 3, 1995, S. 375 (384 f.).
[16] *Schael*, DuD 2018, 547 (548).
[17] *Ertel* (Fn. 2), S. 3.
[18] *Ganapathy/Abdul/Nursetyo*, Neurology India 2018, 934.
[19] *Ganapathy/Abdul/Nursetyo*, Neurology India 2018, 934 (935).
[20] Dazu *Schael*, DuD 2018, 547 (550).
[21] *Ertel* (Fn. 2), S. 321 ff.
[22] *Hoeren/Niehof*, RW 2018, 49.
[23] *Ganapathy/Abdul/Nursetyo*, Neurology India 2018, 934.
[24] *Salzborn,* ZUR 2021, 513; *Martini/Ruschemeier*, ZUR 2021, 515.

Bei der künstlichen Intelligenz hebt *Spindler* zu Recht hervor, dass nicht nur die Algorithmen, sondern auch die eingespeisten Daten von Bedeutung sind.[25] Demnach ist der Datenschutz bei der Interaktion dieser Technologiemodalität mit dem Menschen und seiner Umwelt hinreichend zu gewährleisten. Dieser Ansatz entspricht dem Vorschlag der Europäischen Kommission für eine Verordnung über künstliche Intelligenz. Der Kommissionsvorschlag qualifiziert – innovativ – als „System der künstlichen Intelligenz" ein System, das auf einer Reihe von menschlich gesetzten Zielen basiert und aus dem Ausgabedaten wie Inhalte, Vorhersagen, Empfehlungen oder Entscheidungen erzeugt werden können, welche das mit ihm interagierende Umfeld beeinflussen.[26]

II. Anwendungen

Im Bereich der Anwendungen der künstlichen Intelligenz könnte man von einem technologischen Entwicklungsprozess[27] sprechen. Dieser Entwicklungsprozess wurde wiederum insbesondere durch den Industrialisierungsprozess 4.0 gefördert, der seine Wurzeln in der Hannover Messe im Jahr 2011 findet[28] und auf intelligente Produkte im Internet der Dinge und Dienstleistungen setzt.[29] Der 4.0-Prozess stellt einen Schritt in der technologischen und industriellen Entwicklung[30] dar und erfordert eine Aktualisierung der digitalen Infrastruktur sowie die Verstärkung der digitalen Bildung.[31]

Ausgehend vom Prozess der Industrialisierung 4.0 muss der Prozess der Weiterentwicklung der künstlichen Intelligenz jedoch einen weiteren Schritt in Richtung eines breiten Weges zum Schutz der Menschheit und der Umwelt gehen. Die Förderung einer nachhaltigen wirtschaftlichen Entwicklung[32] mit dem ent-

---

[25]   Vgl. *Spindler*, CR 2021, 361.
[26]   *Spindler*, CR 2021, 361 (362 f.); vgl. KI-VO-Entwurf (Nachweis in Fn. 11), Art. 3 Nr. 1.
[27]   Vgl. zur Entwicklung der KI *Ertel* (Fn. 2), S. 7.
[28]   *Wintermann*, NZA 2017, 537 (538).
[29]   *Bundesverband der Deutschen Industrie*, Gestern war Industrie 4.0 noch Zukunft, heute ist es Realität. Einblick in die vierte Revolution, 2018, abrufbar unter https://bdi.eu/leben-4.0/innovation/#:~:text=Woher%20kommt%20der%20Begriff%20Industrie,Dampfmaschine%20am%20Ende%20des%2018.
[30]   Vgl. *Krause*, NZA-Beilage 2017, 53.
[31]   *Wintermann*, NZA 2017, 537 (538).
[32]   Vgl. Entschließung des Europäischen Parlaments (Nachweis in Fn. 6), lit b), Nr. 37, 46, 82, 137; Vereinte Nationen, Resolution der Generalversammlung, verabschiedet am 25. September 2015 Transformation unserer Welt: die Agenda 2030 für nachhaltige Entwicklung, Ziele 2a, 5b, 7a, 7.b, 8.2., 9.4, 9.5, 9 a-c, 12a, 17.6-9, 17.16, abrufbar unter https://www.un.org/Depts/german/gv-70/band1/ar70001.pdf; Vereinte Nationen, Report of the World Commission on Environment

sprechenden Schutz der Arbeits-[33] und Sozialrechte, der Umwelt und der Nachhaltigkeit der Unternehmen soll ein Bestandteil dieses Fortschritts sein. Demgemäß wird die Anwendung von künstlicher Intelligenz für die nachhaltige Entwicklung an Bedeutung gewinnen. Zudem erstrecken sich die Anwendungen der künstlichen Intelligenz von Haushaltsgeräten bis hin zu nachhaltiger Landwirtschaft[34] und Smart Cities[35], Ernährungssicherheit[36], generierter Kunst und Musik[37], Medizin[38], der Erforschung des Weltraums[39] und so weiter. Dies gilt beispielsweise für das, was *Ganapathy, Abdul und Nursetyo* funktional als „5P-Medizin von morgen" bezeichnen („prädiktiv, personalisiert, präzise, partizipativ und präventiv")[40], sowie für das Informationsmanagement, das durch künstliche Intelligenz im klinischen Kontext gewonnen wird, um einen Aspekt der „Menschlichkeit im Gesundheitswesen wiederherzustellen, indem Ärzte sich auf den Patienten konzentrieren können, anstatt in umfangreichen Daten zu ertrinken".[41] Dieser Ansatz ist unter anderem auch auf Verkehrsstationen, Postämter, Logistikparks und in Datenanalysen erfordernden Berufen anwendbar.

In Anlehnung an die Rechtsliteratur könnte man sich bei der Anwendung der künstlichen Intelligenz auf folgende Zuordnung beziehen:

1. Aufgrund von Spracherkennungsalgorithmen agierende teilautomatisierte Bestellsysteme und automatisierte Agenten.[42] Als Beispiel dienen hier Cortana,

---

and Development: Our Common Future, Our Common Future, Chapter 2: Towards Sustainable Development, 4.8.1987, S. 41, abrufbar unter https://sustainabledevelopment.un.org/content/documents/5987our-common-future.pdf; vgl. auch z. B. *Djeffal*, VEREINTE NATIONEN, 2019, 207 ff.; *Zech*, ZfDR 2022, 123 (129-131); *Ludwigs* (Fn. 6), Einl. A Rn. 11, 12.

[33]   Vgl. *Krause*, NZA-Beilage 2017, 53 ff.; *Groß/ Gresse*, NZA 2017, 990 ff.

[34]   Vgl. *Härtel*, NuR 2020, 439.

[35]   Vgl. *Guckelberger,* Öffentliche Verwaltung Im Zeitalter Der Digitalisierung, 2019, Rn. 103-107, Rn. 99-105; *Braun Binder et al.*, KI-Anwendungsbeispiele in Schweizer Verwaltungen, in: Staatskanzlei Kanton Zürich (Hrsg.), Einsatz Künstlicher Intelligenz in der Verwaltung: rechtliche und ethische Fragen, 2021, S. 24 (27); *von Lucke*, VW 2018, 177 (182, 187, 191). Zu den Herausforderungen von Smart Cities und Societies im japanischen Recht siehe auch den Beitrag von *Rodriguez Samudio* in diesem Band.

[36]   *Zech*, ZfDR 2022, 123 (124).

[37]   Vgl. *Ertel* (Fn. 2), S. 333 ff.

[38]   Vgl. z. B. *Ganapathy/Abdul/Nursetyo*, Neurology India 2018, 934; *Naudé*, AI & Society, 2020, 761; *Kirchberg/Weitz*, Chirurg 2019, 379.

[39]   Vgl. *Chien/Morris*, AI Magazine 2014, 3.

[40]   *Ganapathy/Abdul/Nursetyo*, Neurology India 2018, 934.

[41]   *Ganapathy/Abdul/Nursetyo*, Neurology India 2018, 934 (935).

[42]   *Specht/Herold*, MMR 2018, 40 (41 ff.).

Alexa, Siri und ok-Google,[43] die nach *Schaels* Auffassung (zurzeit) lediglich „eine intelligente Sprachsteuerung" bieten.[44]

2. Autonom agierende Systeme. Es handelt sich um eine sogenannte „[simu-lierte] Intelligenz"[45]. Das zeigt sich z. B. an teilautonom fahrenden Autos.[46]

Darüber hinaus könnte eine weitere Zuordnung eingeführt werden: Über die autonom agierenden Systeme hinausgehende Maschinen. *Keßler* verdeutlicht dies am Beispiel eines Robotraders, „der neben Fremdgeschäften an der Börse (Vermögensverwaltung) parallel Eigengeschäfte abwickelt".[47] Darüber hinaus ermöglicht diese Technologiemodalität die Analyse der Interaktion zwischen Mensch und Maschine und ihre mögliche Anwendung bei Finanzmarktaktivitä-ten.[48]

C. Regulierung

I. Der Regulierungsbegriff

Wie von *Libai et al.* in der Business-School-Literatur hervorgehoben, fordern die Unternehmen eine stärkere Regulierung des Sektors der Entwicklung und An-wendung künstlicher Intelligenz.[49] In diese Regulierung fließen Bedenken zur Stärkung des Datenschutzrechts[50] und der IT-Sicherheit[51] ein. Die Instrumente der Regulierung sowie die Einrichtung von Behörden und Verwaltungskompe-tenzen sind auch angesichts der Entwicklung der künstlichen Intelligenz von we-sentlicher Bedeutung.

---

[43] *Specht/Herold*, MMR 2018, 40; *Schael*, DuD 2018, 547 (551).

[44] *Schael*, DuD 2018, 547 (551).

[45] *Schael*, DuD 2018, 547 (551).

[46] *Specht/Herold*, MMR 2018, 40 (41); *Keßler*, MMR 2017, 589 (593); *Schuster*, RAW 2017, 13 ff.; *Schuster*, DAR 2019, 6 ff.

[47] *Keßler*, MMR 2017, 589 (593).

[48] *le Calvez/Cliff*, EEE Symposium Series on Computational Intelligence 2018, S. 1876 ff., abrufbar unter https://arxiv.org/abs/1811.02880.

[49] *Libai et al.*, Journal of Interactive Marketing 2020, Vol. 51 (1), 44 (53).

[50] *Keßler*, MMR 2017, 589 (590 f.); *Groß/Gresse*, NZA 2016, 990; Verordnung (EU) 2016/679; Ver-ordnung (EU) 2018/1725; KI-VO-Entwurf (Nachweis in Fn. 11), Begründung, 1.2., ErwGr. 7, 24, 72.

[51] *Keßler*, MMR 2017, 589 (591).

Die Regulierung lässt sich als Teil der Typologie des Verwaltungshandelns verstehen.[52] Bei dem Aufbau eines noch zu entwickelnden Rechts der künstlichen Intelligenz könnte man sich auf die von *Schmidt-Preuß* systematisch vorgenommene dreistufige Klassifizierung des Regulierungsbegriffs stützen.[53] Nach dieser von *Merk* dargestellten Klassifizierung befindet sich auf der zweiten Ebene dieser Einstufung die „systematisch-infrastrukturelle Regulierung in volkswirtschaftlich bedeutsamen Sektoren". Als Beispiel dieser Sektoren dienen die Kapitalmarktdienstleister und das Versicherungsgewerbe. Darüber hinaus sind in der dritten Kategorie die Maßnahmen der Wirtschaftspolitik enthalten, die „in sonstigen Wirtschaftsbereichen außerhalb der Netzindustrien und Finanzmärkte Gemeinwohlziele gesteuert werden sollen"[54] und „ihren rechtlichen Niederschlag in Normen und Beschränkungen finden"[55]. Die als Teil der Regulierung zu treffenden Maßnahmen zielen auf die Kontrolle des Marktzugangs und des Marktverhaltens ab.[56]

II. Europäische Vorschlag für eine Verordnung zur Regulierung der künstlichen Intelligenz

Der Vorschlag für eine Verordnung zur Regulierung der künstlichen Intelligenz basiert unter anderem auf dem Ansatz des von der künstlichen Intelligenz verursachten Risikos für den Adressaten ihrer Anwendung oder denjenigen, der an ihrer Interaktion beteiligt ist. Demnach wird zwischen verschiedenen Risikostufen unterschieden.[57] Es kann sich um ein i) unannehmbares, ii) hohes und iii) geringes oder minimales Risiko handeln.[58] Zutreffend betont der Vorschlag, dass auch durch die Anwendung künstlicher Intelligenz Risiken für Grundrechte, die Sicherheit im Rahmen z. B. des Produktsicherheitsrechts[59] sowie Schäden entstehen können, die vom Rechtssystem zu berücksichtigen sind.

Der Vorschlag sieht Anforderungen an hochriskante KI-Systeme vor. Zielt die Regulierung auf hochriskante KI-Anwendungen, sind wie *Spindler* betont, „die Gewährleistung der Grundrechte der betroffenen Nutzer, insbesondere das

---

[52] Ausführlich zur Regulierungsverwaltung zuletzt etwa *Ruthig*, in: Kahl/Ludwigs (Hrsg.), Handbuch des Verwaltungsrechts, Bd. I, 2021, § 22.

[53] Vgl. *Merk,* in: Ludwigs (Hrsg.), FS Schmidt-Preuß, 2018, S. 714 ff.

[54] *Merk*, in: Ludwigs (Hrsg.), FS Schmidt-Preuß, 2018, S. 714 (720).

[55] *Merk*, in: Ludwigs (Hrsg.), FS Schmidt-Preuß, 2018, S. 714 (715).

[56] *Ruthig*, in: Kahl/Ludwigs (Hrsg.), Handbuch des Verwaltungsrechts, Bd. I, 2021, § 22.

[57] *Windoffer*, GewArch 2022, 130 (131).

[58] Vgl. Abschnitt 5.2.2. der Begründung zum KI-VO-Entwurf.

[59] *Spindler*, CR 2021, 361.

Recht auf Meinungsfreiheit, die Nichtdiskriminierung sowie die datenschutz-rechtlichen Grundrechte" zu beachten. Diese Anforderungen betreffen nach *Spindlers* Ansicht die „a) Risikomanagementsysteme", die „b) Voraussetzungen für Daten, insbesondere Trainingsdaten", die „c) Technische Dokumentation und Konformitätsbewertungsverfahren", die „d) Instrumente zur Nachvollzieh-barkeit", eine „e) [menschliche] Aufsicht", die „f) Robustheit, Genauigkeit und IT-Sicherheitsanforderungen", sowie die „g) Transparenz- und Instruktions-pflichten".[60]

Der Vorschlag vereinheitlicht auch die Begriffe von Datenkategorien, ein-schließlich der Eingabedaten für die künstliche Intelligenz. In diesem Zusam-menhang sieht die Verordnung den Schutz der Grundrechte, den Datenschutz (z. B. durch geeignete Daten-Governance- und Datenverwaltungsverfahren zur Beseitigung von Verzerrungen), die Aufdeckung von Mängeln und deren Besei-tigung[61] sowie die Meinungsfreiheit und die Nichtdiskriminierung (z. B. durch die Vermeidung der Verzerrungen in KI-System und die Einbeziehung unab-hängiger nationaler Aufsichtsbehörden) vor.[62]

D. Lateinamerika

I. Statistische Daten

Aus der Statista-Statistik über den Entwicklungsstand im Bereich autonomer Mobilität nach Ländern weltweit ist zu ersehen, dass Chile, Mexiko und Brasilien auf die autonome Mobilität in Lateinamerika am besten vorbereitet sind.[63]

Zudem zeigen Schätzungen, dass sich der Einsatz künstlicher Intelligenz im Umweltbereich auf ein Wachstum des Bruttoinlandsprodukts in Europa um 5,4 %, in Ostasien um 5,1 %, in Nordamerika um 4,2 % und in Mittel- und Süd-amerika um nur 2,2 % auswirken wird. Dies zeigt die Bedeutung der strategi-

---

[60]   *Spindler,* CR 2021, 361.
[61]   Vgl. Art. 10 KI-VO-Entwurf.
[62]   Vgl. ErwGr. KI-VO-Entwurf.
[63]   *Statista,* Autonome Fahrzeuge, 2021, S. 14, abrufbar unter https://de.statista.com/statistik/ studie/id/30065/dokument/autonome-fahrzeuge-statista-dossier/. Die Daten stammen aus dem Autonomous Vehicle Readiness Index von 2020.

schen Ausrichtung der künstlichen Intelligenz in diesem Sektor, die auch in Lateinamerika berücksichtigt werden sollte.[64]

Aus dem Bericht 2020 der Inter-Amerikanischen Entwicklungsbank (IDB) über künstliche Intelligenz für das Gemeinwohl in Lateinamerika und der Karibik geht hervor, dass der (auf die Vermögensteilung bezogene) Gini-Koeffizient in 12 ausgewählten Ländern der Region durchschnittlich 46 % beträgt. Dies zeigt, dass es sich um eine der ungleichsten Regionen der Welt handelt. Daher schlägt die IDB vor, die Möglichkeiten zu untersuchen, wie künstliche Intelligenz dazu beitragen könnte, diese Lücke zu schließen.[65] Die IDB vergleicht vier Kriterien, um das Potenzial für die Entwicklung künstlicher Intelligenz zu bestimmen. Diese Kriterien sind: (1) Regierung mit Digitalisierungsstrategien, (2) Universitäten mit Fachrichtungen mit Bezug zu künstlicher Intelligenz, (3) Förderung des Unternehmertums und (4) Freiheiten der Zivilgesellschaft.[66] Auf dieser Basis sind die Länder mit dem durchschnittlich höchsten Entwicklungspotenzial Uruguay, Brasilien, Chile, Argentinien, Mexiko und Kolumbien.[67] Dies spiegelt einen Teil der Bedeutung der Entwicklung künstlicher Intelligenz in Lateinamerika wider.

II. Eine Herausforderung für die lateinamerikanische Rechtslage

1. Harmonisierung des innerstaatlichen Rechts

So wie die Fortschritte auf der kollisionsrechtlichen Ebene nach der Rom I-Verordnung ein Beispiel für die Vereinheitlichung[68] sind,[69] findet die europäische Vereinheitlichung und die Harmonisierung des innerstaatlichen Rechts der

---

[64] *Statista*, Informe, Inteligencia artificial, Previsión del impacto en el PIB del uso de la inteligencia artificial en el sector medioambiental en 2030, por región del mundo, 2020, S. 4, abrufbar unter https://es.statista.com/estadisticas/1132844/impacto-en-el-pib-de-la-ia-en-el-sector-medioambiental-por-region-mundial/.

[65] *Gómez Mont et al.*, La inteligencia artificial al servicio del bien social en América Latina y el Caribe: Panorámica regional e instantáneas de doce países, 2020, S. 20, abrufbar unter https://publications.iadb.org/publications/english/viewer/Artificial-Intelligence-for-Social-Good-in-Latin-America-and-the-Caribbean-The-Regional-Landscape-and-12-Country-Snapshots.pdf.

[66] *Gómez Mont et al.* (Fn. 65), S. 21.

[67] *Gómez Mont et al.* (Fn. 65), S. 21.

[68] Vgl. *Leible/Lehmann*, RIW 2008, 528 (531).

[69] Vgl. *Lehmann/Krysa*, BRJ 2019, 90; *Lehmann/Leible*, RIW 2008, 528; *Lehmann*, in: Ferrari/ Leible (Hrsg.), Ein neues Internationales Vertragsrecht für Europa, 2007, S. 17 ff.; *Ferrari et al.*, Internationales Vertragsrecht, Rom I-VO, CISG, CMR, FactÜ, Kommentar, 2018.

künstlichen Intelligenz nach der Entschließung des Europäischen Parlaments zur künstlichen Intelligenz im digitalen Zeitalter,[70] dem Vorschlag für eine Richtlinie über KI-Haftung[71] und dem Vorschlag für eine KI-Verordnung[72], eine zukünftige Entwicklung für Europa mit einem universellen Charakter.

Lateinamerika sollte sich auch gemeinsam der Herausforderung der Entwicklung und Anwendung von künstlicher Intelligenz stellen. Hindernisse bei der Erzielung eines Konsenses über Schlüsselfragen in diesem Bereich durch Abkommen oder Mustergesetze können beispielsweise auf verschiedene regionale oder länderübergreifende wirtschaftliche und politische Gründe zurückzuführen sein.[73] Diese Herausforderungen ergeben sich aber auch aus der aktuellen globalen Krisensituation.

Die Organisation Amerikanischer Staaten (OAS) ist diejenige Organisation, die ihre Zuständigkeit auf die meisten Länder der lateinamerikanischen Region ausdehnt. Die Schaffung von Rechtsinstrumenten zur Förderung der Vereinheitlichung oder Harmonisierung wesentlicher Aspekte des Rechts der künstlichen Intelligenz im interamerikanischen Kontext steht im Einklang mit dem Wesen und den Zwecken der Charta der Organisation[74] und sollte auf der politischen Agenda der Mitgliedstaaten Priorität genießen. Darüber hinaus gibt es zahlreiche internationale Organisationen, die sich an die lateinamerikanische Region richten. Die Notwendigkeit, auf interamerikanischer und lateinamerikanischer Ebene z. B. an einem Übereinkommen über die Regelung bestimmter Aspekte der künstlichen Intelligenz und ihrer Entwicklung zu arbeiten, ist vorhanden.

Die Vorschläge der Europäischen Union und die künftigen gemeinsamen Regelungen zum Recht der künstlichen Intelligenz können der OAS als Orientierungspunkt dienen, wobei gleichzeitig die eigene Entwicklung und die Besonderheiten des interamerikanischen Rechts berücksichtigt werden müssen. In jedem Fall muss die Anwendung des bestehenden inländischen privaten und öffentlichen Rechts in den lateinamerikanischen Ländern auf die Herausforderungen

---

[70]   Vgl. Entschließung des Europäischen Parlaments (Nachweis in Fn. 6).

[71]   Vgl. Vorschlag für eine Richtlinie des Europäischen Parlaments und des Rates zur Anpassung der Vorschriften über außervertragliche zivilrechtliche Haftung an künstliche Intelligenz (Richtlinie über KI-Haftung), COM(2022) 496 final.

[72]   Vgl. KI-VO-Entwurf (Nachweis in Fn. 11).

[73]   Das ist z. B. der Fall bei der noch nicht in Kraft getretenen interamerikanischen Konvention von 1994 über das auf internationale Schuldverträge anwendbare Recht, vgl. *Juenger*, The American Journal of Comparative Law 1994, 381; *Samtleben*, IPR 1998, 385, *Pereznieto Castro*, Revista de Derecho Privado 1994, 137; *Hernández-Bretón*, DeCITA 2008, 167; *Leible*, Cuadernos de Derecho Transnacional 2011, 214; *Muriel Ciceri*, AEDIPr 2008, 645.

[74]   Vgl. Carta de la Organización de los Estados Americanos, abrufbar unter https://www.oas.org/es/sla/ddi/docs/tratados_multilaterales_interamericanos_A-41_carta_OEA.pdf.

der Herstellung und Anwendung künstlicher Intelligenz eingehen, um einen effektiven Rechtsschutz zu gewährleisten.

2. Innerstaatliches Recht

Im Bereich des innerstaatlichen Rechts könnten die europäischen Initiativen den lateinamerikanischen Gesetzgebern als Toolbox dienen. Die lateinamerikanischen Länder sollten in den bestehenden öffentlichen Einrichtungen Kompetenzen im Bereich der Regulierung der künstlichen Intelligenz sowie der Regulierung der Produktqualität, der Lieferkette, des Datenschutzes und der Verbraucherschutzstandards schaffen. Ferner soll das bestehende Zivilrecht durch die Gesetzesauslegung, die Rechtsdogmatik und die Analyse der Normen die Lösung von sich aus der Anwendung künstlicher Intelligenz ergebenden Rechtskonflikten bieten. Themen wie das Rechtsgeschäft, die Willenserklärung, die Stellvertretung[75], die Gewährung des Offenkundigkeitsprinzips zum Vertragsschluss[76], die Produkthaftung oder der Verbraucherschutz nehmen in diesem Bereich eine besondere Rolle ein.

Die Rechtsvergleichung könnte dann als Grundlage für eine Analyse des lateinamerikanischen innerstaatlichen Rechts unter Berücksichtigung der eigenen Besonderheiten dienen. In allen Fällen muss die Kompassnadel bei der Entwicklung und den Anwendungen der künstlichen Intelligenz auf den ständigen Schutz der Menschenwürde[77], den entsprechend notwendigen Schutz personenbezogener Daten[78] und einer nachhaltigen Entwicklung[79] ausgerichtet sein.

Wischmayer stellt unter Rekurs auf die Menschenwürde zu Recht fest, dass „der Einzelne durch die Nutzung von KI" durch Regierung und Verwaltung

---

[75] *Specht/Herold*, MMR 2018, 40; *Keßler*, MMR 2017, 589 (592).

[76] *Specht/Herold*, MMR 2018, 40 (42).

[77] *Stern*, Handbuch des Staatsrechts der Bundesrepublik Deutschland, Band 9, 2011, § 184 Rn. 4; *Schuster*, RAW 2017, 13 (16, 18).

[78] *Eifert/Britz*, in: Voßkuhle/Eifert/Möllers (Hrsg.), Grundlagen des Verwaltungsrechts, 3. Aufl. 2022, Bd. 1, § 26 Rn. 102 f., 139 ff.

[79] Vgl. Entschließung des Europäischen Parlaments (Nachweis in Fn. 6), lit b), Nr. 37, 46, 82, 137; Vereinte Nationen, Resolution der Generalversammlung, verabschiedet am 25. September 2015 Transformation unserer Welt: die Agenda 2030 für nachhaltige Entwicklung, Ziele 2a, 5b, 7a, 7.b, 8.2., 9.4, 9.5, 9 a-c, 12a, 17.6-9, 17.16, abrufbar unter https://www.un.org/Depts/german/gv-70/band1/ar70001.pdf; Vereinte Nationen, Report of the World Commission on Environment and Development: Our Common Future, Our Common Future, Chapter 2: Towards Sustainable Development, 4.8.1987, S. 41, abrufbar unter https://sustainabledevelopment.un.org/content/documents/5987our-common-future.pdf; vgl. auch z. B. *Djeffal*, VEREINTE NATIONEN, 2019, 207 ff.; *Zech*, ZfDR 2022, 123 (129-131); *Ludwigs* (Fn. 6), Einl. A Rn. 11, 12.

„nicht zum „Objekt" der maschinellen Entscheidung werden darf".[80] Dieser von der kantischen „Zweck-an-sich-Formel"[81] getragene Ansatz[82] ist ebenso bei der Entwicklung des lateinamerikanischen innerstaatlichen Verwaltungsrechts zu berücksichtigen.

Zum einem dienen die europäischen Vorschläge zu einer Richtlinie über KI-Haftung[83] und zu einer KI-Verordnung[84] hinsichtlich der hochriskanten Systeme der künstlichen Intelligenz für die Grundrechte und die Sicherheit als Vorbild für die Erstellung der lateinamerikanischen inländischen Produktsicherheitsverpflichtungsregelungen der Hersteller oder Betreiber, die ein KI-System entgeltlich oder unentgeltlich in den Markt bringen oder betreiben.[85] Zum anderen sind die Modalitäten des Einsatzes der künstlichen Intelligenz zu unterscheiden. Wenn künstliche Intelligenz bei der Erfüllung von Aufgaben der öffentlichen Verwaltung eingesetzt wird, so muss dieser Einsatz gesetzmäßig, verfassungskonform[86] und mit der Menschenwürde („dignitas humana") vereinbar sein.[87] In *Lorenz'* Sinne ist „der Schutz der Freiheit und der Menschenwürde der Zweck allen staatlichen Handelns" sowie „der Mensch (…) Vorbild und (…) Maßstab der objektiven Rechtsordnung".[88] Der Ansatz des Bundesverfassungsgerichts ist ebenso zutreffend, wonach „jeder Einzelne als gleichberechtigtes Glied mit Eigenwert anerkannt" ist.[89]

Die Anwendung künstlicher Intelligenz ist Bestandteil der Verwaltungsdigitalisierung[90] und damit, wie *Guckelberger* betont, des E-Government.[91] Durch den Einsatz dieser Technologie kann die Effizienz und Entbürokratisierung der öffentlichen Verwaltung[92] in ihrer internen und externen Interaktion mit den

---

[80]   *Wischmeyer*, in: Ebers et al. (Hrsg.), Künstliche Intelligenz und Robotik, 2020, § 20 Rn. 45.

[81]   *Alexy*, Data und die Menschenrechte, 2000, S. 17, abrufbar unter https://www.alexy.jura.uni-kiel.de/de/download/data-und-die-menschenrechte.

[82]   *Kant*, Grundlegung zur Metaphysik der Sitten, 1870, S. 52, 53.

[83]   Nachweis in Fn. 71.

[84]   Nachweis in Fn. 72; näher insb. *Spindler,* CR 2021, 361.

[85]   *Spindler*, CR 2021, 361 (363).

[86]   Vgl. *Bull*, VM 2010, 65 (67 f.).

[87]   *Stern* (Fn. 77), Rn. 4 f., verweist auf die „dignitas humana" als Kern der menschlichen Persönlichkeit, der das Grundgesetz diese Eigenschaft nicht zubilligt, sondern sie als Grundbestandteil seiner Ordnung als „positiviertes überpositives Recht" anerkennt und festschreibt.

[88]   *Lorenz*, Der Rechtsschutz des Bürgers und die Rechtsweggarantie, 1973, S. 50 f.

[89]   BVerfG, Urteil vom 21.6.1977 - 1 BvL 14/76, „jeder Einzelne als gleichberechtigtes Glied mit Eigenwert anerkannt werden"; vgl. auch *Jarass*, in: Jarass/Pieroth (Hrsg.), GG, 17. Auflage 2022, Art. 1 Rn. 12.

[90]   Vgl. *Guckelberger*, VerwArch 111 (2020), 133 (160); *Guckelberger* (Fn. 35), Rn. 99-107.

[91]   Vgl. *Guckelberger*, VVDStRL 78 (2019), 235 (244).

[92]   Vgl. *Bull*, CR 2019, 478 (489).

Behörden,[93] Bürgern, der Wirtschaft und der Gesellschaft[94] gewährleistet werden. *Wischmeyer* stellt insbesondere die Palette der Möglichkeiten für KI-basierte Systeme und die Aussicht auf solche Systeme heraus, die für staatliche und administrative Maßnahmen entwickelt werden könnten.[95] *Eifert* verweist hier insbesondere auf die Diskussion um Wertsicherung und deren Intensität bei der Anwendung Künstlicher Intelligenz. Dies gilt für die Schaffung von Erfahrungsgrundlagen durch Transparenz der Anwendungsbereiche von künstlicher Intelligenz, die über die Risikoinformation hinausgehen. Es geht aber auch um die Schaffung von Alternativen, die es den Nutzern ermöglichen, selbst mit der Nutzung dieser Technologie zu experimentieren und die Ausübung der individuellen Autonomie zu gewährleisten. Schließlich müssen die Entscheidungsfindungsprozesse der künstlichen Intelligenz für die Nutzer klarer werden, damit die Technologie besser kontrolliert werden kann. Auf diese Weise könnte entschieden werden, wie und wo sie eingesetzt werden soll und wie hoch das Schutzniveau sein wird.[96]

Ebenso ist *Gödels* Ansatz in Betracht zu ziehen,[97] demzufolge der vollautomatisierte Erlass von mit Ermessen und Beurteilungsspielräumen verbundenen Verwaltungsakten[98] ausgeschlossen werden könnte. Demnach wäre eine derartige Interessenabwägung für Maschinen nicht zugelassen.

Beim Einsatz der künstlichen Intelligenz bezieht sich *Windoffer* überdies auf staatliche Eingriffe, die sozialstaatlichen Leistungen, die grundrechtsintensiven Entscheidungen Privater und die nicht grundrechtsintensiven Entscheidungen Privater.[99] Die Behörden sollten außerdem über die notwendigen Zuständigkeiten verfügen, um zu verhindern, „dass unannehmbar gefährliche Algorithmen"[100] auf den Markt kommen. Handelt es sich um staatliche Eingriffe in Rechte von Bürgern und Unternehmen, so sind die Schranken des Gesetzesvorbehalts, des Bestimmtheitsgebots, des Verhältnismäßigkeits- und des Gleichheitsgrundsatzes zu berücksichtigen.[101]

---

[93] Vgl. *Eifert*, in: Bultmann (Hrsg.), FS Battis, 2014, S. 421 (430 ff.).
[94] Vgl. *Schoch*, VVDStRL 57 (1998), S. 158 (161 f.).
[95] Vgl. *Wischmeyer* (Fn. 80), § 20 Rn. 13 ff.
[96] Vgl. *Eifert*, in: Bitburger Gespräche: Jahrbuch 2020, 2021, S. 15 ff.
[97] *Evers*, NZSTh 2005, 1017 (108); *Gödel* (Fn. 15), S. 384 f.
[98] Vgl. zu den Grenzen der vollautomatisierten Entscheidungen, *Guckelberger*, VVDStRL 78 (2019), 235 (272); *Guckelberger* (Fn. 35), Rn. 428; zu § 35a VwVfG; *Eifert/Britz* (Fn. 78), § 26 Rn. 90; *Guckelberger* (Fn. 35), Rn. 429. Näher zu vollständig automatisiert erlassenen Verwaltungsakten im deutschen Verwaltungsrecht siehe auch den Beitrag von *Ludwigs/Velling* in diesem Band.
[99] *Windoffer*, GewArch 2022, 130 (132 ff.).
[100] *Molavi*, JRP 2018, 7 (12).
[101] *Windoffer*, GewArch 2022, 130 (132).

Im Fall von sozialstaatlichen Leistungen ist zur Verhinderung eines grund-
rechtswidrigen Ausschlusses Berechtigter eine strenge Regulierung erforderlich.
Demnach wird von *Windoffer* eine „Präventivkontrolle in Gestalt einer Genehmigungspflicht" vorgeschlagen. Somit wäre der entsprechende Verwaltungsträ-
ger von einer Genehmigung abhängig und zur Offenlegung der Programmcodes,
der Datenbasis und des Lernverfahrens sowie zur Erstellung und Übermittlung
einer umfassenden „Risikofolgenabschätzung" verpflichtet.[102] Ebenso sollte der
staatliche Einsatz der künstlichen Intelligenz einer „periodischen und anlassbe-
zogenen nachträglichen Überwachung" seitens der betrieblichen Beauftragten
unterzogen werden. Das Transparenzgebot muss in diesem Zusammenhang ein
permanentes Anliegen darstellen.[103] Sind grundrechtsintensive Entscheidungen
Privater durch künstliche Intelligenz gestützt, wie z. B. im Rahmen des Personal-
managements, des Gesundheits- oder Versicherungswesens oder bei der Erfüllung der Daseinsvorsorgeaufgaben, so ist der Verhältnismäßigkeitsgrundsatz zu
beachten und eine Genehmigungspflicht im Rahmen eines „präventiven Verbots
mit Erlaubnisvorbehalt" zu erwägen.[104] Allerdings müssen im Fall nicht grund-
rechtsintensiver Entscheidungen Privater mit Gewinnerzielungsabsicht die In-
formations- und Transparenzpflichten bestehen bleiben.[105]

Diese Ausgangspunkte könnten u. a. für die Gestaltung von innerstaatlichem
Recht und für die Interaktion der künstlichen Intelligenz mit dem Staat und den
Menschen in Lateinamerika erwogen werden.

E. Fazit

Die Regelung der künstlichen Intelligenz in Lateinamerika hat den dynamischen
Entwicklungsprozess dieser Technologieform zu berücksichtigen. Ihre Anwendung hängt sowohl von Algorithmen als auch von Daten ab[106] und birgt Herausforderungen angesichts der Chancen und Risiken auf lokaler, regionaler und glo-
baler Ebene.[107] Der angesprochene Evolutionsprozess und die Situation, in der
sich die Menschheit und ihre Umwelt befinden, erfordern einen Schritt über die

---

[102]   *Windoffer*, GewArch 2022, 130 (133).
[103]   *Windoffer*, GewArch 2022, 130 (133).
[104]   Vgl. *Windoffer*, GewArch 2022, 130 (133 f.).
[105]   Vgl. *Windoffer*, GewArch 2022, 130 (134).
[106]   Vgl. *Spindler*, CR 2021, 361.
[107]   *Hoffmann-Riem* (Fn. 1), S. 4; *Ertel* (Fn. 2), S. 344; *Guckelberger*, VVDStRL 78 (2019), 235 (275);
        Eifert/Britz (Fn. 78), § 26 Rn. 102 ff.; *Eifert* (Fn. 93), S. 421 (430 ff.); *Eifert* (Fn. 96), S. 15 ff.;
        Schuster, RAW 2017, 13; *Schuster*, DAR 2019, 6; *Spindler*, CR 2021, 361; *Windoffer*, GewArch
        2022, 130; *Wischmeyer* (Fn. 9); *Wischmeyer* (Fn. 80), § 20.

Industrialisierung 4.0 hinaus sowie die Entwicklung eines umfassenderen Weges zur Nachhaltigkeit. In diesem Bereich spielen unter anderem die Regulierung und die Instrumente des Zivilrechts eine wichtige Rolle.

Die Entwicklungen und Analysen des europäischen und des deutschen Rechts können als Leitfaden für den Aufbau eines multidisziplinären Rechts der künstlichen Intelligenz und ihrer Anwendung in Lateinamerika dienen, dessen Eckpfeiler die Menschenwürde,[108] der Datenschutz[109] und die nachhaltige Entwicklung[110] sind. In diesem Sinne müssen die Digitalisierung und die Programmierungsmaßnahmen bei der digitalen Entwicklung dies gewährleisten.

Sowohl in Lateinamerika als auch weltweit ist die Anwendung von künstlicher Intelligenz eine Realität. Sie hat insbesondere das Potenzial, die nachhaltige Entwicklung[111] und die Wettbewerbsfähigkeit des Marktes zu stärken.

Eine Herausforderung für das lateinamerikanische Recht besteht darin, den technologischen Fortschritt mit dem entsprechenden Schutz der Menschheit und ihrer Umwelt in Einklang zu bringen. Diesbezüglich wird die Harmonisierung des innerstaatlichen Rechts entsprechend den globalen rechtlichen Entwicklungen unter Berücksichtigung der eigenen Besonderheiten zur Notwendigkeit. Gleichzeitig müssen die bestehenden innerstaatlichen Rechte dem effektiven Rechtsschutz und dem Justizbedürfnis gerecht werden. Neben anderen Rechtsbereichen müssen auch bestimmte Kategorien des Zivil- und Verwaltungsrechts sowie des Regulierungs- und Haftungsrechts analysiert und gegebenenfalls aktualisiert werden.

Der Kompass muss in jedem Fall auf die Wahrung der Menschenwürde ausgerichtet sein. Der Einsatz von künstlicher Intelligenz kann Brücken zum Wohle der Menschheit, ihrer Zukunft und ihrer Umwelt bauen.

---

[108] Vgl. *Stern* (Fn. 77), § 184 Rn. 4 f.; *Lorenz* (Fn. 50), S. 50 f.; BVerfG, Urteil vom 21.06.1977 - 1 BvL 14/76; *Jarass* (Fn. 89), Art. 1 GG Rn. 12.

[109] Vgl. *Spindler*, CR 2021, 361.

[110] Vgl. Entschließung des Europäischen Parlaments (Nachweis in Fn. 6), lit b), Nr. 37, 46, 82, 137; Vereinte Nationen, Resolution der Generalversammlung, verabschiedet am 25. September 2015 Transformation unserer Welt: die Agenda 2030 für nachhaltige Entwicklung, Ziele 2a, 5b, 7a, 7.b, 8.2., 9.4, 9.5, 9 a-c, 12a, 17.6-9, 17.16, abrufbar unter https://www.un.org/Depts/german/gv-70/band1/ar70001.pdf; Vereinte Nationen, Report of the World Commission on Environment and Development: Our Common Future, Our Common Future, Chapter 2: Towards Sustainable Development, 4.8.1987, S. 41, abrufbar unter https://sustainabledevelopment.un.org/content/documents/5987our-common-future.pdf; vgl. auch z. B. *Djeffal*, VEREINTE NATIONEN, 2019, 207 ff.; *Zech*, ZfDR 2022, 123 (129-131); *Ludwigs* (Fn. 6), Einl. A Rn. 11, 12.

[111] Vgl. Entschließung des Europäischen Parlaments (Nachweis in Fn. 6).

Ludwigs / Muriel Ciceri / Velling (eds.), Digitalization as a challenge for justice and administration, Abhandlungen zum Öffentlichen Recht 1, Würzburg, 2023, pp. 71-88.
DOI: 10.25972/978-3-95826-201-0-71

E-government Challenges in Smart Societies: The Japanese Experience

Ruben E. Rodriguez Samudio

A. Introduction

One is hard-pressed to think of a society that combines technological development and tradition as effortlessly as Japan. With a stable democratic government with a strong economy and solid international relations, Japan is famous for being a safe country that cares for most of its citizens. Though conservative by most standards and not open to change lightly, it nevertheless provides an example of what a well-organized society can achieve.

The country has consistently scored top marks on the OECD fixed and wireless broadband reports.[1] Likewise, it ranks number two on wireless broadband and world robots distribution, number 15 in city management, and number four in e-participation on the International Institute for Management Development's 2021 Digital Competitiveness Ranking.[2] Japan also ranks 14th on the Asia Region UN's 2020 E-Government Survey, being praised for an "integrated approach facilitates the effective dissemination of public-private data and helps to ensure that all stakeholders maintain agreed-upon standards and adhere to compatibility requirements".[3]

With all this high praise and reputation for efficient and smart solutions, Japan has faced and continues to face multiple challenges regarding e-government services. These challenges range from societal, cultural, and institutional to even labor-market related, such as an aging population, lack of effective

---

[1] *Organisation for Economic Co-Operation and Development*, Broadband Portal, available at https://www.oecd.org/digital/broadband/broadband-statistics/. The last access for all web addresses referenced in this chapter was on 27 October 2022.

[2] *International Institute for Management Development*, IMW World Digital Competitivenes Ranking, 2021, available at https://www.imd.org/globalassets/wcc/docs/release-2021/digital_2021.pdf.

[3] *United Nations*, E-Government Survey 2020 - Digital Government in the Decade of Action for Sustainable Development, 2020, p. 154.

communication amongst government agencies, low citizen engagement, and a shortage of IT professionals. Hence, while Japan is often thought of as an example of modernization, it also allows other countries to learn from its past and current setbacks.

The main goal of this chapter is to present, in a brief, simple and accessible manner, how the Japanese government approached the issue of modernizing its administrative services and what we can extrapolate from its successes and setbacks. To this end, we begin with a brief discussion on smart city initiatives focusing on e-government policies. Next, we examine various e-government plans in Japan, discussing some significant reforms. Finally, the last section expresses some comments on why these policies have failed and succeeded in some areas and what can be learned from the Japanese experience.

B. The smartness of a city

Smart cities present themselves as the next step of urban development. By combining the Internet of Things (IoT), Big Data, and Cloud Computing, among other technologies, smart cities aim to provide solutions to urban challenges and improve the lives of the citizens.[4] The origins of *smartness* within urban development can be traced back to the smart growth movement of the late 1990s[5],[6,7] Regardless, there is little consensus on what constitutes a smart city.[8] *Kitchin*

---

[4]   Some authors argue that the imaginary of a city developed in sync with technological advances can be traced back to the 1600s. See: *Cugurullo*, in: Lindner/Meissner (eds.), The Routledge Companion to Urban Imaginaries, 2020, p. 113.

[5]   *Hollands*, City 2008, Vol. 12 (3), 303. However, *Hollands* contends that while the two terms overlap, particularly in relation to the use of information and communications technology, the smart growth agenda utilizes a wider approach.

[6]   Urban planners and geographers have been using quantitative and computational methods to design cities since the 1950s. *Shelton et al.*, CJRES 2015, Vol. 8 (1), 13 (14-15); *Jameson et al.*, Urban Geography 2019, Vol. 40 (10), 1467 (1468). Amsterdam had discussed using computer analysis for census purposes as early the 1960s.

[7]   Research on the necessary technologies for realizing smart cities can be traced back to the late 1980s and consumer-level products appearing by the early 1990s. For example, in 1992, IBM marketed a mobile system capable of combining cell phone functions and management of personal data, in other words, an early version of smartphones. *Rosati/Conti*, Procedia Social and Behavioral Sciences 2016, Vol. 223, 968, *Söderström et al.*, City 2014, Vol. 18 (3), 307 (310).

[8]   The use of the term "smart city" can be divided into two waves. The first wave occurred during the mid-1990s and was used by cities as a means of "self-congratulations" when they introduced functioning information and communications technology infrastructure, e-governance, or high-tech industries to foster economic growth. The second wave began during the late 2000s when IT sector companies, notably International Business Machines Corporation (IBM), began

explains that scholarly discussions can be divided into two camps. The first view defines smart cities based on how pervasive and ubiquitous computing and digitally instrumented devices are integrated into the urban environment. The second view adopts a broader definition and focuses on developing a knowledge economy within a region, i.e. the city's economy and governance are guided by innovation, creativity, and entrepreneurship.[9]

Regardless of the definition, smart cities initiatives share a series of commonalities. *Alexopoulos et al.* conducted a review of smart cities initiatives and literature. They found the following main categories of smart cities development: transportation, environment, tourism, health, waste management & water resources, energy-sustainable development, ICT infrastructure, economic development, security, and e-government.[10] Moreover, any combination of the above can make a city smart; there is no need for an initiative to focus on all areas.

The current model of smart city development revolves around the relationship between the universities, the private sector, municipalities, and citizens. While most projects are financed via public funding, the technologies required are usually developed in academia or the private sector. Citizens, however, are still the main object and pillar that support public initiatives for smart urbanism, which in turn fuel the need for research.

Even with the promise of a safe and sustainable environment that promotes economic growth within a knowledge-based society, smart cities have been criticized for multiple reasons. *Finch and Tene* point out that smart city technologies thrive on constant, omnipresent data flows captured by cameras and sensors throughout the urban landscape, thus raising serious questions about privacy and government accountability.[11] Moreover, there are also issues concerning collecting and storing data collected via ICT, particularly law enforcement at the national and international levels.[12]

The relation between private enterprise and governmental institutions in contracts concerning the design, construction, and administration of smart cities presents unique legal challenges. For one, the private sector is increasingly occupying roles that are traditionally reserved for public institutions, which puts them in a somewhat contradictory position to protect the public interest and their

---

pushing for the use of their technologies in urban development. *Söderström et al.*, City 2014, Vol. 18 (3), 307 (310).

[9] *Kitchin*, GeoJournal 2014, Vol. 79 (1), 1.

[10] *Alexopoulos et al.*, in: Ben Dhaou et al. (eds.), ICEGOV 2019: Proceedings of the 12th International Conference on Theory and Practice of Electronic Governance, 2019, 281 (285).

[11] *Finch/Tene*, Fordham Urb. L. J. 2014, Vol. 41 (5), 1581 (1609).

[12] *Losavio et al.*, Security and Privacy 2018, Vol. 1 (3), 1.

investors.[13] In addition, while national and local governments play a pivotal role in any smart city, the complexity and scale of these projects require specialized knowledge in technology and law; hence, government lawyers might be called to fulfill roles for which they are not trained.[14] *Keymolen and Voorwinden* point out similar issues with contracts concerning smart cities, specifically that these contracts can be open-ended in character, without clear boundaries and agreements on the ownership of data, and are often non-transparent, not public, or incomprehensible.[15]

C. Smart government

One of the main focuses of smart cities projects is the administration of the city, specifically, the use of smart technologies to improve government services, usually under the name of digital government, e-government, e-governance, electronic government, smart government, or other similar. The term emerged in the late 1990s, but the use of computers in government can be traced back to the 1970s to refer to IT in government institutions and later evolved to include services provided to citizens.[16]

Eventually, the term e-government extended to cover government services and governance. *Nam* points out that in current literature, e-government refers to one of the following: service use, general information use, policy research, participation, and co-creation.[17] Moreover, e-government can also be classified based on the user.[18] Under this classification, the first type of e-government prioritizes interactions between government and citizens, encompassing most government services and facilitating the interaction between government and its citizens by providing government information and services regardless of time and place. The second type of e-government focuses on the contact between government and businesses, including many services offered under the first definition (free access to public data, etc.) and a more robust set of tools such as e-procurement and access to a governmental marketplace.

---

[13]   *Rodriguez Samudio*, CES Derecho 2021, Vol. 12 (2), 3 (18).
[14]   *Jefferson-Jones*, U. Tol. L. Rev. 2019, Vol. 50 (3), 447. Discussing how government lawyers in smart cities must fulfill a role of "advisor-evaluator" of new technologies while defending the interests of their municipal clients.
[15]   *Keymolen/Voorwinden*, IRLCT 2020, Vol. 34 (3), 233 (247).
[16]   *Grönlund/Horan*, CAIS 2005, Vol. 15 (39), 713 (714).
[17]   *Nam*, GIQ 2014, Vol. 31 (2), 211 (212).
[18]   *Alshehri/Drew*, IADIS International Conference ICT, Society and Human Beings 2010, 35 (36).

The third type of e-government retakes the original meaning of the term and centers around the communication between government organizations, either at an interdepartmental level or between multiple agencies. The main goal of this type of e-government is to streamline cooperation and coordination and not necessarily to provide direct services to the citizens, even if they benefit in the long run. Finally, the fourth type of e-government emphasizes the relationship between government and public servants. Depending on the context, this might be included as part of the first or third type, as public servants also access government services as private individuals.

Perboli et al. explain that e-government projects use ICT to enhance the efficiency, effectiveness, transparency, and accountability of communications between government and public administration and citizens and businesses.[19] *Alexopoulos et al.* explain that e-government plans focus on e-voting, electronic consultation, electronic signature collection, and converting municipal services online. They also aim to develop applications for reporting problems, online monitoring of municipal meetings, geographic information system applications for building constructions, free access to open data, implementation of a framework for e-government services, evaluation of citizens' sentiment, and metrics to assess city and government performance.[20]

Nam also identifies five specific determinants that influence the use of e-government:[21] psychological predispositions, civic-mindedness, information channels, trust in government, and socio-demographic conditions. Psychological predispositions refer to the end-users' perceived usefulness of the ICT systems and applications. Civic mindedness explains how a particular population uses e-government services as an extension of civic and political involvement via traditional channels. Information channels center on how citizens learn about e-government services, i.e. via interpersonal channels or mass media. Trust in government describes the relationship between government and the use of e-government services by the public. A higher level of trust is associated with more use of e-government tools. Finally, socio-demographic conditions explain how racial, generational, geographical, and economic differences impact e-government services, with older, less educated, and less technically skilled individuals being the ones most reluctant to use them.

Regardless of the implicit benefits for citizens and society in general, the execution of e-government initiatives has always faced multiple challenges. At the European level, *Savoldelli et al.* have identified three periods of e-government

---

[19]   *Perboli et al.*, Tranportation Research Procedia 2014, Vol. 3, 470 (473).
[20]   *Alexopoulos et al.* (Fn. 10), p. 287.
[21]   *Nam* GIQ 2014, Vol. 31 (2), 211 (212-213).

initiatives and various barriers to adoption faced during each period.[22] During the first period (1994-2004), characterized by the optimistic views on the future performance of ICT, the main barriers were the lack of telecommunication infrastructures and communication capacity.

The second period covers from 2005 to 2009. While infrastructural and communication issues such as the lack of integration across government systems were still relevant, the resistance from civil servants, mainly due to the lack of ICT skill, also became an issue. Nevertheless, the most significant challenges were the lack of tools to evaluate e-government services and the difficulties in establishing a firm connection between ICT, benefits, and outcomes.

Lastly, the third period begins in 2010 and extends to 2013, during which the focus shifted to citizens and business empowerment, transparency, and open and collaborative government. During this stage, the main barriers to realizing e-government plans were political/institutional, lack of citizen participation in the policy-making process, and lack of measurement systems on governmental performance.

In addition to the above challenges, concerns regarding privacy, security, the digital divide, and the effect an interconnected government might have on the democratic process, all linked to the previously identified determinants. Furthermore, there are also cultural issues, though this depends on each country or local community's agreed customs and traditions.

Privacy issues are directly linked to trust in government, which then influences citizens' willingness to provide their data to public and private institutions performing a public service. As *van Zoonen* points out, people assess the purpose for which data is used and weigh the benefits received.[23] Most people will share their data when these benefits are of immediate personal relevance, such as medical services or a commercial gain. However, when these benefits are abstract, such as broader social goals, citizens are less likely to provide information.

By contrast, security issues describe a matter of public perception. Using the example of Amsterdam, *Jameson et al.* illustrate how citizens speak about the government as a "monolithic entity" while, in reality, it is composed of multiple departments, agencies, or municipalities, and the communication between them is not seamless.[24] Moreover, while government institutions promote smart government initiatives, the private sector is tasked with actually realizing them in most cases. This dynamic of the private and public sectors in public spaces, par-

---

[22] *Savoldelli et al.*, GIQ 2014, Vol. 31, s63 (s65-s67).
[23] *van Zoonen*, GIQ 2016, Vol. 33 (3) 472 (474).
[24] *Jameson et al.*, Urban Geography 2019, Vol. 40 (10), 1467 (1474).

ticularly those related to citizens' data, creates a series of issues regarding accountability and the role of private companies in government.[25]

D. Japanese E-government

Japan has a long-held reputation as a technological country that predates smart cities initiatives. As such, the country is no stranger to technology in administrative services. Interestingly, while the Japanese government has used IT to improve numerous services through the years, a review of the Japanese literature reveals a distinct lack of the term smart. Indeed, it is not until the early 2010s that we begin to see articles on *smartness*. Nevertheless, this is nothing more than a semantic argument. Not surprisingly, Japan has gone through many of the barriers described by *Salvodelli et al.* in roughly the same order. For example, in 1988, the government passed a law regulating personal data held by public institutions. Later, during the mid-90s, the Headquarters for the Promotion of Advanced Information and Telecommunications Society was established to design and adopt policies to digitize administrative procedures. For example, in 1994, the government presented the Plan for the Advancement of Digitalization of Government Information to create a network that allowed government agencies to exchange information and communication via email.[26]

However, the country does have specific challenges that set it apart from other digital government initiatives. Japanese administrative institutions have always been exceedingly efficient at the national and local levels. Public servant is a highly sought after, well-paid job with high barriers to entry; therefore, the public expects them to be efficient and hard-working individuals. In addition, the national and local governments had streamlined most processes to the point that citizens rarely meet with any delay or obstacle, even before introducing IT into their services. Hence, one of the principal benefits of e-government, improving services efficiency, is not necessarily the same in other countries.

The Japanese government has enacted various policies to facilitate the transition into a digital society with multiple degrees of success. The roll-out of these policies can be roughly divided into four periods, each with its own specific

---

[25] See *Jameson et al.,* Urban Geography 2019, Vol. 40 (10), 1467 (1480); also *Rodriguez Samudio* CES Derecho 2021, Vol. 12 (2), 3.
[26] *Ministry of Internal Affairs and Communications*, Dejitaru Gabamento no Suishinto ni kansuru Chousa Kenkyu no Ukeoi Seika Hokokusho 2021, p. 15.

goal.[27] Early periods focused on one encompassing policy with clear-cut objectives that were achieved with relative ease. However, later periods saw the government revealing more policies in quick succession, which in some cases appear to go against previous goals.

And while these policies, in practice, the changes that led to new forms of e-government within Japan came not from government policy but from technological and societal changes to which the government responded. Hence, even within the various time frames set by the government, we find multiple policy changes that opposed previous goals.

I. The First Period (2000-2003): Infrastructure

The first period focused on building infrastructure and enacting the required legal framework to modernize the government and bring the country to the forefront of internet access. Thus, at the start of the new millennium, the government unveiled a comprehensive policy on digitalization,[28] beginning with the enactment of the IT Basic Law in the year 2000.

In 2001, the government introduced the e-Japan Strategy, a five-year plan to make the required changes to modernize Japan.[29] Under this policy, the government and private sector began an aggressive expansion campaign. As a result, by 2003, they had managed to provide high-speed internet to over 300,000 households and ultra-high-speed internet to over 100,000 homes nationwide at a monthly fee of under 10,000 yen. As a result, Internet users went from less than 20 million people (just over 9 % of the population) in 1997 to over 77 million (more than 60 % of the population).[30] By 2003, over 98 % of businesses had some form of internet.

One of the e-Japan Strategy goals was the establishment of a Digital Government (*denshi seifu*) both at the national and local levels. Under this new digital model, the government strived to digitize all white papers and legal documents, implement a system of online applications for administrative procedures, and promote digital mediums in administrative offices by 2003. As an early step of

---

[27] *Ministry of Internal Affairs and Communications*, Dejitaru de Sasaeru Kurashi to Keizai 2021, pp. 2-10.

[28] *Masami*, Journal of information studies 2013, Vol. 85, 147 (155).

[29] Under the e-Japan Strategy, the government strived to create a society in which all citizens were information literate, promoted economic revolution based on free competition, and actively contributed to the international community to create a knowledge-based at a global scale.

[30] *Ministry of Internal Affairs and Communications*, Heisei 15 Nen Tsushin Riyo Doko Chosa no Seika 2004, p. 1.

this new policy, the government set up the "e-Gov" website in 2001, and by 2003 it had set up a system to receive online applications for over 95 % of administrative processes.[31] The government also began to offer information about various services providing access to government documents via the web, which has continued without significant hiccups throughout the years. However, it soon became apparent that while the physical infrastructure had been laid, the institutional foundations were not up to standard, as many administrative procedures were not compatible with a digital model. Hence, in September 2002, the government decided to revise the e-Japan Strategy to focus on the practical uses of ICT.

Japan had achieved most of its infrastructure-related goals well within the time frame set by the government. It also began the institutional changes required to provide citizens with digital access to various government services. Thus, the first period was a definite success of Japanese ingenuity and perseverance, catapulting the country into the forefront of digital enterprises ahead of its neighbors and some European counterparts. However, this success would prove challenging to maintain in the following years. Tradition, low citizen engagement, and, ironically, the bureaucracy would conspire to create two define types of e-government within Japan, with services aimed at business advancing at a more rapid pace than those aimed at private citizens.

II. The Second Period (2003-2013): Promotion and Expansion

The second period of e-government implementation focused on promoting ICT via multiple national policies. The first one was a follow-up to the e-Japan Strategy, the 2003s e-Japan Strategy II. Regarding e-government, this plan sought to create a society where citizens could access government information and express their opinions, mainly by providing government services 24-hours, 365-days a year by the end of 2005.[32]

The second policy, the New IT Revolution Strategy, was unveiled in 2006 and recognized that previous digital government goals were lagging. Specifically, this plan acknowledged that citizens and businesses were not using e-government services and that many administrative procedures were not adapted to an online environment. Thus, its primary goal was to achieve an e-government use of over

---

[31]   Even though there is no doubt that at one point in time, Japan established a system that allowed for online application of over 95 % of administrative services, there are conflicting reports on the exact date. *Ministry of Internal Affairs and Communications* (Fn. 26), p. 17, sets the date in 2003 while *Ministry of Internal Affairs and Communications* (Fn. 27), p. 114 has it in 2005.

[32]   *Information Technology Strategy Headquarters*, e-Japan II Senryaku 2003, p. 23.

50 % by 2010. In addition, the government also aimed to create a small, cost-efficient government at the national and local levels. Then, in 2009, the government announced the i-Japan Strategy 2015, which aimed to integrate digital services into the citizens' daily lives as meaninglessly as water or air. Finally, in 2010, the New Strategy on Telecommunication Technologies shifted the focus from the government to a citizen-centric society.

In contrast to the infrastructure-focused first period, this period's goals did not entirely depend on government plans and instead hinged upon how well the government could promote its online platforms' benefits. The government first identified those administrative services most used by the citizens, actively promoting online applications by decreasing fees and even offering economic incentives. However, during this period, one of the most recurring challenges faced by the government became apparent: lack of citizen engagement. A seemingly trivial development, one which will be discussed later, contributed to this trend: the appearance of the smartphone in the late 2000s.

Some significant legal changes also took place during this period. The enactment of the Personal Data Protection Law and the Law on the Protection of Personal Information Held by Administrative Organs in 2003 might be the most significant. Both laws established the legal rights and obligations private individuals, businesses, and the government had regarding collecting, using, and transferring personal data. Likewise, the 2004 e-document Law allowed private citizens and enterprises to digitally store tax and financial information. Moreover, the electronic tax declaration service "e-Tax" was also rolled out the same year.[33]

Most successful online administrative services tend to companies and private citizens alike. Systems related to imports and exports illustrate this trend. As an island nation, Japan is highly dependent on maritime trade. Thus, services related to maritime industries such as permits related to crew members, imports, and exports had achieved digitalization by 2003. In addition, by 2010, the system expanded to include air transport and other tariff-associated services. Furthermore, real estate deed registration services are also provided online. Similarly, the one-stop vehicular-service counter allows online access to procedures regarding police, taxes, and other vehicle-related matters and is constantly increasing the number of covered services.

---

[33]   However, this system is also a great illustration of the government's philosophy regarding digital applications. The services are available 24 hours from Tuesday to Friday, and from 8:30 a.m. until midnight on Mondays, Saturdays, Sundays and holidays. *National Tax Agency*, e-tax Riyo Kanona Jikan, available at https://www.e-tax.nta.go.jp/info_center/index.htm.

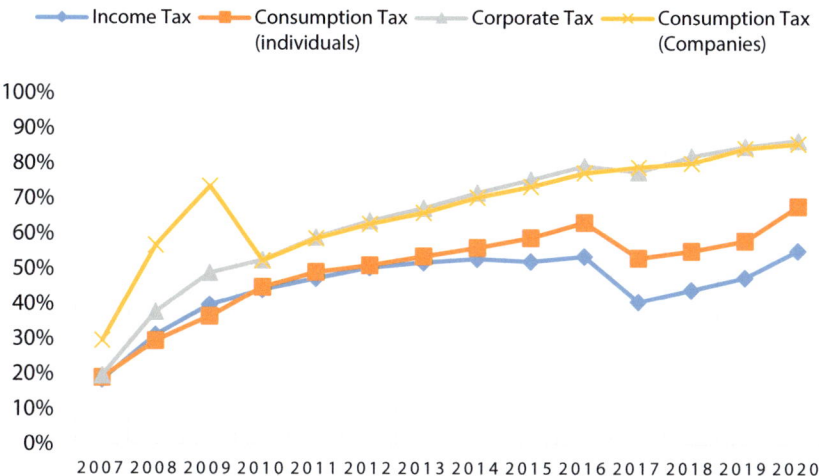

E-tax applications[34]

During this period, it became apparent that there was a lack of coordination between multiple government agencies. There was also a disconnect between national policies and the degree to which prefectural and local governments could implement the changes proposed by the government. Notably, the 2011 Tohoku earthquake and Tsunami revealed significant flaws in how the national government coordinated efforts with prefectural and municipal governments. Thus, the government proposed cooperating with prefectural and local governments by creating standards for various administrative services and relying on the private sector to implement the necessary institutional changes. However, it was not until the arrival of Big Data and Cloud Computing technologies during the early 2010s that the government could finally consolidate various services.

III. The third period (2013-2018): Big Data, Cloud Computing, and reducing costs

If the first period focused on physical infrastructure, the third centered around digital systems. The economic crisis of the late 2000s greatly influenced this

---

[34] Percentage of total tax returns based on the data of the *National Tax Agency* available at https://www.e-tax.nta.go.jp/. In 2020 the government changed the way in which it calculates the data, this resulted in a lower percentage for the years 2017 to 2020.

period; the government began to focus on IoT and personal data and paid close attention to digitalization's economic potential. It also marks a shift in how the government approaches digital government and citizens' data use.

The government also continued its trend of enacting multiples policies in quick succession. The most significant are the 2013s Declaration on Advanced IT Nation, followed three years later, in 2016, by the Basic Law on the Advancement of Public and Private Sector Data Utilization, and the Society 5.0 plan. Moreover, in 2017 the government revealed the Declaration to Be the World's Most Advanced IT Nation Basic Plan for the Advancement of Public and Private Sector Data Utilization. Later the same year, the government launched the Policy on Digital Government Advancement. Finally, in 2018, it presented the Plan to Accomplish the Digital Government Advancement.

Ambitious names aside, the government's goal during this period was to streamline information exchange amongst various national and local government agencies to make full use of citizens' data. In addition, the political landscape of this period also affected government policy concerning smart government. Specifically, Prime Minister *Shinzo Abe's* economic policies, colloquially known as *Abenomics,* placed great importance on supporting the private sector and reducing red tape. As a result, big data and cloud computing became centerpieces of the government strategy to reduce costs, provide businesses with the necessary tools to recover from the economic crisis, and find new uses for citizens' data to modernize administrative services. Specifically, policy shifted from simply making administrative services available online to using citizens' data more efficiently. Hence, cost-cutting measures translated into a reduction of online services, with the government aiming to reduce the number of administrative processes that could be accessed online from 96 % to 52 %.[35]

Thus began a rapid consolidation of government databases, which resulted in the creation of the Joint Government Platform in 2013. The government aimed to reduce online systems from 1500 in 2012 to a half by 2018. It also sought to move around 250 of those systems to the joint platform by 2018. However, by 2016, many of those systems contained large amounts of personal information. In addition, in many cases, the private sector provided the same services, which meant no plan to transfer over 60 % of them to the online platform.[36]

But what is perhaps the government's most ambitious policy concerning e-government, the My Number System, was only tangentially related to the

---

[35]   *Ministry of Internal Affairs and Communications* (Fn. 26), p. 27.
[36]   *Board of Audit of Japan*, Seifu no Joho Shisutem wo Gouryu Shutekitosuru tameno Seifu Kyotsu Puratafo-mu no Seibi oyobi Unyo no Jokyo ni tsuite, available at https://report.jbaudit. go.jp/org/h28/ZUIJI2/2016-h28-Z2017-0.htm.

digitalization of government services. The My Number System is a personal identification system introduced in 2015. It provides Japanese citizens and long-term residents with a unique identification number linked to various government institutions.[37] The identification card includes the person's name, address, date of birth, gender, and an IC chip that can be checked against multiple government databases. Over the years, the government has increased the number of services linked to the My Number System from tax-related, social security, and welfare services. Moreover, there is also an online site that lists all the services connected to the My Number System.

The government has gone to great lengths to convince citizens to obtain and use their cards. However, attempts have met with a lukewarm response at best. Besides the natural reluctance one might expect from mass personal identification policies, there have been several issues with the government's approach. First, obtaining the My Number card is voluntary. Even though every citizen and long-time resident receives a letter with the personal number printed and instructions on receiving the card, there is no obligation. Second, citizens can continue to use government services without acquiring the card; at most, some services that use the identification number will only require a copy of the government notice and not the card itself. Third, initially, the government went to great lengths to communicate that the My Number card contained personal information and had to be closely guarded while at the same time trying to expand the number of services that use the cards. In other words, there have been mixed messages on whether the card should always be carried or left at home to use only for specific purposes.

IV. The fourth period (2018-present)

There is no simple way to describe the fourth period other than *change*. The first two years can be described as a continuation of the consolidation trend that

---

[37]   Mass identification efforts have been taking place in Japan after WWII. Unsurprisingly, the government studied the possibility of assigning personal numbers for tax purposes as early as the 1970s. In 1997, the Pension Number System was created, and soon after, in 1999, the Residential Basic Book Law was reformed to introduce the Resident Certificate Code, an eleven number identification code. While Nationals and long-time residents are part of the National Pension System, it is not a personal identification number. By contrast, even though the Resident Certificate Code is considered a type of identification, citizens must first obtain a copy of their resident registry at the municipal office before using it for administrative procedures. Furthermore, the resident registry only contains basic household information, which would make it inadequate for the government's goal regarding citizen data.

characterized the third period: the government trying to reduce red tape and find better uses of citizens' data to promote economic growth. During this period, the government began to promote its Society 5.0 policy, which was first announced in 2016.[38] In 2018, the government announced its plans to become the World's Most Advanced Digital Nation.

This period also saw some essential legislative and institutional changes. Specifically, the government passed various laws in 2021 to realize its plan as the World's Most Advanced IT Nation, of which the following are worthy of mention. The first is the Basic Law on the Formation of a Digital Society, which aims to improve Japan's competitiveness and solve its most critical social problems, e.g. declining birth rate and aging population. The second is establishing a Digital Agency to promote the measure for forming a Digital Society, particularly the management of the My Number card and information network systems. Lastly, the Law on the Arrangement of Related Laws for the Formation of a Digital Society amends several laws to reflect the government's plans better. Among these changes, the Personal Data Protection Law amendment to allow semi-anonymized and anonymized data and the abolition of the seal system are noteworthy.

Nevertheless, most of the changes that immediately affected how citizens access government services did not come from a political will; instead, they were a reaction to an emergency: the COVID-19 Pandemic. As with every other country, the pandemic greatly impacted the Japanese government's plan. For all the sophistication, technological development, and online services that the government had boasted through the years, it soon became apparent that tradition and bureaucracy were not prepared to deal with radical societal changes. Moreover, the lack of coordination between the national and prefectural governments from the second period became apparent during the pandemic's first month, forcing governors to adopt prefecture-level economic and sanitary measures.

Not surprisingly, the public outcry and health risk helped advance e-government implementation at a pace that everyday politics did not achieve for almost 20 years. However, the most damning indictment of the lack of coordination and ability to address emergencies can be found in the roll-out of the special economic measures to support businesses and citizens. Both national and prefectural

---

[38]   According to official documents Society 5.0 "[A]chieves a high degree of convergence between cyberspace (virtual space) and physical space (real space). In the past information society (Society 4.0), people would access a cloud service (databases) in cyberspace via the internet and search for, retrieve, and analyze information or data. In Society 5.0, a huge amount of information from sensors in physical space is accumulated in cyberspace. In cyberspace, this big data is analyzed by artificial intelligence (AI), and the analysis results are fed back to humans in physical space in various forms." *Cabinet Office*, Society 5.0, available at https://www8.cao.go.jp/cstp/english/society5_0/index.html.

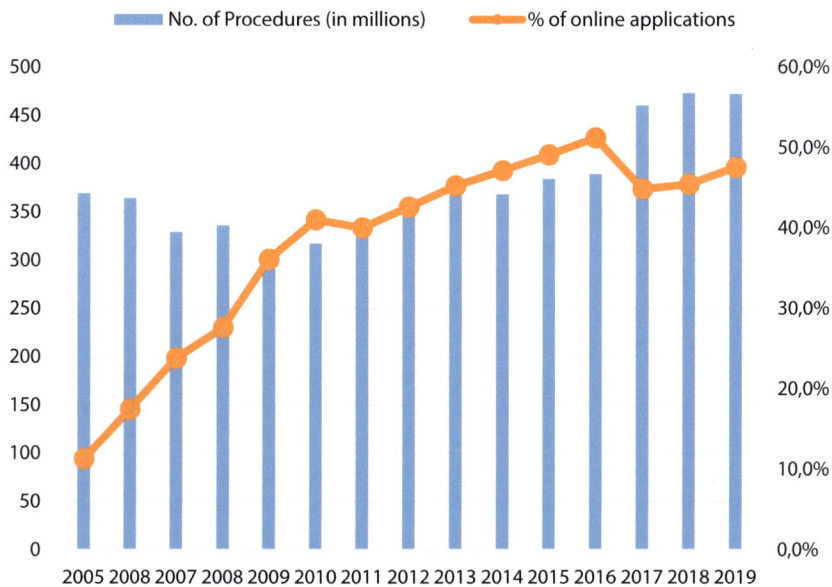

Online applications as a percentage of total applications[39]

governments offered monetary relief to those affected by the pandemic. However, in most cases, applying for this relief had to be done via regular mail, as the
services did not support an online application. Furthermore, citizens had to use
each system, national and prefectural, separately and include a copy of the My
Number card or the notice, which further delayed applications.

E. The Japanese Experience

Japan has achieved some of its e-government goals. Citizens can readily access
government information and essential administrative services online. However,
in reality, these services are underutilized. An industry poll reveals that while
75 % of individuals would like to use online services, only 24 % had accessed
any e-government application services.[40] The main reasons for not using

---

[39] Data from the annual reports published by the *Ministry of Internal Affairs and Communications*,
     available at https://www.soumu.go.jp/menu_seisaku/hakusyo/index.html.

[40] *Trust Bank*, Torasutobanku, Gyosei Tetsuzuki no Dejitaru ka ni kansuru Anketo Kekka wo Hap-
     pyo, Senkoku 1089mei ni Chosa, Yaku 7 Wari ga Gyosei Tetsuzuki ni Fubensa wo Kanjita Keiken
     Ari, Gyosei Tetsuzuki no Onrain Kanketsu Sa-bisu wo Yaku 8 Wari ga Riyoshitai, 2020, available

e-government applications were the limited number of services (33.2 %), the lack of knowledge that the services were offered online (28.7 %), and that the services were too complicated to use (22.6 %).

These results reveal some of the flaws with the government strategy. The top two reasons show that even though the government had digitalized most services by 2005, most citizens were unaware that they could access them online. Thus, it is evident that the government's efforts to promote the virtues of e-government are not reaching the citizens. The cost-cutting measures during the third period might have contributed to the image that there are few services available or the citizen's lack of knowledge. To be fair, the government adopted these measures after considering which services were being used the most. However, it is not clear whether the lack of use is the immediate reason, or it is a result of poor promotion. Hence, there is the possibility that these services would have been kept online if better promoted.

The third reason is not related to any campaigning efforts; instead, perhaps surprisingly, it has its genesis in a disconnect between government policy and how citizens access the internet. Most of the e-government systems were designed during the early to mid-2000s. Therefore, most of these services presuppose access from laptop or desktop computers. Moreover, many government pages only support older browsers. It is not uncommon to receive a message that more recent ones are not supported and might result in errors. However, the debut of smartphones in the late-2000s completely changed the way Japanese people access the internet. According to a 2021 report[41], over 89 % of polled individuals have smartphones. By contrast, only 48 % of respondents have laptops, and a lower percentage of people (26.5 %) use desktop computers.

The government is aware of this issue and is expanding the number of services accessed via smartphones beginning, unsurprisingly, with tax declaration. It also has announced that it is studying the possibility of creating a My Number card application for smartphones. Nevertheless, it is not clear how this would work in practice, as it continues its effort to consolidate various services into the My Number System.

In addition, critics point out that, while the national government pushed for further digitalization, the actual labor of implementing it falls upon prefectural and local governments. Furthermore, the adoption rate of the My Number

---

at https://www.trustbank.co.jp/newsroom/newsrelease/press365/. While this poll is quoted in official reports, the total number of participants was rather low, only 1089 people.

[41]   *Ministry of Internal Affairs and Communications*, Reiwa 2 Nendo Uizu Korona ni okeru Dejitaru Katsuyo no Jitsumu to Riyosha Ishi no Henk ani kansuru Chosa Kenkyu no Ukeoi – Hokoku-sho – , 2021, p. 101.

System is still low, with no indication that it will increase in the near future.[42] Hence, local governments face the economic risk of preparing for a system that might be underused. A proposed solution to this issue is the standardization of the most common services, with a simple user interface that allows for a countrywide adoption.[43]

The solution to this issue might prove challenging, as Japan scores relatively low on digital literacy for all its technological and scientific achievements. Thus, while Japan ranks 14th out of 64th on E-government in the International Institute for Management Development's 2021 Digital Competitiveness Ranking, it places 62nd in the digital/technological skill department.[44] Moreover, the lack of specialized skills extends to professionals. An industry report reveals that in 2019, over 89 % of businesses considered a shortage of IT experienced employees.[45]

Therefore, the number of professionals who could help solve the issue is relatively low. Those with the required knowledge and skills are most likely to go to the private sector for better benefits, leading to the government contracting from the private sector to develop IT systems. While this is not necessarily a shortcoming, it might further contribute to fragmenting online services, as each company uses its vision of how to design them. Hence, every new policy brings forward a new type of online service that fails because it does not integrate with other systems. An example of this is the latest iteration of the Joint Government Platform, handed to Amazon's Webs Services in late 2020 and discontinued less than a year after in 2021 in favor of a government-run system.[46]

Societal factors also play a role. For example, Japan is an aging society; thus, many citizens are not digitally literate enough to utilize online government services. Also, even though it might seem a contradiction when talking about technological development, the truth is that Japan is a conservative society that is famous for being resistant to change. It is not uncommon for households to have a fax machine, and even official institutions still make important announcements, like the new Emperor's coronation, via fax.[47]

---

[42] *Mori,* Jurist 2021, Vol. 1556, 44 (46).
[43] *Mori,* Jurist 2021, Vol. 1556, 44 (46).
[44] *International Institute for Management Development* (Fn. 2), p. 105.
[45] *Ministry of Internal Affairs and Communications* (Fn. 27), p. 25.
[46] *Nikkei Xtech,* Shodai no Seifu Kyotsu Kuraudo Dai 2 ki PF ha Haishi he, 2 Daime Gabakura he Daitogo suru Riyu, 2021, available at https://xtech.nikkei.com/atcl/nxt/column/18/01869/112400001/.
[47] *Denyer,* Japan wants to shred its paper habit. Could it finally leave the fax behind?, The Washington Post, 2020, available at https://www.washingtonpost.com/world/asia_pacific/japan-fax-paper-suga/2020/10/16/fc6fcdd8-06ef-11eb-8719-0df159d14794_story.html. In 2021 the government announced its plans to abolish the use of fax machines. However, there was fierce opposition by several government agencies and the government was forced to suspend the program.

So, what can the Japanese e-government experience teach us? For one, modernization for modernization's sake is not enough to convince citizens to use digital services, especially if analog services are efficient. Second, Japanese citizens do not differ from their counterparts in other countries: they are willing to provide their data and use online services if they perceive a concrete personal benefit, as posited by *van Zoonen*. There is enough evidence of this within official data. For example, a 2021 report on the use of the My Portal services reveals that an overwhelming number of applications had to do with services related to economic support for child-rearing families, followed by nursing or disaster relief.[48] Hence, any e-government initiative must communicate the immediate benefit presented in clear and straightforward terms.

The second lesson we can learn from the Japanese experience is the importance of understanding the technological priorities of a target population. The government has just recently begun to make its systems smartphone friendly. Currently, it is not clear if the Japanese private sector has the human resources required for the task. And, even if it does, tradition might once more prevent a full implementation at all government levels. The last lesson demonstrates the importance of effective communication between national and local governments, lest all efforts cause more confusion and chaos than any potential benefit. The Japanese bureaucratic system is efficient enough to endure and overcome these setbacks. However, other countries' systems might collapse or, at the very least, greatly inconvenience the general population. Therefore, any government trying to implement e-government strategies must ensure effective backup measures during the transition period and even after that.

This work was supported by JSPS KAKENHI Grant Number JP 22K13274.

The Guardian, Japanese fax fans rally to defence of much-maligned machine, 2021, available at https://www.theguardian.com/world/2021/jul/07/japanese-fax-fans-rally-to-defence-of-much-maligned-machine; *The Mainichi*, Japanese gov't requires ministries, agencies to eliminate faxes by end of June, available at https://mainichi.jp/english/articles/20210612/p2a/00m/0na/006000c.

[48]   *Ministry of Internal Affairs and Communications* (Fn. 26), p. 65.

Ludwigs / Muriel Ciceri / Velling (eds.), Digitalization as a challenge for justice and administration, Abhandlungen zum Öffentlichen Recht 1, Würzburg, 2023, pp. 89-110.
DOI: 10.25972/978-3-95826-201-0-89

La digitalización del proceso civil japonés: ventajas y desafíos

Maeda Michiyo

A. Introducción

I. Desde la codificación hasta la enmienda de 2004 del Código de Procedimiento Civil

El primer Código de Procedimiento Civil en Japón fue promulgado en 1890 bajo una fuerte influencia de la Zivilprozessordnung (ZPO) de Alemania.[1] Este código fue sustituido en 1996 por el actual Código de Procedimiento Civil (en adelante CPC), que entró en vigor en 1998. El objetivo de esta reforma integral fue el de modernizar los procedimientos civiles a fin de que fuesen más accesibles y fáciles de comprender por parte de los ciudadanos. Los principales puntos de la reforma de 1996 fueron los siguientes: (1) optimizar los procedimientos referentes a alegatos y pruebas; (2) extender el alcance de la obligación de presentar documentos; (3) la introducción de un procedimiento especial sobre las demandas de menor cuantía; y (4) la restricción de las apelaciones ante la Corte Suprema.[2] Igualmente, y aunque no eran puntos principales de la reforma, el código de 1996 aportó algunas inovaciones en lo referente a la digitalización del proceso civil como el sistema de teleconferencia (art. 170, párr. 3 y art. 176, párr. 3 del CPC[3]) y el de videoconferencia para interrogar a los testigos (art. 204 del

---

[1] *Jauffret-Spinosi*, El Derecho Japonés, en Los Grandes Sistemas Jurídicos Contemporáneos, 2017, p. 411, disponible en https://archivos.juridicas.unam.mx/www/bjv/libros/6/2792/54.pdf. La última recuperación de todas las direcciones web mencionadas en este capítulo es el 27 de octubre 2022.

[2] *Inomata*, en: *Orpeza* (coord.), Japón. Una visión jurídica y geopolítica en el siglo XXI, 2019, p. 268.

[3] La traducción al inglés del Código de Procedimientos Civiles está disponible en el sitio web https://www.japaneselawtranslation.go.jp/en/laws/view/2834.

CPC). En aquella época, no habían muchos códigos en el mundo que utilizaran estos sistemas.

El código de 1996, en su enmienda de 2004, permitió presentar diversas solicitudes en línea (art. 132, párr. 10 del CPC) y, a partir de 2006, se estableció en los tribunales un sistema de pago en línea donde los acreedores pueden presentar la solicitud para que les paguen y hacer consulta de trámites por internet.

En cuanto a la presentación de solicitudes en línea, en el mismo año, una operación experimental se inició en el tribunal distrital de primera instancia en Sapporo, Hokkaido. Sin embargo, no llegó a ocupar un lugar prioritario en la gestión del tribunal porque se admitía presentar solicitudes para fijar la fecha de audiencia, cambio de fecha, práctica de pruebas, pericias, etc. pero no incluía la presentación de demandas. Además, se requería también la presentación física de los escritos impresos, por lo que no había mucha diferencia entre el sistema en línea y el tradicional (art. 132-10, párr. 5 del CPC[4]). La prueba se suspendió en marzo de 2009, desde entonces se continua con el sistema tradicional.

II. Preocupación en la comunidad económica japonesa por la situación actual del procedimiento civil

Según el Informe del Doing Business, una publicación insignia del Grupo Banco Mundial, que mide la facilidad para hacer negocios en 190 países, Japón ocupó el lugar 24 en 2013[5]. En aquel momento, el gobierno japonés estableció un objetivo para alcanzar los tres primeros puestos en la clasificación hasta 2020. Sin embargo, en la edición 2018 del mismo, Japón ocupó la posición 34 entre los 35 países desarrollados.[6]

---

[4]   Código de Procedimientos Civiles, Art. 132-10 (5) (disponible en el sitio web https://www. japaneselawtranslation.go.jp/en/laws/view/2834): When a Petition, etc. filed pursuant to the provision of the main clause of paragraph (1) (excluding a Petition, etc. filed during demand procedures; the same applies in the following paragraph) has been recorded in the file prescribed in paragraph (3), the court as referred to in paragraph (1) shall output the contents of the data recorded in said file in the form of a paper document.

[5]   *Banco Mundial/Banco Internacional para la Reconstrucción y el Desarrollo,* Doing Business 2013, 2013, p. 3, disponible en https://www.doingbusiness.org/content/dam/doingBusiness/media/Annual-Reports/English/DB13-full-report.pdf.

[6]   *Banco Mundial/Banco Internacional para la Reconstrucción y el Desarrollo,* Doing Business 2018. Reforming to Create Jobs, 2018, p. 4, disponible en https://www.doingbusiness.org/content/dam/doingBusiness/media/Annual-Reports/English/DB2018-Full-Report.pdf.

El reporte analiza diez indicadores que miden el número de procedimientos, tiempos, costos y calidad de regulaciones federales y locales que impactan el ambiente de negocios para las PYMES (Pequeñas y Medianas Empresas), como apertura de empresas, obtención de permisos de construcción, pago de impuestos, registro de la propiedad, resolución de insolvencia, obtención de electricidad, obtención de crédito, protección a inversionistas minoritarios, comercio transfronterizo y cumplimiento de contratos. Entre estos indicadores, Japón sufrió un gran retroceso en cumplimiento de contratos, un área altamente ligada al procedimiento civil.

Al respecto, el informe del Banco Mundial considera aspectos tales como los costos y tiempos requeridos y la calidad de los procesos judiciales. Los tribunales con sistemas automatizados, proveen mayor eficiencia y dinamismo al proceso; este es el caso de países como los EEUU, Inglaterra, Australia, Alemania, Singapur, Corea del Sur, China y Malasia.[7]

No hay duda de que estamos en una época en la que los retos de la transformación digital son importantes para los sectores públicos y privados, incluyendo administración de justicia. Por ello, implementar buenas estrategias para la transformación digital se hace hoy más necesario que nunca.

En 2017, el gobierno japonés tomó la decisión de la digitalización de los procesos civiles y administrativos en su Plan de Acción para Estrategia de Crecimiento (*Action Plan of the Growth Strategy Japan*) publicado en el mismo año.[8] Un paso esencial es la optimización de la administración de justicia mediante procesos de transformación digital para mantenerse y seguir

---

[7] *Sugimoto*, Minjisaibantetsuzuki no ITka, Hogaku Kyoshitsu, n° 460, 2019, pp. 51-58. En los Estados Unidos existe el sistema *PACER* desde 1988 y otro sistema *CM/ECF* de e-Filing desde 1996. En Inglaterra existe el sistema de *CE-File* (Courts Electronic Filing) donde la presentación en línea es obligatoria en algunos casos como los mercantiles, de insolvencia, de propiedad intelectual, etc. desde abril de 2017. En Australia existe el sistema de *ECF* (Electronic court file) desde 2014 y también cuenta con el sistema de *eLodgement* (electronic lodgment of documents system). En Alemania había reforma del CPC en 2001 para posibilitar la digitalización de los expedientes de casos. Hasta 2022 se plantea realizar digitalización obligatoria en las demandas presentadas por los abogados. En Singapur existe el sistema de *EFS* (Electronic Filing System) de e-Filing desde 1998 y el sistema totalmente reformado que se llama *e-Litigation system* desde 2013. En Corea del Sur existe el sistema de *ECFS* (Electronic Case Filing System) desde 2003 y se inició la digitalización de los procedimientos judiciales desde 2010. En China empezó una reforma de comunicación de informaciones de juicios desde 2013 y tienen sus plataformas en materia de procedimiento civil, ejecución civil, insolvencia, propiedad intelectual, comercio externo y casos marítimos. En Malasia es obligatorio la utilización del sistema de *e-Filing System* en el Tribunal de Kuala Lumpur en los casos civil, mercantil, de familia y de insolvencia desde marzo de 2011.

[8] *Gobierno de Japón,* Growth Strategy, 2017, p. 37, disponible en https://www.kantei.go.jp/jp/singi/keizaisaisei/pdf/miraitousi2017_summary.pdf.

evolucionando en todos los aspectos, por lo que es muy importante contar con estrategias para implementar la digitalización.

III. Creación del equipo del proyecto para la digitalización del procedimiento judicial

El 30 de octubre de 2017, se organizó un comité oficial dentro del gabinete integrado por profesores, abogados, representantes de la empresa privada y consumidores, con la finalidad de elaborar los planes de transformación digital de los procedimientos judiciales. Para el 30 de marzo de 2018, se celebraron ocho reuniones que culminaron en un reporte de planes para la digitalización de los procedimientos judiciales (*Torimatome*[9]). Según el reporte, la digitalización de los procesos judiciales se iniciaría con el proceso civil, con el objetivo final de digitalizar todos los procedimientos judiciales, incluyendo procesos contencioso administrativos y todos los documentos y piezas procesales. La razón por la que se iniciaron el procedimiento civil es una parte fundamental del procedimiento judicial en general. Además, se espera aumentar los beneficios de los usuarios del sistema, mejorar la eficiencia del proceso, y garantizar el acceso a la justicia ya que en Japón una gran porcentaje de los litigantes se autorepresentan.

IV. Panorama general de planes de acción 2018 (Torimatome)

La planificación estratégica del plan de acción 2018 se basa en las "tres 'e's": "presentación en línea (*e-Filing*)", "gestión judicial de casos en línea (*e-Case Management*)" y "juicio en línea (*e-Court*)".

El proceso de planificación estratégica consta de tres fases que incluyen las siguientes acciones: (1) uso de los sistemas de teleconferencia y videoconferencia actualmente consagrados en el CPC; (2) reforma del CPC para responder a los requerimientos del juicio digital; y (3) reforma de las leyes y reglamentos correspondientes para admitir "presentación de documentos judiciales en línea" y "gestión judicial del caso en línea".

A continuación, analizamos cada uno de las palabras claves de las "tres 'e's" y tres fases, comparando las reglas propuestas con las actuales.

---

[9]   *Grupo de Estudios de la Digitalización de los Procedimientos Civiles de la Corte,* Resumen de In-
        formática para los Procedimientos Civiles de la Corte, 2018, pp. 2-6, disponible en
        https://www.kantei.go.jp/jp/singi/keizaisaisei/saiban/pdf/report.pdf (disponible sólo en japo-
        nés).

B. "Las tres 'e's" como palabras clave en el plan de acción 2018

I. Presentación en línea (e-Filing)

1. Reglas actuales

a. Exigencias de forma escrita

En general, una demanda comienza mediante la presentación de una denuncia escrita ante un tribunal (art. 133, párr. 1 del CPC). Sin embargo, una demanda puede presentarse oralmente ante un tribunal sumario (art. 271 del CPC).[10] Aunque la oralidad es uno de los principios del proceso civil, se exige la presentación física de la denuncia como una excepción al principio de oralidad. Además, debe observarse esta exigencia de forma escrita en los actos procesales importantes como sustitución de la demanda (art. 143, párr. 2 del CPC), retiro de la acción (art. 161, párr. 1 del CPC), recurso de apelación (art. 286, párr. 1 del CPC), recurso de casación (art. 314, párr. 1 del CPC), etc. La contestación de la demanda (art. 80 de la ley Reglamentaria del Procedimiento Civil (RPC)[11]) y la presentación de alegatos (art. 161 del CPC y art. 79 de la RPC) por parte de demandado, también deben ser por escrito. A la hora de presentar una demanda, se deben acompañar las copias del escrito de demanda y de las pruebas, así como el poder, las copias del registro de personas jurídicas o físicas, las copias del registro de propiedad inmueble, etc (art. 55 de la RPC).

Como bien se mencionó, nuestro CPC, enmendado en 2004, introdujo presentación en línea de algunas solicitudes. Sin embargo el hecho de que no existe ningún reglamento correspondiente y que se requiere también imprimir las informaciones presentadas en línea, generó como resultado que este sistema no sea utilizado en la medida que se esperaba.

b. Tasas y costas judiciales

Para abonar una tasa judicial al inicio del litigio, se debe entregar el escrito inicial de la demanda debidamente sellado (art. 8 de la Ley de Tasas Judiciales (LTJ)[12]).

---

10   *Inomata*, en: *Orpeza* (coord.), Japón. Una visión jurídica y geopolítica en el siglo XXI, 2019, p. 275.
11   La traducción al inglés de la Ley Reglamentaria de Procedimiento Civil está disponible en el sitio web https://www.japaneselawtranslation.go.jp/en/laws/view/3865.
12   No hay traducción disponible en inglés de la Ley de Tasas Judiciales.

Se puede pagar en efectivo en caso de que la cantidad total de tasa judicial sea más de 100 millones de yenes (art. 8 de la LTJ). Otras costas judiciales deben ser abonadas en efectivo (art. 12 de la LTJ) o mediante sellos postales (art. 13 de la LTJ).

En el caso del sistema de cobranza judicial en línea donde los acreedores pueden presentar sus solicitudes y hacer consulta de trámites por internet, los interesados pueden pagar a través de los servicios de banca y pago de cuentas en línea o mediante cajero automático. En este último caso considera ello, como un pago en efectivo.

c. Notificación

Si el juez que preside encuentra que la demanda escrita cumple con todos los requisitos[13], el tribunal entregará la demanda por escrito al demandado (art. 138, párr. 1 del CPC). La entrega de la demanda por escrito se realiza por correo, aunque el art. 101 del CPC establece la entrega personal de oficio por tribunales (art. 98 del CPC). También existe la modalidad de citación por publicación a través de edicto fijado en el tribunal en el supuesto de que se ignore el domicilio del demandado (art. 111 del CPC).

d. Pruebas

La mayoría de procedimientos utilizan pruebas documentales. Sin embargo, solo se consideran documentos aquella información impresa en papel. Es decir, que, si bien se permite aportar evidencias tecnológicas al proceso, esto no incluye los metadatos de archivos digitales ya que estos no se pueden materializar en las audiencias. En lo que atañe a las grabaciones sonoras, estas permiten materializarse en las audiencias por lo que se incluyen en los medios de prueba documental (art. 231 del CPC y arts. 147-149 de la RPC).

---

[13] *Inomata,* en: *Orpeza* (coord.), Japón. Una visión jurídica y geopolítica en el siglo XXI, 2019, p 275. El Código de Procedimiento Civil prescribe los temas que deberán ser expuestos en una denuncia escrita, estos son: i) las partes, y los agentes estatutarios, si existiera alguno; y ii) la sentencia específica exigida y el fundamento de la demanda (art. 133, párr. 2 del CPC). Un papel básico de una denuncia escrita es especificar los alegatos del demandante; bajo el CPC, se espera que describa otros hechos suplementarios, hechos importantes y relevantes, además del conjunto concreto de hechos sobre los alegatos de la demanda y las evidencias que serán probadas (art. 53, párr. 1 del CPC), con el fin de revelar todos los hechos y evidencias importantes y de llevar a cabo el procedimiento de manera más eficiente.

2. Reglas propuestas

a. Unificación del sistema integrado de la presentación de demandas en línea

La redacción actual del art. 132, párr. 10 del CPC se basa en la existencia de un expediente físico. Por ende, no permite un sistema completamente en línea, sino que es un sistema dualista: físico-en línea. Las reglas nuevas propuestas como modelo no son una simple ampliación de lo que se admite en línea, sino la unificación del sistema integrado de la presentación de demandas en línea disponible las 24 horas.[14] Sin embargo, actualmente hay tres propuestas de digitalización.

La primera, y la más estricta, busca la unificación total del sistema integrado de presentación de demandas en línea, sin excepciones. La segunda propuesta sólo se exige la presentación de demandas en línea cuando sean presentadas por parte de abogados, excluyéndose los litigantes autorepresentados. La tercera propuesta es similar al sistema actual donde admite la presentación tanto en línea como de manera física. En este último caso, la única diferencia entre el sistema actual y el propuesto sería la prevalencia o no de la presentación por escrito. En el tercer sistema propuesto la presentación en línea es de igual importancia que la presentación física, por lo que siempre se requiere realizar conversiones entre los expedientes digitales y los escritos en papel.[15] A mi juicio, esto supone una carga enorme para los operadores de justicia y puede fragmentar nuestro sistema unitario de jurisdicciones. Por ello, el primer tipo del sistema propuesto (el de unificación total sin excepciones) sería el más adecuado para evitar situaciones más complicadas.

Por otra parte, hay que prestar atención a la población japonesa que carece de alfabetización digital. Debido al avance de las Tecnologías de la Información y Comunicación (TIC), el derecho de acceso a la justicia a través de entornos digitales afecta a las personas adultas mayores que carecen o no cuentan con alfabetismo digital que posibilite dicho acceso. Por ende, resulta indispensable que el Estado atienda con políticas públicas efectivas y con responsabilidad social a este grupo etario para garantizar sus derechos, implementando programas

---

[14] *Sugiyama*, e Teishutsu/ e jikenkanri to sono rironteki kadai, Horitsu Jiho 2019, n° 91-6, pp. 10-15.

[15] *Gobierno de Reino Unido*, Practice Direction 510 – the electronic working pilot scheme, disponible en https://www.justice.gov.uk/courts/procedure-rules/civil/rules/part51/practice-direction-51o-the-electronic-working-pilot-scheme. En Inglaterra, sólo se admite la presentación de algunas demandas en línea en determinados tribunales, por lo que también es necesario realizar conversiones entre los expedientes digitales y los escritos en papel si quieren transferir los casos entre los tribunales.

adecuados de capacitación para generar las competencias básicas que les permita su libre acceso fácil y rápido al sistema de justicia. Será indispensable algún sistema de apoyo en los casos de litigantes autorepresentados si quieren exigirles la presentación obligatoria de demandas.[16]

b. Presentación de demandas en línea

La técnica concreta que se propone para presentar demandas en línea es subir los expedientes del caso; como el escrito inicial, contestación, documento de acreditación de la representación etc., en el sistema del tribunal que se denomina "MINji saibansyorui denshi Teisyutsu System" (MINTS). Los tribunales de primera instancia en Kofu y en Otsu de la provincia de Shiga iniciaron pruebas de estos sistemas desde febrero de 2022.

Uno de los problemas en la operación del sistema MINTS es la forma de verificar las identificaciones personales. Una solución efectiva sería instalar aplicaciones de firma en el sistema operativo para realizar la firma electrónica, pero esta exigencia de la firma electrónica podría resultar en barreras al acceso al sistema. Por el contrario, la implementación del sistema de presentación de demandas en línea podría conducir a un aumento del número de demandas presentadas, lo que puede resultar en la acumulación de procesos o de demandas pendientes ante un mismo tribunal.[17]

c. Pago electrónico de tasas y costas judiciales

Se propuso un sistema que admita la realización del pago electrónico de tasas y costas judiciales al momento de interponer demandas en línea. Se espera que este sistema provea la facilidad tanto para los usuarios como para los operadores del tribunal, por lo que debería unificar los medios de pagos al electrónico sin admitir los abonos en efectivo (art. 12 de la LTJ) o por sellos postales (art. 13 de la LTJ).

d. Notificación electrónica

Cuando el secretario del tribunal sube los documentos en el sistema de MINTS, la parte demandada podrá acceder al sistema para descargarlos electrónicamente. Para poder tener acceso al sistema, las partes deberán registrar con antelación sus

---

16 *Kakiuchi*, Honninsosho ni okeru ITka no kadai to kaiketsu no hoko, Horitsu Jiho 2019, n° 91-6, pp. 23-28; *Kobayashi*, Minjisaiban ITka no Pabucome kekka kohyo wo uketemo yahari online moushitate tou no gimuka niha dannkotoshite hantai subeki dearu, Shohisha Ho News 2021, n° 129, pp. 27-29.

17 Existen opiniones optimistas que se refieren a las elevadas costas judiciales que restringen la presentación de las demandas, pero también existen los demandantes que acuden a la asistencia legal para la presentación gratuita de las demandas.

direcciones de correo electrónico. A través de estas direcciones el secretario del tribunal les notificará a las partes sobre los documentos presentados. Los efectos de citación se producen en el momento del acceso al contenido del acto notificado o bien, si este acceso no se efectúa, se presentan tales efectos por el transcurso del plazo de una semana desde su puesta a disposición en dicha dirección electrónica. Transcurrido el plazo indicado, se entenderá hecha la notificación y se enviará constancia al buzón electrónico.

En cuanto a la notificación mediante edicto fijado en el tribunal, se propone un formato visible en línea como la publicación en el sitio web del tribunal. En este caso, aunque se puede garantizar más eficientemente el debido proceso, debe prestarse especial atención a la privacidad de las partes, de modo que no se revele a los terceros datos confidenciales o sensibles.

e. Sentencia en rebeldía

Dentro de las propuestas no acogidas se presentó una que buscaba permitir sentencias condenatorias en los casos donde no existan puntos controvertidos, siempre que se confirme la falta de voluntad por parte del demandando a responder al caso presentado contra él. Esto tiene su fundamento en el principio del contradictorio, inherente al derecho de defensa, bajo el cual las partes tienen el derecho a participar en el proceso.

II. Gestión judicial del caso en línea (e-Case Management)

1. Reglas actuales

Una vez hecha la notificación, el juez que preside el proceso designará una fecha para los argumentos orales y convocará a las partes para que se presenten (art. 139 del CPC). Para la fijación de fechas de audiencias, se admite utilizar teléfono y fax (art. 149 del CPC y art. 63 de la RPC) en el caso de las fechas que programan audiencias donde participan las dos partes (demandante y demandado). Ahora bien, si una de las partes reside en un lugar lejano y sólo el otro puede presentarse en el tribunal, se admite fijar estas fechas por teléfono (art. 96 de la RPC).

Los documentos que integran el expediente del caso, como el escrito inicial, la contestación de la demanda, etc., se conservan en el archivo para que puedan consultarlos las partes y los terceros (art. 91, párr. 1 del CPC). Las partes y los terceros interesados pueden fotocopiar los expedientes (art. 91, párr. 3 del CPC), pero es necesario que realice su solicitud por escrito en la secretaría del tribunal (art. 33-2 de la RPC). En los casos de secretos comerciales o de privacidad contenidos en los expedientes, es posible limitar el acceso por parte de terceros a dichas informaciones. En el caso del sistema de pago en línea, los expedientes deben ser imprimidos para consulta (art. 401 del CPC).

Las sentencias judiciales se dictan con base en sus documentos originales (art. 252 del CPC) y se transmiten a las partes personalmente en el tribunal o por correo en sus domicilios (art. 255 del CPC).

2. Reglas propuestas

a. Comunicación entre el tribunal y las partes
Actualmente todas las comunicaciones necesarias entre el tribunal y las partes se realizan a través de teléfono y fax. Sin embargo, en las reglas propuestas se realizarán las comunicaciones también por webinario y chat del sistema MINTS. En el mismo sistema electrónico, también se deberán poder compartir todas las informaciones necesarias para la realización de audiencias, tales como: los resultados de procedimiento de audiencia preliminar para organizar los alegatos de la demanda y las evidencias que serán probadas, la elaboración del plan de etapas del juicio, el plan de citación de los testigos, la fijación de día y hora de los alegatos orales, y los plazos para dictar sentencia.

b. Digitalización de los expedientes de caso y su publicación
A lo largo de la instalación de la gestión judicial del caso en línea, los documentos análogos pueden digitalizarse para que las partes y sus abogados puedan accederlos en línea, siempre que lo requieran. Esto servirá para una mejor administración de los documentos judiciales tanto por las partes y sus abogados, como por los operadores del tribunal. De esta forma, no hará falta que los abogados lleven todos los documentos físicos al tribunal, ni que los operadores del tribunal tengan que archivarlos. Ello ayudará también a fomentar una organización rápida y eficiente de alegaciones controvertidas y las evidencias que serán probadas, ya que varias partes pueden consultar los documentos en línea simultaneamente además de poder realizar las búsquedas.

En lo que atañe a la publicación de los expedientes en línea, las partes y sus abogados pueden visualizar, descargar e imprimirlos sin ninguna restricción desde sus computadoras. [18] Por otra parte, se propone que los terceros soliciten a los funcionarios del tribunal, la visualización y la fotocopia de esos documentos

---

[18] En los casos de violencia doméstica, será restringida la consulta del domicilio, aunque éstas sean entre las partes.

desde las computadoras del tribunal. Estas diferencias de tratamiento entre las partes y los terceros se pueden justificar por la exigencia establecida de aclarar la existencia de interés para que los terceros puedan consultar los documentos no publicados e incluso imprimirlos aunque sean publicados (art. 91, párrs 2 y 3 del CPC).

III. Juicio en línea (e-Court)

1. Reglas actuales

a. El procedimiento de audiencia preliminar para organizar los alegatos de la demanda y las evidencias que serán probadas

Como se mencionó anteriormente, el CPC aportó algunas inovaciones en lo referente a la digitalización del proceso civil, tales como el sistema de tele-conferencia (art. 170, párr. 3 y art. 176, párr. 3 del CPC) y el de videoconferencia para interrogar a los testigos (art. 204 del CPC).

En relación con el sistema de teleconferencia, existen dos requisitos concurrentes para su utilización. Primero, una de las partes debe residir en un lugar lejano u otros casos razonables que el tribunal admita. En estos casos, el tribunal debe escuchar las opiniones de las partes. Segundo, una de las partes pueda comparecer ante el tribunal en la fecha fijada (art. 170, párr. 3 del CPC).

Otra modalidad donde se utiliza el sistema de teleconferencia es el procedimiento de audiencia preliminar de forma escrita (art. 175 del CPC). En este caso, se admiten discusiones por teléfono a través del sistema de teleconferencia (art. 176, párr. 3 del CPC). El requisito para que pueda hacerse el procedimiento de audiencia preliminar de forma escrita es que una de las partes resida en un lugar lejano, además de otros casos especialmente admitidos por el tribunal.

Otros procedimientos secundarios para programar las audiencias (art. 96, párr. 1 de la RPC) o el juicio de expertos (art. 96-3 de la RPC), se pueden realizar a través del sistema de teleconferencia.

b. Interrogatorio de los testigos (art. 204 del CPC) y las partes (art. 210 del CPC)

El sistema de videoconferencia se puede utilizar al interrogar a los testigos y las partes, pero se requiere comparecer ante el tribunal más cercano, porque este sistema sólo está disponible dentro de la red interna de los tribunales (art. 123 y art. 127 de la RPC).

Para la utilización del sistema de videoconferencia, se necesitan los mismos requisitos que para el sistema de teleconferencia (residencia lejana de los testigos, etc.), además de las situaciones específicas donde los testigos se encuentren en riesgo de inestabilidad emocional. Un ejemplo de esta última situación, sería el caso de la víctima del crimen que será escuchada en el procedimiento.

Con respecto a los procedimientos de pequeñas causas, se utiliza el sistema de teleconferencia a la hora de interrogar a los testigos a solicitud de las partes y con su admisión por parte del tribunal (art. 372, párr. 3 del CPC).

c. Declaración oral de los expertos
Las declaraciones orales de los expertos se pueden hacer a través del sistema de videoconferencia desde los tribunales cercanos u otros lugares, como por ejemplo, su lugar de trabajo, siempre que el experto resida en un lugar lejano y el tribunal lo considere razonable (art. 215-3 del CPC).

d. Valor probatorio de evidencias digitales
Aunque por regla se establece la presentación obligatoria de documentos físicos (art. 219 del CPC), en la práctica se admiten medios electrónicos. Este es el caso de discos ópticos, tarjeta de memoria flash, etc. como objeto de prueba, siempre que se imprima en soporte de papel su contenido, al igual que en cintas magnetofónicas (art. 231 del CPC y art. 144 de la RPC), o que tales documentos electrónicos, como el conjunto de impulsos eléctricos que recaen en un soporte de computadora, permitan su traducción natural a través de una pantalla. En este último caso, los medios electrónicos (no documentos digitales *per se*) se consideran como cuasi-documentos. Por lo tanto, tienen el mismo valor que los documentos originales.

De esta forma, en la práctica actual, se admite presentación de copias auténticas en lugar de documentos originales, siempre que la parte contraria no tenga objeciones, ni argumente la existencia o exija la presentación del documento original.

2. Reglas propuestas

a. Directriz básica de planificación de juicio en línea
Según el informe, se propone un aumento considerable de la utilización de teleconferencias y videoconferencias en todas las etapas del procedimiento. Estos serían los casos de la primera audiencia oral, el procedimiento de audiencias preliminares para organizar los alegatos de la demanda y las evidencias que serán aportadas además del interrogatorio de testigos. Ello servirá sin duda para la fácil

fijación de fechas de audiencias y en general para la economía procesal. Lo ideal sería contribuir a la conveniencia de las partes y los testigos, sin exigirles la comparecencia ante el tribunal.

A pesar de lo expuesto, se debe afirmar que no se supone que literalmente todas las etapas de procedimiento se operan a través de videoconferencias. A diferencia de la directriz para la presentación en línea (*e-Filing*) y la gestión judicial del caso en línea (*e-Case Management*) donde se supone la unificación del sistema enteramente en línea, el juicio en línea permite la subsistencia de ambas formas: audiencias tradicionales y audiencias digitales. Con base en la especialización y la separación de las funciones, las audiencias digitales operarían mejor en la esfera de primera audiencia oral y de los procedimientos de audiencias preliminares para la organización de los alegatos de la demanda y de las evidencias que serán probadas. Por otra parte, las audiencias tradicionales funcionan mejor y de forma adecuada en la etapa de interrogatorio de testigos, porque el juez estudiará la prueba según su libre valoración. Al mismo tiempo es necesario asegurar en forma efectiva el derecho a repreguntar a testigos de la contraparte.[19]

Respecto a las sentencias, estas se redactarán en forma digital con la firma electrónica del juez que la dicta.

En cuanto a la amigable composición, esta tendrá lugar en cualquier momento, incluso a través de videoconferencia.

b. Nuevos requisitos para audiencias preliminares

Como hemos mencionado, para poder utilizar el sistema de teleconferencia según la regla actual, se requiere que una de las partes resida en un lugar lejano o el tribunal lo admita en los casos razonables. Sin embargo, consideramos que el requisito de residencia debe eliminarse a fin de fomentar las prácticas digitales del juicio que ambas partes estimen convenientes. El requisito de razonalibilidad, por otra parte, debe permanecer para garantizar el control de procedimientos por parte del tribunal. Sin embargo, actualmente tal como lo establece la ley, el tribunal debe escuchar opiniones de las partes para asegurar la razonabilidad de los casos admitidos y también para respetar principios de iniciativa de las partes y de su conducta procesal. Cuando las partes tengan motivos razonables para querer comparecer personalmente ante el tribunal, no puede realizarse el juicio a través de los sistemas de teleconferencias y videoconferencias. Tampoco son adecuados estos sistemas cuando el tribunal no puede realizar el control de procedimientos.

---

[19]   *Kasai*, e Hotei to sono rironteki kadai, 2019, Horitsu Jiho, n° 91-6, pp. 16-22.

c. Interrogatorio de testigos y partes

Bajo la regla actual, para utilizar el sistema de videoconferencia en el interrogatorio de testigos y partes, se necesitan los mismos requisitos que para el sistema de teleconferencia (residencia lejana de los testigos o admisión formada por el tribunal en los casos razonables[20]) (art. 204 del CPC).

Respecto a la admisión más amplia para la utilización del sistema de videoconferencia en el interrogatorio de los testigos y las partes, la comisión llegó a la conclusión de que no debería ampliarla sin límite, aunque quieran fomentar las prácticas digitales del juicio. Se admite tal práctica, siempre que todas las partes estén de acuerdo con su utilización y el tribunal lo considere razonable.

Hay ciertos principios jurídicos que regulan la prueba en el proceso, como son los principios de inmediación, de contradicción y de libre valoración de la prueba. Todos estos principios tienen que ver con el sistema de libre valoración de prueba, donde el juez es libre para obtener su convencimiento, porque no está vinculado a reglas legales sobre la prueba. En este sentido, el juez puede convencerse por lo que le diga un único testigo frente a lo que digan varios.

La necesidad del fiel respeto a estos principios nos lleva a concluir que, respecto a la interpretación del art. 204, párr. 1 del CPC que establece los requisitos para la utilización de videoconferencia, sólo puede ser ampliada su aplicación, hasta donde haya dificultad de comparecencia ante el tribunal y este último lo considere razonable. Si fuera un testigo hospitalizado, el juez le visitará en el hospital y se realizará el interrogatorio, por ejemplo, en la sala del director en consideración a la dificultad de comparecencia ante el tribunal. Aparte de estos casos donde existe tal dificultad, se necesitará el consentimiento de las partes para poder realizar el interrogatorio por fuera del tribunal.

Por último, no hay ninguna razón para distinguir entre los testigos y las partes para la aplicación de estos principios, tal como lo establece el art. 210 del CPC.

d. Declaración de los expertos

Para la utilización del sistema de videoconferencia en la declaración de los expertos, existe el requisito de su residencia lejana, según nuestra regla actual. No obstante, se propone eliminar este requisito, de modo que el tribunal puede considerar razonable la aplicación de este sistema, aún cuando el testigo esté ocupado y quiera utilizar el sistema de videoconferencia.

---

[20] Las situaciones específicas donde los testigos se encuentren en riesgo de inestabilidad emocional.

e. Valor probatorio de los documentos electrónicos

En la práctica actual, no se reconoce el valor legal del documento electrónico, pero sí se reconocen los medios electrónicos presentados ante el tribunal, siempre que sean impresos o visualizados a través de una pantalla.

Según la propuesta para la gestión judicial del caso en línea (*e-Case Management*), todos los expedientes del caso serán digitalizados. Por ello es necesario permitir la aportación de pruebas de origen digital en el juicio y reconocerles directamente el valor legal, sin la intermediación de los medios electrónicos. Para la autenticidad de estos documentos digitales, estos deberán llevar la firma digital según lo que establece la ley de firmas digitales. En la comisión se presentaron opiniones para el establecimiento de sanciones en el caso de falsificación de los documentos digitales.

No obstante, aún después de todas las fases concluidas en la digitalización del proceso civil, lo que permanece inalterable es la importancia de los documentos originales. Sólo excepcionalmente, siempre que la parte contraria no lo objete, ni argumente la existencia o formación del documento original, se permite la presentación de copias auténticas y documentos digitales, en lugar de documentos originales. El fundamento legal sería una clase de contrato de pruebas entre las partes con base en el principio de oralidad. Si las partes solicitan la confirmación de la existencia o la formación del documento original ante el tribunal, no se permite realizar un juicio en línea, porque ello carece de la razonabilidad exigida por el art. 204 del CPC para la utilización del sistema de videoconferencia.[21]

---

[21]   *Kasai,* e Hotei to sono rironteki kadai, 2019, Horitsu Jiho, n° 91-6, p. 21.

C. Las tres fases del proceso estratégico de planes de acción 2018

I. Uso ampliado de los sistemas de teleconferencias y videoconferencias ya consagrados en nuestro Código de Procedimiento Civil

1. Procedimiento de audiencia preliminar de forma oral (art. 170, párr. 3 del CPC)

La primera fase de plan de acción 2018 es la implementación del juicio en línea (*e-Court*) antes que las otras dos ramas, que son la presentación en línea (*e-Filing*) y la gestión judicial del caso en línea (*e-Case Management*).

En lo que respecta al juicio en línea, se busca llevar a cabo audiencias a distancia a través del sistema de videoconferencia. De hecho hay tres supuestos de audiencia a distancia admisibles según la regla actual: (1) Una de las partes participa digitalmente a través del sistema de videoconferencia y otra parte comparece ante el tribunal (procedimiento de audiencia preliminar de forma oral); (2) las dos partes participan digitalmente a través del sistema de videoconferencia (procedimiento de audiencia preliminar de forma escrita); y (3) las dos participan digitalmente a través del sistema de videoconferencia admisible sólo para programar las audiencias. Los dos últimos supuestos no contemplan los requisitos que establece el art. 170, párr. 3 del CPC para dar forma y constituir el procedimiento de audiencia preliminar de forma oral, por lo que se considera ello como procedimiento de audiencia preliminar de forma escrita.

El art. 170, párr. 3 del CPC establece dos requisitos para la utilización de la teleconferencia. Primero, una de las partes reside en un lugar lejano u otros casos razonables que el tribunal admite. En estos casos, el tribunal debe escuchar opiniones de las partes. Segundo, una de las partes puede comparecer ante el tribunal en la fecha fijada (art. 170, párr. 3 del CPC).

2. Procedimiento de audiencia preliminar de forma escrita (art. 175 y art. 176, párr. 3 del CPC)

El procedimiento de audiencia preliminar de forma escrita (art. 175 y art. 176, párr. 3 del CPC), es la única forma admisible por la regla actual para realizar la audiencia preliminar para organizar los alegatos de la demanda y las evidencias que serán probadas sin comparecer ninguno ante el tribunal.

Sin embargo, este procedimiento se considera realizado fuera de las fechas de la audiencia, por lo que no es posible hacer alegaciones o practicar pruebas. Las partes deberán confirmar los hechos que sean objeto de practicar pruebas en la primera audiencia oral después de la conclusión del procedimiento de audiencia preliminar de forma escrita (art. 177 del CPC).

3. Operación experimental del sistema de videoconferencia desde 2020

Desde febrero de 2020, la operación experimental del sistema de video-conferencia se inició en ocho tribunales de primera instancia y en el tribunal de apelación en materia de propiedad intelectual.

Se utiliza esta operación, en los casos donde las partes residen en un lugar lejano del tribunal competente para su audiencia preliminar y que se destina a organizar los alegatos de la demanda así como las evidencias que serán probadas. La conexión se establece entre el tribunal y el despacho de abogados, pero en el futuro será posible conectarse desde el departamento de asuntos legales de empresas donde está el abogado. Antes del inicio de esta operación experimental, tal y como se comentó, se utilizaba sólo el sistema de teleconferencia donde no se podían compartir los expedientes del caso.

En fin, como ya sabemos, el COVID-19 aceleró el uso del sistema de teleconferencia, al igual que la teconología y el teletrabajo en muchos sectores de la industria.

4. Interrogatorio de testigos y declaración de expertos

Actualmente es posible utilizar el sistema de videoconferencia para interrogar a los testigos, pero se requiere comparecer ante el tribunal más cercano, porque este sistema sólo está disponible dentro de la red interna de los tribunales.

Para la utilización del sistema de videoconferencia, se necesitan los mismos requisitos que para el sistema de teleconferencia (residencia lejana de los testigos, etc.), además de las situaciones específicas donde los testigos se encuentren en riesgo de inestabilidad emocional. Un ejemplo de esta última sería el caso de víctima del crimen que será escuchada en el procedimiento.

Igual que los testigos, el tribunal admite a los expertos a declarar sus opiniones a través del sistema de videoconferencia, siempre que el experto reside en un lugar lejano o que el tribunal lo considere razonable (art. 215-3 del CPC).

II. Reforma del Código de Procedimiento Civil necesaria para la realización de juicio en línea

1. La Comisión oficial para la reforma del Código de Procedimiento Civil

La Comisión oficial para la reforma del CPC creada por el Ministerio de Justicia, publicó el esquema básico propuesto (*Yoko-An*[22]) para la reforma del CPC en enero de 2022. Antes de esta publicación, existió un borrador provisional (*Chukan-Shian*[23]), el cual se publicó por la misma comisión en febrero de 2021 con la finalidad de obtener opiniones públicas al respecto. Aparte de estas publicaciones oficiales, el Profesor *Kazuhiko Yamamoto* de la Universidad de Hitotsubashi, y presidente de la comisión, conformó un grupo privado de investigadores, el cual publicó el reporte del procedimiento digital en materia de proceso civil, en el mes de diciembre de 2020.[24]

2. Creación del procedimiento especial con la duración establecida

Según el esquema básico propuesto (*Yoko-An*) publicado en 2022, se plantea crear un procedimiento especial con duración establecida. Esto tiene por objetivo lograr menos tiempo en el tramite del proceso y en el proferimiento de la sentencia respectiva.

Desde hace tiempo, el público japonés tiene la idea que la justicia en Japón es tardía, por lo que muchas personas se muestran reacias a tramitar procesos. Por ello, si es posible predecir la exacta duración del proceso, aumentará el número de usuarios del servicio de justicia. Con la utilización del sistema MINTS será mucho más facil de programar audiencias a través del sistema de video-conferencia. La digitalización del proceso posibilita la creación del nuevo procedimiento especial con la duración establecida. Esto será utilizado en los casos donde no hay conflicto sobre situaciones concretas y sólo falta determinar

---

[22] *Grupo de Estudios de la Digitalización de los Procedimientos Civiles de la Corte,* Resumen de Informática para los Procedimientos Civiles de la Corte, 2022, disponible en https://www.moj.go.jp/shingi1/shingi04900001_00119.html (disponible sólo en japonés).

[23] *Grupo de Estudios de la Digitalización de los Procedimientos Civiles de la Corte,* Resumen de Informática para los Procedimientos Civiles de la Corte, 2021, disponible en https://www.moj.go.jp/shingi1/minji07_00178.html (disponible sólo en japonés).

[24] *Grupo Privado de Estudios de la Digitalización de los Procedimientos Civiles de la Corte,* Resumen de Informática para los Procedimientos Civiles de la Corte, 2020, disponible en https://www.shojihomu.or.jp/kenkyuu/saiban-it (disponible sólo en japonés).

la interpretación de cláusulas contractuales o la aplicación de ley. Por último, serán excluidos de la utilización de este procedimiento especial, los casos en materia de derecho de consumidor y del derecho del trabajo.

III. Reforma de las leyes y reglamentos correspondientes para realizar "presentación en línea (e-Filing)" y "gestión judicial del caso en línea (e-Case Management)"

1. Implementación anticipada de la fase 3 en lugar de la fase 2

El sistema MINTS del tribunal (fase 3) comenzó a prestar servicios desde febrero de 2022 antes de la reforma del CPC (fase 2). Por ello, el sistema funciona según el actual CPC, concretamente su art. 132, párr. 10 introducido en la enmienda del año 2004, para permitir presentación de solicitudes en línea.

2. Opiniones contrarias a las reglas propuestas

La Federación Japonesa del Colegio de Abogados, manifestó su inconformidad con la idea de elegir entre las tres opciones propuestas sobre presentación de demandas en línea: (1) La presentación obligatoria de todas las demandas en línea sin excepción; (2) la presentación obligatoria de las demandas en línea siempre que sean representadas por los abogados; y (3) la presentación optativa de las demandas en línea y en papel físico. Lo ideal sería entonces, la implementación paso a paso desde la opción (3) hasta la opción (1). [25]

Según la regla del sistema MINTS, se utilizará el sistema siempre que sean demandas representadas por los abogados y estos quieran utilizarlo en lugar de la audiencia tradicional.

Según el esquema básico propuesto (*Yoko-An*) publicado en 2022, existen tres categorias de demandas que deben ser presentadas en línea: (1) Las demandas representadas por los abogados; (2) las demandas relacionadas al interés del Estado; y (3) las demandas relacionadas al interés de los municipios.

---

[25] Federación Japonesa del Colegio de Abogados, 2021, p. 10, disponible en https://www. nichibenren.or.jp/library/pdf/document/opinion/2021/210318_8.pdf (disponible sólo en japonés).

3. Litigantes autorepresentados

Como se ve, se excluyen de las demandas que deben ser presentadas en línea, las de los litigantes autorepresentados. Con base en los datos de la estadística judicial de 2017, el 15,7 % de todas las demandas de la primera instancia son las de ambos litigantes autorepresentados y el 55,7 % son las de uno de los litigantes autorepresentados. En el último caso, el demandado suele ser litigante autorepresentado (50,3 %).[26] En el tribunal sumario, más del 90 % de demandas son las de ambos litigantes autorepresentados.[27]

Respecto a las capacidades de uso de los recursos y medios tecnológicos para acceder y manipular la información en internet, hay cierta división digital con relación a las personas adultas mayores, personas discapacitadas y a los residentes de bajos ingresos.[28]

En consideración de estas situaciones actuales, se plantea la exclusión de las demandas de los litigantes autorepresentados tanto en el sistema MINTS, como en el esquema básico propuesto (*Yoko-An*) de 2022.

D. Conclusiones

I. Principio de publicidad del proceso

El principio de publicidad establecido en la Constitución japonesa (art. 82, párr. 1) está dirigido a garantizar la transparencia, la imparcialidad y la rectitud en la administración de justicia. Para cumplir con esta exigencia, deben ser públicas la audiencia oral y el pronunciamiento de la sentencia (fase 2). Sin embargo, los procedimientos de la audiencia preliminar en las formas oral y escrita en línea bajo el actual CPC (fase 1) se pueden realizar sin contemplar la exigencia del principio de publicidad.

En concreto, la audiencia oral y el pronunciamiento de sentencia se realizarán a través de la pantalla grande en la sala del tribunal donde están presentes una de las partes, los jueces y el público. Tampoco se considera inconstitucional si se

---

[26] *Ministerio de Justicia de Japón,* disponible en https://www.courts.go.jp/app/files/toukei/909/011909.pdf (disponible sólo en japonés).

[27] *Ministerio de Justicia de Japón,* disponible en https://www.courts.go.jp/app/files/toukei/910/011910.pdf (disponible sólo en japonés).

[28] *Ministerio de Justicia de Japón,* disponible en https://www.soumu.go.jp/johotsusintokei/whitepaper/ja/r03/html/nd111430.html (disponible sólo en japonés).

tratara de sólo audio sin imagen, lo que se emite en la pantalla (art. 372, párr 3 del CPC).

El pronunciamiento de la sentencia debe ser realizado en la sala del tribunal y las partes pueden escucharlo por internet, lo cual aumentará mucho sus conveniencias. Sin embargo esta conveniencia no será ampliada al público por el momento. Por ello, el público siempre tiene que asistir al tribunal para participar en el juicio en línea a través de la pantalla grande, en la sala del tribunal.

II. Principios de oralidad y de inmediación

Los principios de oralidad y de inmediación son los principios jurídicos que regulan la prueba en el proceso. En nuestro ordenamiento jurídico es en el juicio oral en donde hay que practicar las pruebas, porque sólo lo que ha sido oralmente debatido en el juicio puede ser fundamento legítimo de la sentencia; así lo exige tanto el carácter público del proceso (art. 82, párr. 2 de la Constitución japonesa), como el derecho de defensa. Por otra parte, el principio de inmediación exige que el tribunal haya percibido por sí mismo la producción de la prueba. Es por eso que en nuestro proceso, la exigencia de forma escrita de los actos procesales (art. 161, párr. 1 del CPC) se considera secundaria, sólo para organizar las alegaciones controvertidas de ambas partes. Además en la regla propuesta, no se plantea ampliar sin límite la utilización del sistema de videoconferencia en el interrogatorio de testigos, sustituyéndolo totalmente por la lectura de las actas que recogen sus declaraciones.

Estos principios vinculan al sistema actual de libre valoración de la prueba. El juez debe apreciar las percepciones durante el juicio según las reglas del criterio racional, es decir, según las reglas de la lógica, y dentro de ellas, el principio de no contradicción, así como según los principios generales de la experiencia.

III. Consulta de los expedientes del caso por los terceros

El art. 91, párr. 1 del CPC permite a los terceros consultar los expedientes del caso con base en el espíritu del principio de publicidad del proceso.

Según la regla propuesta de digitalización del proceso civil, las partes y sus abogados pueden visualizar, descargar e imprimir los expedientes, sin ninguna restricción desde sus computadoras. Por otra parte, en cuanto a los terceros, se propone la exigencia de solicitar a los funcionarios del tribunal la visualización y la fotocopia de documentos desde las computadoras del tribunal. Estas diferencias de tratamiento entre las partes y los terceros se pueden justificar, por el requisito establecido de aclarar la existencia de interés, para que los terceros puedan consultar los documentos no publicados e incluso imprimirlos aunque sean publicados (art. 91, párrs 2 y 3 del CPC).

Con respecto a la publicación en línea de los expedientes del caso, es necesario encontrar un equilibrio entre privacidad y acceso. Aunque es necesario que se atienda al principio de publicidad del proceso, se debe prestar especial atención a las formas de archivar y publicar las informaciones de acceso restringido como secretos comerciales, intimidad o datos personales de las víctimas de violencia doméstica.

This work was supported by *JSPS KAKENHI* Grant Number JP 18K01224.

Ludwigs / Muriel Ciceri / Velling (eds.), Digitalization as a challenge for justice and administration, Abhandlungen zum Öffentlichen Recht 1, Würzburg, 2023, pp. 111-120.
DOI: 10.25972/978-3-95826-201-0-111

Taking Notice and Service of Process Digital

Robin J. Effron

A. Introduction

In the United States, notice and opportunity to be heard is a cornerstone of due process – the constellation of rights guaranteed by the Fifth and Fourteenth amendments to the U.S. Constitution. Lawsuits typically end in binding judgments enforceable in all U.S. jurisdictions. In order to litigate, adverse parties must know about the existence of pending litigation. Where are they being sued? For what? And what remedy is demanded? Awareness of the lawsuit is a cornerstone of due process. In the worst-case scenario, a court might enter a default judgment against an absent party in which it is now responsible for the judgment, regardless of the merits of the underlying claims. Even in the absence of default judgment, adverse parties need adequate time and key information to begin mounting a defense.

Given that notice and service of process plays such a vital function, one would expect American jurisdictions to be at the forefront of developing and deploying cutting edge technology for finding and serving parties to lawsuits, as well as other parties entitled to notice in litigation, such as absent class members in certain types of class action lawsuits. Indeed, many jurisdictions and private entities have developed sophisticated technologies and platforms that facilitate the conduct of litigation once it is underway. But notice and service of process itself remains trapped in a mostly pre-digital space. Moving forward requires an historical and doctrinal understanding of why notice practices remain so stubbornly analog as well as an attentiveness toward the needs of all litigants so that digitization efforts make service of process a healthy addition to our system of notice rather than a wholesale replacement.

B. The Origins of Lagging Digitization

The constitutional boundaries of acceptable notice practices are governed by a 1950 Supreme Court decision, *Mullane v. Central Hanover Bank & Trust Co.*[1] There the Court announced that "notice must be reasonably calculated under the circumstances to apprise interested parties of the pendency of the action and afford them an opportunity to present their objections." At first glance, this standard appears to be both flexible and adaptable to changing circumstances in the law, as well as innovations in communication practices and technology which comprise the social and economic background against which modern litigation occurs. But since the mid-twentieth century decision, the United States' constitutional test of notice has not sufficiently adapted to broader social and societal changes to the circumstances in which modern litigation proceeds.

In its time, *Mullane* signaled procedural innovation and a liberalization of the methods of notice. *Mullane* was an equitable action for accounting of a trust fund, the outcome of which would produce a binding judgment affecting the rights of many trust beneficiaries. The Supreme Court held that notice could be given to beneficiaries by delivering notices to known beneficiaries via first class mail accompanied by publication of the notice in a periodical for successive weeks. In so doing, the Court acknowledged the utility of first-class mail (as compared with formal service of process or notice), and also affirmed that the suit could proceed without expensive and likely impossible efforts to identify, locate, and notify unknown beneficiaries. The "reasonable under the circumstances" language would presumably allow courts in the coming decades to evaluate rules and practices of notice and service of process. Yet, despite *Mullane's* ostensibly flexible doctrine, courts and lawmakers have been slow to adapt to the rapid changes in communication and litigation that have marked the seven decades since *Mullane* was decided.

Law practice and the business of adjudication look quite different than they did in the mid twentieth century. Lawyers research, draft, and exchange documents electronically. Parties communicate electronically with each other and with courts, many of which have developed electronic document management systems. Drafting, exchanging, and even consuming documents electronically is (usually) cheaper and more efficient than in person transmission of physical documents. This is why many court systems offer and even sometimes *require* e-filing. But notice and service of process are left behind. Until the proverbial lawsuit ball is rolling, parties are locked out of systems of electronic transmission.

---

[1]   Mullane v. Central Hanover Bank & Trust Co., 339 U.S. 306 (1950).

In earlier work I have hypothesized why this is so. The *Mullane* framework encourages judges make factually specific decisions about the adequacy of notice against a background of older methods. This allows them to consider the individual issues, costs, and logistics of particular notice practices in a given case. But context-specific analyses limited to the facts of notice in a given case often exclude attention to the broader changes to the societal circumstances and background within which litigation takes place.

Judges and lawmakers are beholden to certain "invisible circumstances" of notice that stymie the expansion of acceptable and encouraged service to include digitized methods.[2] These are a set of shared assumptions about what "real" or "good notice" is, namely it involves physical documents transmitted by and to human beings. Digitization is not a solution for all litigants and litigation. When jurisdictions begin to offer and promote digitized notice and service of process it must not be done in a way that disadvantages vulnerable populations. But the status quo, which still privileges older, analog methods of transmission, fails to serve many litigants.[3] Courts need to understand how the invisible circumstances of notice have created barriers to e-notice reform, not only to ensure that the actual notice given is more effective, but also to bring notice procedure into the 21st century.

C. Moving Beyond the Primacy of Paper and the Dominance of Service by and on Natural Persons

In the Anglo-American legal tradition, service of process serves two distinct purposes. The term "process" refers to any judicial notice by which a court obtains jurisdiction over a person or property. In a lawsuit, process is most commonly the "summons," which along with the complaint informs adverse parties of the pendency of an action and the claims asserted against it. These, then, are the two functions of process: the state's assertion of power and the provision of notice. As such, the tangible quality of a paper document has special significance in American jurisdictions. The in-hand, personal service of process on a defendant replaced a much older practice of physically arresting and detaining a defendant while awaiting a civil trial.[4] So the transmission of a tangible document still carries with it the significance of the state exercising adjudicative power over the party. Thus, service of process by intangible means ("e-service") requires a

---

[2] *Effron*, N. C. L. Rev. 2021, 1527.
[3] *Gottshall*, Arkansas Law Review 2018, 813; *Budzinski*, U. Colo. L. Rev. 2019, 167.
[4] Pennoyer v. Neff, 95 U.S. 714 (1878).

conceptual leap. Electronic transmission lacks the tangible and territorial quality of in-hand service, or even service of a summons using the postal service.

When *Pennoyer* and *Mullane* were decided, physical transmissible documents were the gold standard of notice, with other forms of notice such as notice by publication and notice by posting on property were considered second-best alternatives. Publication notice in particular has long been treated by courts and lawmakers as sub-optimal, a last resort method of notifying a defendant or large group of absent parties of pending litigation. This skepticism helped to ground assumptions about tangible paper-based notice, that paper forms of process documents are ideal, and any alternative form should hew as closely as possible to paper summons (or other forms of legal process).

For many persons and entities, paper is no longer the dominant or even default mode of written communication, but courts and lawmakers have been slow to adapt to these realities. Email, secure forms of electronic document transmission, and even text messages and social media are, in many places, ubiquitous and an easy means of reaching people. While paper is still a necessary and important means of communication for many Americans, there is no reason to categorically privilege its use over electronic means, especially to the point where any use of electronic means of service is considered exceptional and requiring of extra permission or extraordinary circumstances.

Just as tangible documents have been the default form of process, transmission by and on natural persons has been the default and preferred form of service. In-hand personal service on the adverse party has the supposed advantages of ensuring that the litigant actually received service of process, and thus courts assumed that service using persons instead of systems was more reliable and even ultimately cost effective. Even substituted service on another natural person, usually an appointed agent of a person or business, or a person of "suitable age and discretion"[5] meant that two humans, the server and the recipient, could verify delivery and receipt via affidavit or other means of affirmation.

Service using systems instead of persons requires verification to confirm that process has been delivered to and received by the correct parties. Nevertheless, jurisdictions err in assuming that service by systems, especially electronic systems, are inherently less trustworthy. Just as jurisdictions have developed protocols for ensuring that service by postal service is not complete until the adverse party has formally acknowledged receipt, so can they develop comparable electronic systems for acknowledgement and verification. As this Chapter will elaborate, most jurisdictions already have such systems in place for the transmission and receipt of documents filed in an ongoing lawsuit.

---

[5]   Federal Rules of Civil Procedure (Fed. R. Civ. P.), Rule 4 (e) (2) (B).

More importantly, the casual assumptions about the reliability of natural persons have resulted in a surprising level of indifference to problems with service of process. The problems affect plaintiffs and defendants alike. For defendants, personal service is not a guarantee of receipt. The phenomenon of "sewer service" in which process servers falsely claim to have served process is alive and well, and its victims are usually Americans from marginalized communities living in economically disadvantaged neighborhoods.[6] Some members of immigrant communities are wary of interacting with law enforcement officers or persons who appear to be deputized by governments to transmit legal papers. For plaintiffs, the use of natural persons is also suboptimal. Aside from the high expense of paying a process server (or the sophistication needed to attain government assistance in process serving), plaintiffs must contend with defendants who attempt to evade service by absenting themselves from the jurisdiction. States have long recognized these problems, thus the history of methods of substituted service and the ability to use first-class mail for service or waiver of formal service. Yet somehow, the paradigm of in hand service by and on natural persons persists and stymies efforts to harness technology for newer electronic alternatives.

Some jurisdictions purport to be at the vanguard of modernizing the tools of service of process, but they still are remarkably conservative in their approach. For example, the Texas state legislature amended its procedural rules in 2019 to explicitly permit service of process "via social media, email, or other technology".[7] This made Texas among the first states to codify a pattern of *ad hoc* decisions by American courts to allow certain forms of e-service. Most of these decisions came from statutes or rules that permitted e-service in "exceptional circumstances". The Texas rule attracted some attention for being among the first to explicitly name email and social media as distinct methods for service of process. But in reality, the Texas rule did not do much to enable or encourage parties to use and explore e-service beyond existing practices. Parties must still demonstrate by motion that in-hand personal service and service by mail has failed. And to the extent that one of the benefits of e-service is that it is inexpensive, requiring parties to make a motion before using any e-service method means that parties cannot capture the benefits of avoiding the high costs of in-hand service.

E-service should be on par with the existing alternative of first-class mail. E-service is not without risks and difficulties, but that is also true of using first-class mail. In the United States, all jurisdictions have procedures by which parties can transmit process by mail instead of by in-hand personal service. Some jurisdictions, such as the federal court system, use a "waiver" system in which parties use

---

[6]   *Gottshall*, Arkansas Law Review 2018, 813 (816-818).
[7]   Texas Rules of Civil Procedures (Tex. R. Civ. P.), Rule 106 (b) (2) (rule adopted in 2020).

the mail to request that the adverse party waive formal service of process. For many persons and entities, a failure or refusal to waive formal service of process means that the serving party can demand that the adverse party bear the costs of formal service.[8] Other jurisdictions, such as Texas, directly authorize service of process by first-class mail. In all systems, although the details and nomenclature differ, the rules amount to the same type of procedure. The serving party uses mail to transmit the summons, complaint, and other relevant documents to the adverse party. The adverse party is generally required to respond. But service of process is not considered complete until the adverse party has acknowledged receipt of the service (or documents accompanying a waiver request). The challenge for the future is to translate current modalities of using public and private postal service transmission into electronic systems that are cost-effective, reliable, and accessible to most persons and litigants.

D. Choice of Digital Modalities or Platforms

There are a number of ways in which court systems can harness newer technologies to expand on the possibilities for service of process and move to a digitized system, but despite the ubiquity of the internet and electronic media, the use of electronic ("intangible") notice is still treated as suspect by the courts. Overcoming the hesitancy to endorse e-notice is the first step, and as this Chapter has shown, this requires lawmakers to embrace the distinct benefits of e-notice, but also engaging in an honest assessment of the shortcomings of traditional in-person and mail or waiver notice.

The most straightforward way to enable e-service is for lawmakers to amend the statutes and rules governing service of process to allow for electronic transmission. The Texas approach is still contingent on a showing that other methods of service, including service by mail, are unavailable or have failed. A wholesale adoption of electronic service as a method on par with other service methods would be a step further.

This method has some advantages. First, it would mirror traditional service in that it would be conducted by the parties, thus allowing both courts and litigants to adapt new technologies to existing systems. Aside from formal recognition of the acceptability of electronic methods, this path would not require courts, court systems, or legislatures to pass new rules and laws or to create new administrative infrastructure. This method is also cost effective in that parties can trans-

---

[8]   Fed. R. Civ. P. Rule 4 (d).

mit multiple copies of lengthy documents to several email, text, or social media addresses at very little additional cost.

There are, however, some disadvantages to the approach of simply adding e-service as an acceptable method. Using direct communication to a party's email, cellular phone number, or social media profile is the least secure method of transmission. Parties may be understandably hesitant to transmit documents with sensitive information to and from unconfirmed and unsecured accounts. An email address or phone number may be long discarded, unused, or unchecked by the intended recipient. And the possibility for typographical errors to misdirect communications are heightened when entering only a string of numbers, letters, or relying on databases that might also have data entry errors.

Given the potential pitfalls, jurisdictions giving serious consideration to enabling parties to serve process electronically on par with postal mail should enact rules aimed at ameliorating these risks. Right now, states like Texas have it exactly backwards – by viewing e-service as less trustworthy, Texas has put it in the category of exceptional service. While this makes e-service less accessible, it does little to address the problems behind the intuitions of riskiness. Instead, rules for e-service should include guardrails for efficiency and reliability. For example, a rule might state that e-service should be made on any and all known email, phone, or social media accounts belonging to a party, and require the serving party to identify the latest known active account held by the adverse party. The rule might specify that service be made using a secure and encrypted email service in which the receiving party must log into a separate system and server in order to view the message and download attachments. Finally, the rules might specify a uniform system of response and acknowledgement by the receiving party. Although these requirements raise the cost of e-service such that it is not a completely seamless alternative to traditional service, the parties would still retain many of the cost and efficiency benefits of using electronic means. The purpose of e-service is not to eliminate cost altogether, but to offer secure and reliable lower cost digital alternatives alongside personal service and mail service.

The "allow electronic delivery just like mail" approach is simple because it extends a known system (service or waiver by mail) to a new format. But the digitalization of judicial administration should be more than just making the analog digital. Rulemakers should explore how electronic formats can create new methods of service altogether. One such possibility would be for the state to provide an electronic portal or platform through which parties can transmit and receive service of process.

Most states already have e-filing systems which typically requires parties to have counsel with access to such filing system. For example, New York state uses the NYSCEF system to allow litigants with access to NYSCEF to file court documents electronically.[9] Filing documents to be served during a lawsuit, however, is distinct from service of process, making New York one of many American jurisdictions that have constructed e-*filing* systems, but not e-*notice* systems. New York is an example of a court system's hesitancy to adapt to a fully digitized system. Such a system would not be mandatory given the importance of protecting parties whose access to digital systems is still limited or burdensomely costly. It would, however, enable digitized service of process via a platform accessible to all litigants, regardless of whether their attorney has access to an e-filing system.

An e-notice system could be an independent portal system or could be built out as an extension of existing e-filing systems. The most important feature would be that process itself (the summons, complaint, and any other relevant or required documents) would not be transmitted directly by electronic means to the recipient. Instead, they would be stored on a secure server and available for download. The recipient would receive a message from the state system via email, text, social media, or other electronic means, notifying them of service of process in a legal proceeding. Similar to service by mail, service would not be complete until the recipient formally acknowledged receipt through the system itself, or by opting for more traditional service (hard copies by mail or in person service). Just as with existing methods of service, rules drafters should be attentive to classes of persons needing special protection such as minors and incompetent persons. Moreover, rules drafters might create similar incentives for litigants to accept service of process in which the receiving party must pay for traditional service if electronic service is declined.

Private companies might also develop and offer such portal systems. This would be a natural extension of the services that registered agents for service of process offer,[10] or of the claims administration systems that third-party class actions administration firms offer.[11] It would be possible for a number of such companies to offer portal-based e-notice systems within a given jurisdiction, giving litigants choices for which service to use. A system of for-profit administrators, however, would make it harder to integrate e-service with existing e-filing platforms. Moreover, a well-designed public system might be seen as a more trustworthy vehicle for the transmission of e-service. Experience with the private notice and claims administration systems in class action practice have shown that class members are often suspicious of communications from private claims

---

[9]   See *N.Y. State Unified Court System*, Authorized for E-Filing, available at https://iapps.courts.state.ny.us/nyscef/AuthorizeCaseType (accessed on 27 October 2022), choose the relevant court from drop-down menu and press "select".

[10] *Jennings*, JCL 46 (2020), 76 (89-90).

[11] *Federal Trade Commission*, Consumers and Class Actions: A Retrospective Analysis of Settlement Campaigns, 2019, p. 6 et seqq.

administrators and will not engage in those systems for fear of spam or even fraud.[12]

E. Technology and the New "Notice By Publication"

At the far frontiers of digitalization of notice, one moves beyond service of process in ordinary lawsuits and even beyond e-notice in mass litigation to the prospect of using modern tools of media, targeting advertising, and social media algorithms to rethink the very old concept of notice by publication. Notice by publication has been an acceptable means of notice in American jurisprudence since the founding of the Republic, but it has always been considered a method of last resort. Although large companies and law firms have always had employees comb the legal notices for items relevant to their businesses and clients, notice by publication was never realistically meant to reach a high number of average litigants. Media consumed over the Internet might change that balance. Although that future is still in the distance, it is worth considering the following anecdote to illustrate how viral social media posts and algorithmic processing might accelerate and sharpen the uses of notice by publication.

In 2017, a major credit rating agency, Equifax, announced that it had been the target of one of the largest data breaches of the past decade. Several lawsuits by public officials and a consumer class action lawsuit ensued. When the parties reached a settlement in the Equifax consumer class action litigation in 2019, major news outlets reported the settlement to the public and urged them to claim their settlement proceeds. One reporter implored readers that it was a "moral obligation" to file a claim and get the proposed $100 settlement from Equifax.[13] Popular New York Congresswoman Alexandria Ocasio-Cortez then posted on her Twitter account to encourage consumers to cash in on their available proceeds and included a link to the settlement administrator.

The news items and a congresswoman's tweet brought so much attention to the settlement that consumers flocked to the site to file claims. A rather unofficial "notice by publication" had achieved what ordinary class action notice practices had been failing at for years—a high claims participation rate in the class action settlement. In fact, so many consumers filed claims that the portion of the settlement allocated to consumer claims made it impossible for the fund to actually

---

[12] *Rose*, UCLR 2021, 487 (489-453).
[13] *Wolff*, You Have a Moral Obligation To Claim Your $125 from Equifax, 2019, available at https://slate.com/technology/2019/07/equifax-settlement-money-how-to-claim.html (accessed on 27. October 2022).

pay all valid claimants the promised $100 per claim. This suggests that the parties in the case agreed to the settlement because they had expected and counted on poor participation from class members, and that better notice practices could lead to fairer class action settlements with more equitable distributions of those settlements to aggrieved parties.

Viral tweets are hard to predict, and savvy journalists sometimes strike gold, but more often are competing in a fierce market for attention. Thus, a true revolution in notice by publication might be in the works but it is still not a realistic present-day option. Nonetheless, rules drafters, claims administrators, and those designing systems of notice for ordinary litigation might take note about the new and dynamic ways in which Americans interact with technology and information and how this can and should continue to shape the future of notice and service of process.

Ludwigs / Muriel Ciceri / Velling (eds.), Digitalization as a challenge for justice and administration, Abhandlungen zum Öffentlichen Recht 1, Würzburg, 2023, pp. 121-140.
DOI: 10.25972/978-3-95826-201-0-121

Matrimonio: una aproximación al consentimiento electrónico ante la autoridad administrativa registral

Arán García Sánchez

A. Introducción

Cuando nos referimos al consentimiento matrimonial entre ausentes pensamos en el matrimonio por mandato, dicho consentimiento se expresa, ante la autoridad administrativa registral (Registro Civil de las Personas), lo que sin duda nos hace reflexionar entre su regulación internacional y en la multijurisdiccionalidad del derecho de familia mexicano, en contraste con el orden de la realidad jurídica y tecnología de México.

En el ámbito internacional, la Declaración Universal de los Derechos Humanos (en adelante, la Declaración) considera el derecho al matrimonio en su art. 16. En cuanto al consentimiento matrimonial es regulado por la Convención sobre el consentimiento para el matrimonio, la edad mínima para contraer matrimonio y el registro de los matrimonios (en adelante, la Convención).

Por ello es importante reflexionar sobre la realidad tecnológica mundial, al momento de la entrada en vigor de la Declaración y la Convención, con el contexto tecnológico y de salud que vivimos actualmente.

El sistema jurídico matrimonial mexicano es regulado por 32 legislaciones locales y una de orden federal. En ellas se regula al matrimonio por medio de los requisitos de forma y fondo. En estos últimos señala el requisito de presencialidad de los pretensos ante la autoridad administrativa registral y, en caso de no ser posible, puede ser subsanada con un mandato especial para contraer matrimonio. Lo anterior también es motivo de reflexión, en cuanto a conectividad, los servicios de videoconferencias y el sistema de firmas electrónicas disponibles en México.

Otra situación a destacar es la disminución de la nupcialidad en México, en los últimos 20 años, los factores que incidieron en dicha disminución son: el concubinato, el divorcio, la minoría de edad, el matrimonio utópico, los matrimonios religiosos y por supuesto, el matrimonio entre ausentes.

Lo anterior conduce al análisis de la derrotabilidad del matrimonio entre ausentes, con base en el orden de la realidad jurídica y tecnológica en México, a partir de los tres puntos conclusivos que plantea *Stern* en su artículo "Matrimonios por poder en México".[1]

El principal objetivo en el presente trabajo es analizar la derrotabilidad de la presencialidad, es decir, del matrimonio por poder, al momento de celebrar el matrimonio ante autoridad administrativa registral, en caso de ausencia de los pretensos. En dicho cometido, se analiza el orden de la realidad jurídica y tecnológica frente al sistema jurídico mexicano. Finalmente, se propone la celebración de matrimonios entre ausentes a través de un consentimiento electrónico con plena validez por medio de un sistema de videoconferencia, de modo que se evite la presencialidad de los pretensos y se proponga a la firma electrónica como un medio fiable y eficaz para autenticar la voluntad de estos.

B. El consentimiento matrimonial

I. El consentimiento matrimonial en el contexto internacional

El matrimonio es un Derecho Humano y considerado como una de las formas de fundar una familia y de que los cónyuges puedan disfrutar de la igualdad de derechos a partir de su celebración y posterior a su disolución.[2] Lo anterior es posible a partir de lo señalado por el art. 1 de la Convención al señalar en su primer párrafo:

> No podrá contraerse legalmente matrimonio sin el pleno y libre consentimiento de ambos contrayentes, expresado por éstos en persona, después de la debida publicidad, ante la autoridad competente para formalizar el matrimonio y testigos, de acuerdo con la ley.[3]

---

[1] *Stern*, Revista de la Escuela Nacional de Jurisprudencia, tomo VII, núm. 31 (1946), 213.

[2] *Declaración Universal de los Derechos Humanos*, art. 16, consultado en https://www.un.org/es/about-us/universal-declaration-of-human-rights. La última recuperación de todas las direcciones web mencionadas en este capítulo es el 27 de octubre 2022.

[3] *Convención sobre el consentimiento para el matrimonio para el matrimonio, la edad mínima para contraer matrimonio y registro de los matrimonios*, art. 1, disponible en https://www.ohchr.org/sp/professionalinterest/pages/minimumageformarriage.aspx.

Ahora, es importante reflexionar sobre el orden de la realidad tecnológica y la presencialidad de los contrayentes, al momento de la entrada en vigor de la Convención de 9 de diciembre de 1964, de conformidad con el art. 6 de la misma, ya que dichas condiciones son diferentes a nivel global y nacional.

II. El consentimiento matrimonial en México

En México, el matrimonio y el consentimiento matrimonial entre ausentes son regulados por las legislaciones locales (32), ya sea en su codificación civil (18) o familiar (14), más la codificación civil federal, conformando una multijurisdiccionalidad en materia de matrimonio y por consecuencia de consentimiento matrimonial entre ausentes.

Además, existe una legislación civil federal que también regula al matrimonio. Dicha legislación omite una concepción del matrimonio (situación que también acontece en algunas legislaciones locales, otra más cuenta con una concepción matrimonial), pero su art. 146 señala que debe celebrarse ante los funcionarios y las formalidades que exige la ley.[4]

Los funcionarios ante quien se celebrase el matrimonio son los jueces o encargados del Registro Civil, que es la autoridad administrativa reconocida por el art. 130 de Constitución Política de los Estados Unidos Mexicanos.[5]

En cuanto a las formalidades, en ese sentido se debe visualizar al matrimonio como un acto jurídico, al ser definido como:

> Acto voluntario y solemne celebrado conforme a las disposiciones de la ley ante el representante del Estado (Autoridad administrativa registral, es decir, Registro Civil de las Personas, representado por el Juez del Registro Civil, al momento de la celebración del matrimonio), es decir, constituye el ámbito de los requerimientos imprescindible para su realización legal.[6]

---

[4] *Código Civil Federal*, art. 146: "El matrimonio debe celebrarse ante los funcionarios que establece la ley y con las formalidades que ella exige", *Cámara de Diputados del H. Congreso de la Unión*, 2022, disponible en http://www.diputados.gob.mx/LeyesBiblio/pdf/2_110121.pdf.

[5] *Constitución Política de los Estados Unidos Mexicanos*, art. 130, párrafo 7: "Los actos del estado civil de las personas son de la exclusiva competencia de las autoridades administrativas en los términos que establezcan las leyes, y tendrán la fuerza y validez que las mismas les atribuyan". *Cámara de Diputados del H. Congreso de la Unión*, 2022, disponible en: https://www.diputados.gob.mx/LeyesBiblio/pdf/CPEUM.pdf.

[6] *Buenrostro/Baqueiro*, Derecho Familiar, 2019, pp. 68, 70.

Los requerimientos imprescindibles a que se refiere la cita anterior se dividen en requisitos de fondo y de forma. Para su estudio nos referiremos al Código Civil de la Ciudad de México, que es más explícito que la codificación civil federal.

1. Requisitos de fondo

Los de fondo son tres: la mayoría de edad de los pretensos, su libre consentimiento y la ausencia de impedimentos.[7]

Respecto del primero es importante señalar que, en México, está prohibido el matrimonio entre personas menores de 18 años, derivado de la promulgación de la Ley General de los Derechos de las Niñas, Niños y Adolescentes (2014) y en especial de su art. 45.[8]

En cuanto al consentimiento matrimonial es la "manifestación de la voluntad de dos personas que han decidido casarse para formar una familia".[9] Esta debe ser externada de forma libre, es decir, sin ningún vicio del consentimiento como la violencia y el error y manifestarse de forma expresa y verbal de forma personal o por medio de mandatario especial, ya que el matrimonio en México no es un acto jurídico personalísimo.

Por último, los impedimentos para contraer matrimonio son mencionados en los art. 156, 157 y 159 del Código Civil de la Ciudad de México.

2. Requisitos de forma

Los requisitos de forma son de dos tipos, previos a la celebración y propios de la celebración. En el primero de ellos se requiere presentar una solicitud ante el Juez del Registro Civil, que contenga los atributos de la personalidad de los pretendientes, la manifestación de no tener impedimento para celebrar el matrimonio, la manifestación de que es su voluntad, firma y huella digital de los pretendientes, confirmar y verificar su voluntad de contraer matrimonio ante el Juez del Registro Civil.[10] De lo antes mencionado, cabe destacar, con relación al presente trabajo de investigación, que la solicitud debe contener una firma grafológica y hue-

---

[7] *Buenrostro/Baqueiro* (nota al pie 6), p. 70.
[8] *Gobierno de México*, Decreto por el que se expide la Ley General de los Derechos de Niñas, Niños y Adolescentes, entró en vigor en 2014, disponible en http://www.dof.gob.mx/nota_detalle.php?codigo=5374143&fecha=04/12/2014.
[9] *Buenrostro/Baqueiro* (nota al pie 6), p. 73.
[10] *Código Civil para el Distrito Federal*, art. 98, disponible en: http://www.aldf.gob.mx/archivo-0bd3121a0334f53844d2fe92b52fb5a2.pdf.

lla digital, cómo si en la actualidad no tuviéramos firmas electrónicas avanzadas, que permiten acreditar la identidad y la aceptación de un documento.

El art. 98, señala que deben acompañar a la solicitud el acta de nacimiento certificada de los pretendientes, la constancia de que los pretendientes otorgaron de manera indubitable su consentimiento, el documento que acredite su identidad, la declaración de los pretendientes de no haber sido sentenciados por violencia familiar y las capitulaciones. En caso de que alguno de los pretendientes sea viudo debe acompañarse el acta de defunción. Asimismo, en caso de que alguno de los pretendientes haya concluido el proceso para la concordancia sexo-genérica.[11] Ahora bien, se propone valorar un sistema que permita subir todos los requisitos solicitados por los artículos en comento, mudando a un Registro Civil cero papel y socialmente responsable. Un ejemplo es lo que sucede en Costa Rica, dónde los notarios cuentan con Sistema de inscripción de matrimonio civil digital.[12] Cabe mencionar que la propuesta es para que los ciudadanos lo realicen. En México, los notarios no están facultados para celebrar matrimonios, pero en algunos Estados tienen la facultad de divorciar.

Una vez cumplidos los requisitos previos a la celebración del matrimonio, el encargado de la autoridad administrativa registral civil (Juez del Registro Civil) señalará día y hora, en un término de ocho días para la celebración del matrimonio, en la que deberán estar presentes, ante él, los pretendientes o sus apoderados especiales. Acto continuo dará lectura en voz alta al acta respectiva y les hará saber sus derechos y obligaciones matrimoniales y así preguntarles a los pretendientes si es su voluntad la de unirse en matrimonio, en caso de estar conformes los declarará unidos en matrimonio en nombre de la ley y la sociedad.[13]

Como podemos deducir de los requisitos de forma, en sus dos momentos la presencialidad de los pretendientes es de suma importancia. En caso de no ser posible y derivado de que el matrimonio no es un acto personalísimo, la presencialidad puede ser subsanada por mandatarios especiales para contraer matrimonio.

Es necesario reflexionar respecto al orden de la realidad mexicana en este momento, con relación a la conectividad, el servicio de videoconferencia y el sistema de firma electrónica. Lo anterior permitirá conectar, a través de internet y de una video conferencia, a todos los intervinientes en tiempo real, sin necesidad de estar

---

[11] *Código Civil para el Distrito Federal*, art. 98.

[12] *Centro de información jurídica en línea*, Matrimonio digital, Informe de investigación, disponible en: https://cijulenlinea.ucr.ac.cr/portal/descargar.php?q=MzQzNQ==.

[13] *Código Civil para el Distrito Federal*, art. 100-102, disponible en https://www.congresocdmx.gob.mx/media/documentos/ad63a5bd2aef33e50ef1ed68d82450cf368578c0.pdf.

presentes físicamente y los consortes firmen el acta de matrimonio con una firma electrónica.

C. La nupcialidad en México

En América Latina, los países con mayor número de población son: Brasil 211,049,519, México 127,575,529 y Argentina 44,938,712 habitantes.[14] En consecuencia, la nupcialidad en la región va de la mano con este indicador, que hasta el 2019 era Brasil con 1,024,676, México con 504,923 y Argentina con 123,397.[15] También es importante señalar que en cuanto a la celebración de matrimonios por cada 1,000 habitantes en la región México ocupa la séptima posición con cuatro matrimonios por cada 1,000 habitantes.[16]

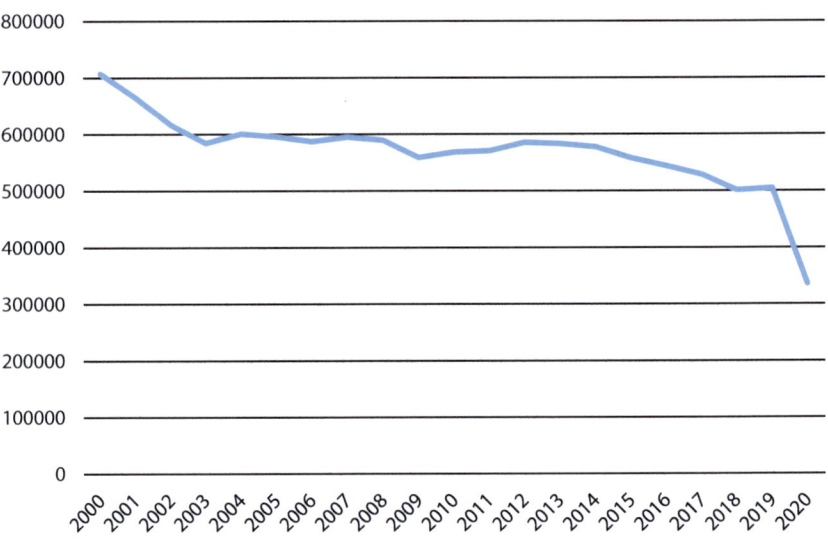

Figura 1: Gráfica de matrimonios en México 2000-2020. Fuente: Nupcialidad, INEGI[17]

---

[14] *Banco Mundial*, Población total América Latina y el Caribe, 2022, disponible en: https://datos.bancomundial.org/indicador/SP.POP.TOTL?locations=ZJ.
[15] *Statista*, El matrimonio en América Latina, 2021, disponible en; https://es.statista.com/.
[16] *Statista* (nota al pie 15), p. 3.
[17] *INEGI* (nota al pie 18).

En México, en el periodo del año 2000 a 2020, se evidenció un decrecimiento en cuanto a la nupcialidad civil. Lo anterior se demuestra con los datos estadísticos generados por el Instituto Nacional de Estadística y Geografía (INEGI). En el año 2000 se celebraron 707,422 matrimonio civiles, con referencia a la cifra anterior. En 2020 se observa una disminución del 52.57 % ya que al cierre del año se presentaron 335,563 matrimonios[18].[19]

En el año 2020, derivado de la pandemia COVID-19 y del confinamiento decretado por el gobierno mexicano, se observa una disminución aún más drástica. En cuanto a la nupcialidad en México, consistente en un decrecimiento del 33.55 % con referencia al año anterior, ya que, en 2019, se celebraron 504,923 matrimonios y en 2020, 335,563.[20] El factor primordial de dicha disminución fue la presencialidad de los futuros cónyuges al momento de externar su conocimiento, ante la autoridad administrativa registral, es decir, el Registro Civil, requisito indispensable para la celebración del matrimonio.

Lo anterior nos lleva a deducir que existen dos supuestos de falta de presencialidad al momento de consentir. La primera es debido a que uno de los futuros cónyuges no se encuentre dentro del territorio nacional, la segunda es la imposibilidad de asistir ante la autoridad administrativa registral, derivado del aislamiento a consecuencia de caso fortuito o fuerza mayor, postergando con ello el consentimiento matrimonial.

D. Disminución del matrimonio

En el presente apartado analizaremos los factores que inciden en la disminución de la nupcialidad en México.

I. El concubinato

De acuerdo con la Encuesta Nacional de Ocupación y Empleo (ENOE), en México, la población de 15 años y más se encuentra unida de la manera siguiente: 57.6 % se encuentra en situación conyugal (incluye casado y unión libre), el

---

[18]   *Instituto Nacional de Estadística, Geografía e informática* (INEGI), Nupcialidad, 2020, disponible en: https://www.inegi.org.mx/temas/nupcialidad/.

[19]   De conformidad con la metodología empleada por el INEGI en México, las estadísticas de nupcialidad aquí resaltadas comprenden la contabilización de matrimonios y divorcios. Cf. https://www.inegi.org.mx/programas/nupcialidad/.

[20]   *INEGI* (nota al pie 18).

31.7 % está soltera y el 10.7 % ya estuvo en una situación conyugal anterior, es decir, se encuentran separada, divorciada o viuda. Es importante señalar que en el periodo del año 2008 a 2018 las personas de entre 15 a 29 años unidas disminuyó la proporción de las casadas, pasó de 59.7 a 42.8 % y en contraposición, las personas que declararon estar en unión libre pasaron de 40.3 a 57.2 %, en el mismo periodo[21]. Lo antes señalado, es una muestra de que la población mexicana se sigue uniendo para conformar familias, pero de la mano de instituciones jurídico-familiares que se adecuen al orden de la realidad social, como lo es el concubinato, dejando de lado al matrimonio.

Lo anterior nos lleva a determinar qué tipo de relaciones conforma la situación conyugal no casadas, ya que la encuesta las denomina unión libre.[22] En términos generales, dicha denominación es considerada como sinónimo de concubinato.[23] En consecuencia, el concubinato incide en la disminución de matrimonios, subsistiendo de forma colateral ante éste y cada vez con mayor certeza jurídica.

II. El divorcio en México

En la actualidad el matrimonio no garantiza estabilidad y permanencia, prueba de ello es que, en los últimos 20 años, la disolución del matrimonio a través del divorcio aumentó considerablemente en México tal y como se desprende de las estadísticas generadas por el INEGI.

En el año 2000 se realizaron 52,358 divorcios, diez años después se consumaron 86,042. Lo anterior permite demostrar un aumento del 64.33 % en dicho

---

[21]   *INEGI*, Comunicado de prensa número 104/19, 2019, p. 3, disponible en: https://www.inegi.org .mx/contenidos/saladeprensa/aproposito/2019/matrimonios2019_Nal.pdf.

[22]   "Al referirme a la unión libre abarcó las relaciones sexuales que existen entre varones y mujeres no comprometidos en una vida conyugal. Están como posibles las relaciones concubinarias y la habidas esporádicamente. Excluyo a las adulterinas por la especial ilicitud de ellas y el daño que causan a la vida conyugal." *Chávez Asencio*, La familia en el derecho, Derecho de familia y relaciones jurídicas familiares*, 2003, p. 210.

[23]   Los tribunales federales mexicanos reconocen distintas concepciones doctrinales al señalar: "En la doctrina el concubinato es denominado matrimonio contractual no solemne, matrimonio por comportamiento, matrimonio de hecho, matrimonio consensual: dicha relación suele revestir la apariencia del matrimonio pues los concubinos viven con frecuencia en la misma casa, tienen hijos y se presentan ante la sociedad como verdaderos cónyuges, siendo así que la única diferencia que se presenta entre el matrimonio y el concubinato es la inexistencia de un documento denominado acta de matrimonio." Pleno en Materia Civil del Tribunal Colegiado de Circuito del Primer Circuito, Décima Época, libro 9, tomo I, 29.08.2014, disponible en: https://sjf.scjn.gob. mx/SJFSem/Paginas/DetalleGeneralScroll.aspx?id=25185&Clase=DetalleTesisEjecutorias.

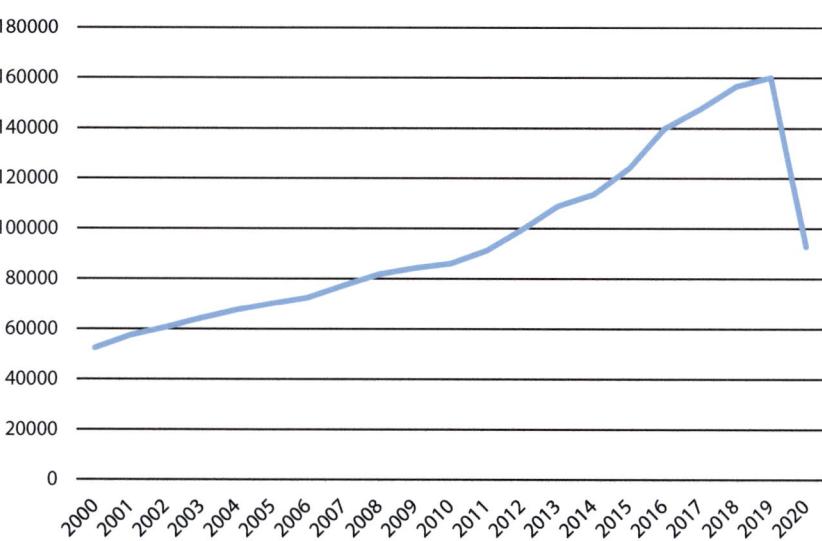

Figura 2: Gráfica de divorcios en México 2000-2020. Fuente: Nupcialidad, INEGI[24]

periodo. Realizando un análisis similar hasta el año 2018, el incremento es de casi el 200 % ya que en este año se llevaron a cabo 156,556 disoluciones matrimoniales,[25] equivalente al 199.01 %.

Por último, es necesario analizar el número de divorcios por cada 100 matrimonios en el mismo periodo, es decir, del año 2000 al 2018. En ese sentido, al iniciar el siglo, teníamos un 7.4 % de divorcios por cada 100 matrimonios y en el año 2018 la cifra se elevó hasta un 31.2 %.[26] Lo anterior demuestra un incremento del 321.62 % en los últimos años. Por lo tanto, el divorcio incide en la disminución de matrimonios posteriores a su celebración.

III. La minoría de edad

Al analizar la situación conyugal de las personas de 15 a 19 años en un periodo de diez años (2008-2018), se observa un descenso considerable en los tipos de unión: casados y unión libre. Los casados disminuyeron de un 36.6 a un 15.9 %,

---

[24]   *INEGI* (nota al pie 17).
[25]   *INEGI*. Estadística de Nupcialidad, 25.5.2020, disponible en: https://www.inegi.org.mx/temas/nupcialidad/default.html#Informacion_general.
[26]   *INEGI* (nota al pie 17).

en unión libre aumentaron de 63.4 a 84.1 %.[27] Cabe aclarar que la información vertida es anterior a la reforma de prohibición de matrimonio infantil en México.[28] Lo expuesto, permite deducir que antes de la reforma eran considerados los matrimonios celebrados entre menores en las estadísticas y al prohibir el matrimonio infantil impacta en la disminución estadística de matrimonios.

IV. La carencia económica y cultural[29]

La carencia económica tiene su origen en la falta de capacidad económica por parte de las parejas para sufragar los gastos económicos derivados de la celebración del matrimonio ante el Registro Civil.[30]

La segunda derivada de una falta de cultura de la legalidad matrimonial,[31] es decir, un escaso conocimiento de los derechos y obligaciones que emanan de la relación jurídica matrimonial. Esto es provocado por una falta de cultura jurídica *externa*, cuyo responsable es la población en general e *interna*, que les

---

[27] *INEGI* (nota al pie 18).

[28] El matrimonio infantil en México se encuentra prohibido a partir del día siguiente de la publicación del Decreto por el que se reforman y derogan diversas disposiciones del Código Civil Federal, en materia de prohibición del matrimonio infantil, publicado el 3 de junio de 2019 y entrando en vigor al día siguiente de su publicación. Las principales reformas sustanciales son: reforma del artículo 148 anteriormente señalaba: "Para contraer matrimonio el hombre necesita haber cumplido dieciséis años y la mujer catorce. A partir de la reforma señala: Para contraer matrimonio es necesario haber cumplido dieciocho años de edad." Otra reforma importante fue la derogación de los art. 149 al 155, en ellos se contemplaban la licencia (por parte de los padres, cuando los contrayentes no cumplieran con la edad legal, pero si con la pubertad legal) y la dispensa (por parte de las autoridades correspondientes, cuando los contrayentes no cumplan con la pubertad legal). *Gobierno de México*, Diario Oficial de la Federación, Decreto; se reforman y derogan diversas disposiciones del Código Civil Federal, en materia de prohibición del matrimonio infantil, 2019, disponible en: https://dof.gob.mx/nota_detalle.php?codigo=5561717&fecha=03/06/2019.

[29] Cfr. *Barros Álvarez*, El matrimonio en el mundo actual, 2001, p. 60.

[30] En la Ciudad de México, los costos para la celebración del matrimonio son de $1,367.00 pesos mexicanos. (en oficina del Registro Civil), $2,745.00 celebración de matrimonio (a domicilio), $8,398.00 celebración de matrimonio (fuera de la circunscripción) *Gobierno de la Ciudad de México/Secretaría de Administración y Finanzas*, Pagos en línea, 2022, disponible en: https://data.finanzas.cdmx.gob.mx/formato_lc/conceptos/registro_civil/grupo.

[31] En el presente supuesto, es necesario definir a la cultura de la legalidad: "… es un término que trata de explicar la importancia del derecho no sólo en la obediencia de la ley por temor a una sanción, como tradicionalmente se entendió, sino como una conformación cultural de la sociedad de que se trata." *Friedman*, en: Fix Fierro et al., (coords.) Los mexicanos y su constitución, Tercera encuesta nacional de cultura constitucional, Centenario de la Constitución de 1917, 2017, p. 30.

corresponde a los operadores jurídicos.[32] Un ejemplo del impulso a la cultura de la legalidad matrimonial es la Ciudad de México, ya que uno de los requisitos para contraer matrimonio ahí es la participación de los contrayentes en un curso prenupcial ante los jueces del Registro Civil, cuyo objetivo es dar a conocer los derechos y obligaciones de los cónyuges.

V. El matrimonio utópico

El matrimonio utópico es una perspectiva donde se considera al matrimonio como modelo único de situación conyugal y que la familia gira en torno a él. De lo anterior, podemos señalar algunas manifestaciones como la siguiente: "El matrimonio está en crisis. La crisis de la familia y el matrimonio es la manifestación más visible de la crisis en que se encuentra el hombre de nuestra época."[33]

Además, es la base para formular críticas respecto a otros modelos de convivencia. Esta visión del matrimonio provocó que parejas sin impedimentos, decidan no celebrarlo ya que lo consideran como una intromisión e imposición estatal en su vida de pareja. Considero que en la actualidad el matrimonio no es la única unión que permite conformar una familia. De acuerdo con un estudio realizado por el Instituto de Investigaciones Sociales de la UNAM existen once tipologías familiares en México y las agrupa en tres grupos: Familia tradicional representa el 50 % de los hogares, familia en transición representa el 42 % de los hogares y familias emergentes, con un porcentaje del 8 %.[34] Lo anterior, representa que el matrimonio no es la única forma de situación conyugal, y tampoco la única forma de conformar una familia.

VI. Los matrimonios religiosos

En México, de acuerdo con el censo más reciente del año 2020, cuenta con 126,014,024 habitantes. Del total de la población el 77.7 % se declara católico, el

---

[32] *Friedman* (nota al pie 31), p. 30.
[33] *Friedrich/Herr*, en: Chávez Asencio, La familia en el derecho: derecho de familia y relaciones jurídicas familiares, 2003, p. 209.
[34] *Instituto de Investigaciones Sociales*, En México existen once tipos de familia, señala investigación de la UNAM, 2017, disponible en: https://www.dgcs.unam.mx/boletin/bdboletin/2017_335.html.

11.2 % protestante o cristiano evangélico, 0.2 % de otra religión, 2.5 % se declara creyente sin definir una religión y 8.1 % sin religión.[35]

El matrimonio religioso no produce ningún efecto legal en México y sus efectos se equiparán a los del concubinato, siempre que cumpla con los dos supuestos señalados por la hipótesis normativa: el tiempo o la procreación de alguna hija(o).[36]

Además, puede ser una alternativa para los pretendientes, que tengan algún impedimento para contraer matrimonio civil. Un ejemplo de ello es la edad legal para contraer matrimonio (18 años). En la gráfica siguiente se realiza un comparativo entre la celebración de matrimonios civiles y religiosos en la población de 12 a 19 años,[37] demostrando cómo los matrimonios religiosos, antes de los 18 años, tienen un incremento a consecuencia de la prohibición de los matrimonios infantiles a través de la reforma del Código Civil de 2019. A partir de los 18 años el efecto es contrario: los matrimonios civiles incrementan y los religiosos disminuyen considerablemente.

A partir de los 20 años el efecto es diferente. El matrimonio civil disminuye relativamente en proporción a la edad de los contrayentes y el matrimonio religioso disminuye por debajo de los diez puntos porcentuales sin importar la edad de los contrayentes, como se observa en la siguiente gráfica.

---

[35] *INEGI*, Comunicado de prensa núm. 24/21 de 25 de enero de 2021, disponible en: https://www. inegi.org.mx/contenidos/saladeprensa/boletines/2021/EstSociodemo/ResultCenso2020_Nal. pdf.

[36] *Código Civil de la Ciudad de México*, art. 291 bis: Las concubinas y los concubinarios tienen derechos y obligaciones recíprocos, siempre que, sin impedimentos legales para contraer matrimonio, hayan vivido en común en forma constante y permanente por un período mínimo de dos años que precedan inmediatamente a la generación de derechos y obligaciones a los que alude este capítulo. No es necesario el transcurso del período mencionado cuando, reunidos los demás requisitos, tengan un hijo en común.

[37] *INEGI*, Censo de Población y Vivienda 2020, 2020, disponible en: https://www.inegi.org.mx/ programas/ccpv/2020/#Tabulados.

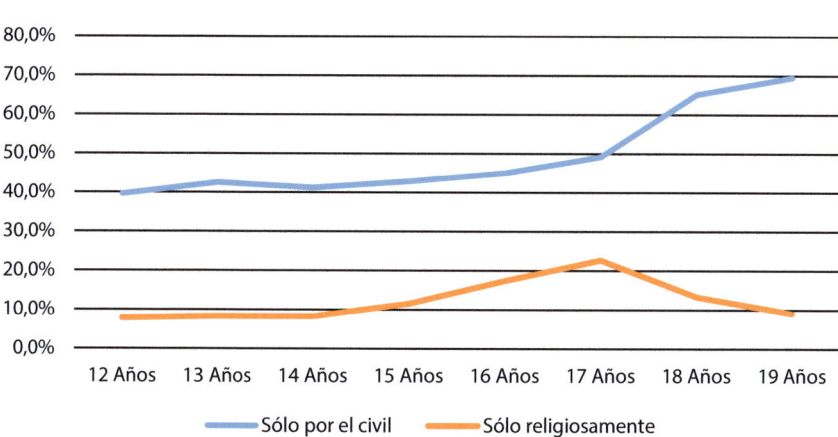

Figura 3: Gráfica de comparación entre matrimonios civiles y religiosos por edad. Fuente: Religión, INEGI[38]

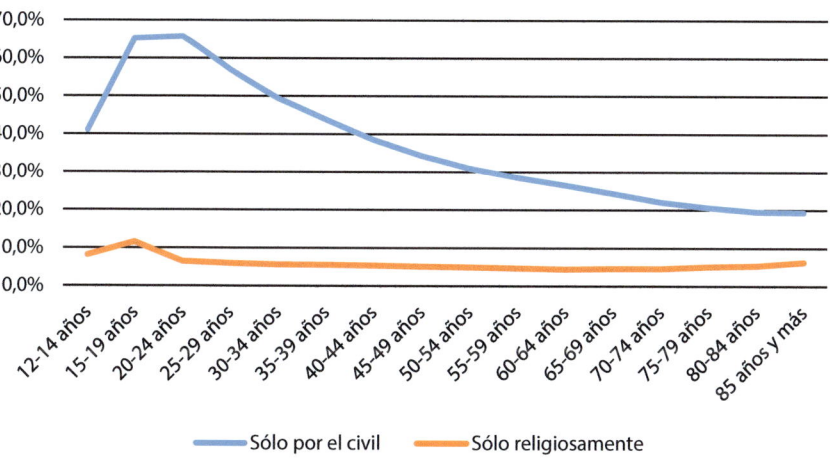

Figura 4: Gráfica de comparación entre matrimonios civiles y religiosos. Fuente: Religión, INEGI[39]

---

[38]   *INEGI*, Religión, 2020, tabulados del Cuestionario Básico. Información agregada disponible para el caso de situación conyugal, disponible en: https://www.inegi.org.mx/contenidos/programas/ccpv/2020/tabulados/cpv2020_b_eum_11_situacion_conyugal.xlsx.

[39]   *INEGI* (nota al pie 38).

VII. Los matrimonios entre ausentes

El origen y práctica del matrimonio entre ausentes se remonta a Roma, ya que su ordenamiento jurídico reconocía que cuando un varón estuviera ausente y quisiera contraer matrimonio, la única modalidad matrimonial posible, era el matrimonio por carta o por nuncio y surtiría sus efectos a partir de la entrada de la mujer a la casa de su futuro cónyuge.[40] Lo anterior permite remontarse a los orígenes del matrimonio por poder.[41]

En el sistema jurídico mexicano, el consentimiento matrimonial entre ausentes es regulado por la multi jurisdiccionalidad civil que es congruente con la legislación civil federal, que en este apartado será referencia y en su art. 44 señala:

> Cuando los interesados no puedan concurrir personalmente, podrán hacerse representar por un mandatario especial para el acto, cuyo nombramiento conste por lo menos en instrumento privado otorgado ante dos testigos. En los casos de matrimonio o de reconocimiento de hijos, se necesita poder otorgado en escritura pública o mandato extendido en escrito privado firmado por el otorgante y dos testigos y ratificadas las firmas ante Notario Público, Juez de lo Familiar, Menor o de Paz.[42]

La codificación civil federal de 1928 sigue vigente. En el año 2000 fue la fuente formal del Código Civil del Distrito Federal, hoy Ciudad de México, el cual en su art. 44 al igual que en la codificación federal regula el consentimiento matrimonial entre ausentes.

Dentro de la legislación federal encontramos otro artículo que abona en cuanto a la regulación del consentimiento matrimonial entre ausentes dentro del capítulo sobre actas de matrimonio, es el art. 102. En su primer párrafo señala:

> En el lugar, día y hora designados para la celebración del matrimonio deberán estar presentes, ante el Juez del Registro Civil, los pretendientes o su apoderado especial constituido en la forma establecida en el artículo 44.[43]

---

[40]   *Pumar-Santana*, Ius Canonicum, tomo 36, núm. 72 (1996), 595.
[41]   A dichos mandatos se les denominó matrimonios por poder y es definido como: Este término hace referencia a una de las formas que puede asumir el matrimonio entre ausentes, en el cual el consentimiento es prestado a través de un representante o mandatario. *Martínez*, Matrimonio por Poder, 2015, disponible en: https://diccionario.leyderecho.org/matrimonio-por-poder/.
[42]   Código Civil Federal, art. 44, disponible en: http://www.diputados.gob.mx/LeyesBiblio/pdf/2_110121.pdf.
[43]   Código Civil Federal, art. 102.

Otra situación que debe considerarse es el número de matrimonios que por mandato se celebraron en los últimos años, previo a la pandemia y posterior a ella.

Número de mandatos otorgados para la celebración de matrimonios entre ausentes por parte de la red consular mexicana antes de la pandemia (2016-2019)

Año	Cantidad
2016	10
2017	2
2018	7
2019	9
Total	28

Tabla 1: Tabla de mandatos para el matrimonio entre ausentes. Fuente: Secretaría de Relaciones Exteriores, 2020[44]

Considerando la información anterior, se puede señalar que, antes de la pandemia del COVID-19, (a pesar de que la multijurisdiccionalidad de la regulación civil en México, quien regula al matrimonio entre ausentes) el mandato especial para contraer matrimonio era poco utilizado, lo anterior podría generar su desuso y convertirlo en una ficción jurídica.

Posterior a la pandemia, se solicitó información en relación al número de mandatos especiales otorgados para contraer matrimonio en el periodo comprendido desde el año 2019 y hasta el 8 de abril del 2022, y la respuesta por parte de la Secretaría de Relaciones Exteriores de México fue de 109 mandatos.[45] Lo anterior lleva a deducir que, al restringirse la movilidad de los ciudadanos en el mundo, en específico los mexicanos viviendo en el extranjero y al no poder regresar a su país a otorgar su consentimiento matrimonial de forma presencial

---

[44] *Secretaría de Relaciones Exteriores/Unidad de transparencia,* solicitud de información 500113020, respuesta con oficio número UDT- 3139/2020, 2020.

[45] *Secretaría de Relaciones Exteriores/Unidad de transparencia,* solicitud de información 330026822000622, respuesta con oficio número UDT- 2179/2022, 2022.

ante la autoridad administrativa registral (Registro Civil), recurrieron a otorgar mandatos ante el servicio consular mexicano y enviarlos a México, subsanando el requisito de la presencialidad. Lo anterior no significaba que el matrimonio entre ausentes fuera la solución, sino por el contrario era la única opción consecuencia de la inexistencia de un matrimonio a través de medios electrónicos.

Sin embargo, otras figuras jurídicas como el testamento, derivado de la pandemia en México, se tuvieron que adaptar al nuevo orden de la realidad. El 4 de agosto de 2021 fue publicado en la Gaceta de la Ciudad de México el decreto que permite la celebración del testamento público por medios electrónicos, al señalar en su art. 1520bis:

> El testamento público abierto también podrá realizarse por medios electrónicos, siempre que el testador cuente con la posibilidad de comunicarse con el notario a través de un dispositivo electrónico y el notario pueda ver y oír al testador, así como hablar con él de manera directa, simultánea y en tiempo real durante todo el acto del otorgamiento.[46]

También, fue reformada la Ley del Notariado para la Ciudad de México, con la intención de que la actuación del Notario sea digital (art. 2 fracción II) a través de medios electrónicos, ópticos o de cualquier otra tecnología en el entorno de protocolo digital, con equivalencia funcional al protocolo ordinario.[47]

Ahora es pertinente proponer algo similar a lo establecido por el art. 1520 de la Codificación Civil Capitalina en cuanto a la presencialidad de los consortes al momento de la celebración del matrimonio, evitando el mandato especial para celebrar el matrimonio entre ausentes. En cuanto a la autoridad administrativa registral (Registro Civil) es necesario mudar su actuación al ámbito digital en beneficio de los consortes, que no se encuentran presentes al momento de la celebración del matrimonio y toda la población en la realización de los distintos registros y trámites ante dicha autoridad.

Para concluir es necesario plantear la siguiente pregunta: ¿Acaso se presenta una derrotabilidad del matrimonio entre ausentes en México?

---

[46] *Gobierno de la Ciudad de México*, Decreto por el que se modifican y adicionan diversas disposiciones para el Código Civil del Distrito Federal y la Ley del Notariado para la Ciudad de México, 2021, disponible en: https://data.consejeria.cdmx.gob.mx/index.php/gaceta.

[47] *Gobierno de la Ciudad de México* (nota al pie 46).

E. La derrotabilidad del matrimonio entre ausentes en México

La derrotabilidad de matrimonio entre ausentes parte de dos situaciones específicas: la derrotabilidad de la norma jurídica y el orden de la realidad en México.

I. La derrotabilidad de la norma jurídica

El estudio de la derrotabilidad del consentimiento matrimonial lo iniciamos se-
ñalando que "con frecuencia se sostiene que una reconstrucción sistemática del
derecho basada en la noción clásica de consecuencias nos compromete con una
visión distorsionada de las normas jurídicas".[48] Aplicado a la presencialidad de
los contrayentes en el consentimiento matrimonial, considero que el ordenamiento jurídico fue superado por el orden de la realidad digital y sanitaria, lo que
permite visualizar de forma distorsionada a los mandatos especiales derivados
del matrimonio entre ausentes.

Navarro y Rodríguez señalan que el problema surge cuando se admite que las
calificaciones normativas ofrecidas por las normas jurídicas pueden ser supera-
das o derrotadas por una modificación.[49] En este sentido se concluye con la propuesta, ya que lo que se pretende es la derrotabilidad de la presencialidad de los
contrayentes en el consentimiento matrimonial, a partir de la reforma y adiciones
al art. 1803 de la codificación federal, en materia de modalidades del consentimiento expreso al señalar en su primera fracción: "Será expreso cuando la voluntad se manifiesta verbalmente, por escrito, por medios electrónicos o por cualquier otra tecnología, o por signos inequívocos".[50] Por lo tanto, se debe valorar y
reflexionar sobre la pertinencia de seguir regulando una ficción jurídica (matrimonio por mandato) en la legislación civil mexicana o adecuarse al orden de la
realidad jurídica en materia de consentimiento electrónico. Los autores en comento concluyen:

> Nuestro propósito ha consistido en mostrar que la relevancia de la mo-
> dificación del contexto fáctico en el que se plantea un problema norma-
> tivo puede ser analizado sin dificultad en una concepción clásica de los
> sistemas normativos. En este sentido, si la objeción de la derrotabilidad

---

[48]   *Navarro/Rodríguez*, Derrotabilidad y sistematización de normas jurídicas, 2000, pp. 61-85, dis-
       ponible en: https://www.scielo.org.mx/pdf/is/n13/1405-0218-is-13-00061.pdf.
[49]   *Navarro/Rodríguez* (nota al pie 48).
[50]   *Código Civil Federal*, reforma del 29.5.2000, disponible en: http://www.diputados.gob.mx/
       LeyesBiblio/ref/ccf/CCF_ref44_29may00_ima.pdf.

está íntimamente ligada a la modificación del universo de propiedades relevantes para resolver un problema normativo, entonces no hay conflicto entre derrotabilidad y reconstrucción sistemática del derecho.[51]

II. El orden de la realidad en México

El orden de la realidad mexicana se analizará a partir de los tres puntos conclusivos que plantea *Stern* en su artículo "Matrimonio por poder en México".[52]

1. Primer punto conclusivo: "El derecho mexicano ha autorizado los matrimonios por poder en mucho mayor extensión que cualesquiera otros países de derecho civil o de common law".[53]
La apreciación es correcta, como se menciona en el apartado: El consentimiento matrimonial en México, tanto las entidades federativas como la federación regulan al matrimonio y su consentimiento entre ausentes hasta la fecha.

2. Segundo punto conclusivo: "Los matrimonios por poder tienen su lugar adecuado en los países cuyas líneas de comunicación se hallen sin desarrollar y en aquellos en que los juristas recurren a ficciones legales, tales como la presencia de un ausente, con objeto de preservar conceptos tradicionales".[54]
Se considera que en México se puede dejar de recurrir al mandato para contraer matrimonio, ya que se tiene un porcentaje de conectividad del 67 % de la población mexicana y se pronostica que para el año 2027 será de un 71 %.[55] En el mismo sentido, se señaló que en 2020, 84.1 millones de la población mexicana eran usuarios de internet lo que representaba el 72 % de la población a partir de los seis años; y que los tres medios para la conexión a internet fueron: los smartphones con un 96 %, las computadoras portátiles con 33 % y con un 22.2 % a través de televisiones con acceso a internet. El objetivo principal de las personas usuarias a internet en 2020 fue comunicarse con un 93.8 %, búsqueda de información 91 % y acceso a redes sociales 89 %.[56]

---

51 *Navarro/Rodríguez* (nota al pie 48).
52 *Stern* (nota al pie 1).
53 *Stern* (nota al pie 1).
54 *Stern* (nota al pie 1).
55 *Statista*, porcentaje de la población con acceso a internet 2015 a 2026, 2022. Base de datos: https://es.statista.com/.
56 *INEGI*, Comunicado de prensa núm. 352/21 de 22 de junio de 2021, pp. 1-2, disponible en: https://www.inegi.org.mx/contenidos/saladeprensa/boletines/2021/OtrTemEcon/ENDUTIH_2020.pdf.

De la segunda parte del punto conclusivo en comento, se concluye que se debe dejar de recurrir al matrimonio entre ausentes a través del mandato especial, en la medida de las posibilidades y las necesidades de los ciudadanos mexicanos, ya que en la actualidad el consentimiento expreso puede manifestarse por medios electrónicos, ópticos o por cualquier otra tecnología, o por signos inequívocos. De acuerdo con lo señalado por la fracción I del art. 1803 del Código Civil Federal.

Lo anterior permite que la tecnología sea la vía para expresar el consentimiento en los actos jurídicos con plena validez. Al mismo tiempo facilita la posibilidad de celebrarlos, sin la necesidad de la presencialidad, debiendo cumplir con requisitos especiales que permitan autenticar que los consortes, manifestaron su voluntad.

En consecuencia, el medio idóneo para autenticar que los consortes manifestaron su voluntad y firmado del acta de matrimonio ante la autoridad administrativa del Registro Civil (Juez del Registro Civil) a la distancia, es la firma electrónica,[57] que es fiable[58] y eficaz.[59]

En el caso de la autoridad administrativa registral, es decir, los jueces o encargados del Registro Civil, en cuanto a su firma, no tienen la facultad expresa de firmar electrónicamente, pero en la actualidad, en nuestro sistema jurídico, ya existen leyes federales[60] y estatales (14 de las 32 entidades federativas cuentan con leyes que regulan el uso de la firma electrónica simple) que regulan la firma electrónica para los funcionarios públicos. En dichas leyes, no se contempla la posibilidad de firmar electrónicamente los actos del Estado Civil de las personas.

3. Tercer punto: "El pedir una reglamentación legal de los matrimonios por poder en algunos de nuestros Estados, haría pensar que los matrimonios por carta o

---

[57] Firma Electrónica: Los datos en forma electrónica consignados en un Mensaje de Datos, o adjuntados o lógicamente asociados al mismo por cualquier tecnología, que son utilizados para identificar al Firmante en relación con el Mensaje de Datos e indicar que el Firmante aprueba la información contenida en el Mensaje de Datos, y que produce los mismos efectos jurídicos que la firma autógrafa, siendo admisible como prueba en juicio. Código de Comercio, art. 89, disponible en: https://www.diputados.gob.mx/LeyesBiblio/pdf/CCom.pdf.

[58] Requisitos de la firma electrónica en México. Código de Comercio, art. 97.

[59] Código de Comercio, Art. 89bis: "No se negarán efectos jurídicos, validez o fuerza obligatoria a cualquier tipo de información por la sola razón de que esté contenida en un Mensaje de Datos. Por tanto, dichos mensajes podrán ser utilizados como medio probatorio en cualquier diligencia ante autoridad legalmente reconocida, y surtirán los mismos efectos jurídicos que la documentación impresa, siempre y cuando los mensajes de datos se ajusten a las disposiciones de este Código y a los lineamientos normativos correspondientes."

[60] Ley de firma electrónica avanzada (federal), disponible en: https://www.diputados.gob.mx/LeyesBiblio/pdf/LFEA_200521.pdf.

televisión, o el cumplimiento de determinadas ceremonias por cada una de las par-
tes, están más a tono con una visión realista del derecho que la ficción que informa
el principio del matrimonio por poder".[61]

En este sentido, es importante mencionar que las conclusiones fueron realizadas en la primera mitad del siglo XX. Respecto a esta última, coincido con el
autor, es necesario ir acabando con ficciones jurídicas como el mandato especial
para celebrar el matrimonio entre ausentes, ya que desde hace 20 años en México
contamos con un consentimiento electrónico reconocido por nuestra legislación
civil federal.[62]

F. Conclusiones

Se debe afirmar que el consentimiento matrimonial entre ausentes se encuentra
regulado a nivel internacional y por una multijurisdiccionalidad de ordenamien-
tos jurídicos civiles y familiares en México, que no son congruentes con el orden
de la realidad jurídica y tecnológica actual. Lo anterior es uno de los factores que
inciden en la disminución de la nupcialidad, independientemente del concubinato, divorcio, la edad para contraer matrimonio, la carencia económica y cultural, el matrimonio utópico y el matrimonio religioso.

En consecuencia, se puede dejar de recurrir al mandato para contraer matrimonio por falta de presencialidad por parte de los pretensos, ya que el 67 % de la
población cuenta con acceso a internet y se pronostica que para 2027 será de un
71 %. Además, la mayoría de las y los mexicanos cuenta con medios de conexión.
Lo anterior permite que el consentimiento matrimonial se pueda expresar a través de medios electrónicos y la forma para autenticar dicho consentimiento sería
la firma electrónica en el acta de matrimonio ante la autoridad administrativa del
Registro Civil.

Derivado de los argumentos anteriores, se propone la derrotabilidad de la
norma jurídica, en cuanto presencialidad de los pretensos al momento de celebrar el matrimonio y del mandato especial para contraer matrimonio en caso de
ausencia. Lo anterior con fundamento en el orden de la realidad jurídica y tecnológica, a partir de la reforma al art. 1803 del Código Civil Federal, llevada a cabo
el 29 de mayo del año 2000, permitiendo la posibilidad de consentir a la distancia
a través de medios electrónicos, ópticos o por cualquier otra tecnología.

---

[61] *Stern* (nota al pie 1).
[62] *Código Civil Federal*, reforma del 29.5.2000, disponible en: http://www.diputados.gob.
      mx/LeyesBiblio/ref/ccf/CCF_ref44_29may00_ima.pdf.

Ludwigs / Muriel Ciceri / Velling (eds.), Digitalization as a challenge for justice and administration, Abhandlungen zum Öffentlichen Recht 1, Würzburg, 2023, pp. 141-152.
DOI: 10.25972/978-3-95826-201-0-141

La administración digital de la decisión judicial penal en México

Juliana Vivar Vera

A. Introducción

La justicia penal contiene en su esencia responsabilidad estatal sobre el control de la violencia. Sin embargo, cuando la tecnología invade la cotidianeidad y se hace necesaria su utilización, el cuidado de la comprensión algorítmica es de sumo cuidado. La pandemia de COVID-19 trajo consigo que el Estado Mexicano implementara de forma abrupta la digitalización de expedientes y la tramitología procesal. Esto evidenció los beneficios que la intervención de la tecnología tiene en el acceso a la justicia, pero, por otro lado, mostró que, en un país desigual, estos beneficios están centrados en los que tienen acceso a dicha tecnología.

El presente capítulo tiene como objetivo mostrar que en México durante la pandemia de COVID-19 y para cumplir con las medidas sanitarias, la aceleración en la implementación de tecnología para el acceso a la justicia penal tuvo contrapuestos de impacto a la dinámica social, los cuales ayudan a prever un escenario de sustitución humana.

Para lograr lo anterior, se inicia con la contextualización del escenario de México en la implementación de la transparencia digital de la justicia penal, a fin de identificar la complejidad de una decisión judicial y los mecanismos administrativos que requiere su publicidad; en un segundo momento, se muestra el escenario de implementación durante la pandemia de COVID-19 a fin de resaltar que lo acelerado en su introducción tuvo afectación en el acceso a la justicia en igualdad social; por último, se destaca el papel de la justicia penal digital ante la desigualdad social existente, a fin de que pueda ayudar a identificar elementos de análisis interseccionales que combinen armónicamente con la propuesta de una implementación digital eficaz.

B. La transparencia digital de la decisión judicial sobre la violencia

La interna convicción del caso penal es una tarea humana que se traslada a un sinnúmero de realidades que luego tendrán que ser expuestas al escrutinio social. Es en este sentido que, en lo interno, la decisión judicial penal implica esfuerzo intelectual humano de razonamiento formal y material. El principio de legalidad que resulta en la decisión judicial es el "hecho que la ley señala como delito" de acuerdo al artículo 20 de la Constitución Política de los Estados Unidos Mexicanos. Así la subsunción del hecho al tipo penal descrito en la ley bajo el apotegma *nullum crimen, nulla poena, sine lege y* bajo un modelo estructural dogmático de teoría del delito, conlleva la imposición de una pena o la absolución de responsabilidad penal que transforma la vida de la persona destinataria y de su familia. Este control estatal de la violencia se materializa con instituciones que deben actuar con fundamento legal y cuya máxima expresión de impartición de justicia es la decisión penal.

Así lo que corresponde es que el Poder Judicial exponga ante la sociedad la interna decisión humana de quien fue contratado como su ejecutor. Las y los jueces al ser evaluados deberían evidenciar su calidad humana además del conocimiento técnico y capacidad argumentativa, una actuación judicial verdaderamente pública, sin tener al Estado como patrón, sin que los juzgadores se representen como seres especiales y etéreos – aunque su función lo sea. Deben rendir informe a la sociedad, no sobre el número de sentencias resueltas con fundamentaciones legales, sino sobre el resultado del contraste de la realidad y las implicaciones actuales y a futuro de sus resoluciones que, de lo contrario, constituye un desdén. Por ello la importancia de crear condiciones necesarias de trabajo en conjunto, con compromisos y responsabilidades a cumplir para crear un ejercicio cíclico de justicia, concebir a la sentencia no como simple instrumento jurídico sino como un arma poderosa de decisión de vidas, que actúa para afectar y no para beneficiar a su víctima; es un parteaguas de la violencia pues culmina la violencia procedimental y marca el inicio de una nueva que durará toda la vida.

La burocracia en la práctica judicial permite apreciar:

> Las rutinas programadas que sostienen su propia progresión. La capacidad administrativa y organizativa de los expedientes los muestra más allá de meras inscripciones mecánicas sobre el papel: constituyen las bases materiales para la creación del derecho y se manifiestan como las herramientas cognitivas de los sujetos de la burocracia judicial articuladas en un régimen de verdad en el que los documentos establecen los límites

materiales y epistemológicos... los expedientes son capaces de generar múltiples y contingentes estados afectivos en los sujetos que los crean.[1]

Tal vez pudiera pensarse que el juez dicta sentencia con previo plan estructurado, sin embargo, no es así, pues la cantidad de expedientes no permiten contemplar tal posibilidad "...aun cuando varios de ellos insistían con aquella metáfora de la Corte como un almacén de ramos generales, imagen más que elocuente para reflejar sus quehaceres cotidianos, metáfora que parecía corporizarse en la cantidad de expedientes acumulados en escritorios, sillas y hasta los pisos de sus oficinas."[2] Pero es más sencillo ampararse en artículos legales para evitar la acumulación del trabajo, no importa si se percibe como burocracia y política.[3]

Pues como lo observan *Berger y Luckmann*, "las instituciones por el hecho mismo de existir, también controlan el comportamiento humano estableciendo pautas definidas de antemano que lo canalizan en una dirección determinada, en oposición a las muchas otras que podrían darse teóricamente."[4] Las instituciones parecieran ser el medio de control entre la subjetividad y la objetividad para la justa de imparcial decisión judicial, resisten todo intento de cambio o evasión, ejercen sobre él un poder de coacción, tanto de por sí, por la fuerza pura de su facticidad, como por medio de los mecanismos de control habitualmente anexos a las más importantes.

Vale decir que los jueces son artistas, pues combinan técnica con creatividad; cuando aplican la ley, técnica, cuando ejercen su facultad discrecional, creatividad al crear derecho, tal como los novelistas de manera inconsciente.[5] Sin embargo, la diferencia importante entre ellos es el sueldo seguro del que goza un juez. Pero de ello se desprende que hay dos clases de jueces: los líderes y los

---

[1]   *Barrera,* La Corte Suprema en escena. Una etnografía del mundo judicial, 2012, p. 155.

[2]   *Barrera* (nota al pie 1), p. 95.

[3]   *Barrera* comparte una experiencia propia de solicitud de información ante el Tribunal que fue negada con fundamento el art. 280, lo que generó un fuerte efecto simbólico respecto a la autoridad de la Corte. *Barrera* (nota al pie 1), p. 76.

[4]   *Berger/Luckmann,* La Construcción Social de la Realidad, 1968, p. 82.

[5]   "Un novelista escribe un pasaje de una manera en vez de en otra porque siente que esa es la manera adecuada; incluso puede que sea incapaz de explicar el porqué de su parecer. A menudo sucede que un juez ve con claridad cómo ha de ser resuelto un caso, pero cuando trata de motivar su decisión al redactar la sentencia, su explicación por lo general, será una racionalización de un resultado alcanzado sobre fundamentos inarticulados, aunque a veces el esfuerzo de tener que motivar le llevará a refinar, y quizá a invertir, el sentido de intuición que le condujo inicialmente a sostener una determinada opinión como fundamentación del fallo (...) Los distintos géneros de arte, del mismo modo que las decisiones judiciales, son gobernados pro normas y, en ambos casos, las normas son controvertibles." *Posner,* Cómo Deciden los Jueces, 2011, p. 77.

seguidores[6] según la calidad y qué tanto trabajen. Sin embargo, como *Posner* señala, "El 'miedo a la revocación' les crea a los jueces un conflicto entre lo que se espera de su rol y sus sentimientos personales."[7] Ello hace que cada uno ponga su mayor esfuerzo y ya sea que ellos mismos o con ayuda, cumplan el compromiso estatal, actuando en sus decisiones como se esperaría de un "buen" juez.

Es por eso que el escrutinio social es el objetivo de la llamada transparencia y acceso a información relativa a la impartición de justicia, pues representa una herramienta particularmente importante que permite a la ciudadanía mejorar la comprensión del sistema de justicia y de los recursos legales que tienen a su disposición para el pleno ejercicio de todos sus derechos y evaluar el desempeño de las autoridades jurisdiccionales.

Una reforma estructural al sistema de justicia penal que contemple algunos de estos factores y que incluso otorgue alternativas para que no llegue la responsabilidad de la sentencia penal, ha sido insuficiente para la certeza de la seguridad jurídica, como fue el caso *Rubí* en el estado de Chihuahua México[8], no obstante, la publicidad como principio contenido en el art. 20 de la Constitución Política de los Estados Unidos Mexicanos , evidenció el momento procesal del dictado oral de la sentencia que luego fue revisada y revertida. El llamado error judicial bajo el escrutinio social, dio cuenta de la función latente del sistema penal que se vuelca implacable contra la vulnerabilidad en la desigualdad social, tal como fue expuesto en la disculpa pública dictada por la Procuraduría General de la República el 21 de febrero de 2016 en un caso alterno paradigmático, el de *Jacinta Francisco Marcial*.[9]

De acuerdo con este principio de publicidad, la Ley General de Transparencia y Acceso a la Información Pública indica que las sentencias deben ser publicadas.

---

[6] Afirma *Posner* (nota al pie 5) que hay artistas obreros-especializados, así como hay jueces obreros-especializados.

[7] *Posner* (nota al pie 5), p. 85.

[8] Donde el Tribunal de primera instancia dictó sentencia absolutoria y el de alzada una sentencia condenatoria de 50 años. Para mayor referencia de este caso véase *Ríos Espinosa,* en: Cienfuegos Salgado/Froto Madariaga (coords.), Los Derechos Humanos en el Momento Actual, 2012, p. 404.

[9] En el caso de *Jacinta Francisco Marcial*, *Alberta Alcántara Juan* y *Teresa González Cornelio*, mujeres indígenas otomíes de Santiago Mexquititlán, condenadas a 21 años de prisión en agosto de 2006 por posesión de cocaína y secuestro de seis agentes de la extinta Agencia Federal de Investigación (AFI). Pasaron tres y cuatro años de prisión. Después de once años, el Estado reconoció haber violado el principio de presunción de inocencia y conculcado el debido proceso por no contar con un traductor y una defensa adecuada, sin que la Comisión Nacional para el Desarrollo de los Pueblos Indígenas y la Comisión Nacional de los Derechos Humanos interviniera. *Centro de Derechos Humanos Miguel Agustín Pro Juárez A.C.*, Dossier de prensa de Doña Jacinta Francisco Marcial, 2017, disponible en: https://bit.ly/35K4nHB. La última recuperación de todas las direcciones web mencionadas en este capítulo es el 27 de octubre 2022.

Así en mayo de 2015, esta obligatoriedad fue en el sentido de publicar las sentencias que hayan causado estado y que el propio poder judicial considerara de interés público, disponiéndose como plazo un año para armonizar las legislaciones locales y cumplir con esta obligación. Esto generó incertidumbre jurídica sobre el precepto que debe atenderse para que el Poder Judicial cumpliera su obligación.[10] Por tal motivo, se reformó en 2020 la fracción II del art. 73 de la Ley General, en los siguientes términos: "…II. Las versiones públicas de todas las sentencias emitidas."[11]. Sin embargo, al intentar dar cumplimiento, surgió la problemática de no contar con ellas de forma digitalizada, por lo que la generación de la versión pública implicaba obtener una fotocopia simple de cada expediente, testar los datos personales y escanear nuevamente la copia testada a efecto de generar el archivo digital. Así también había resistencia de publicitar las sentencias penales que representaban para los jueces la actuación con secrecía, como fue la solicitud de las versiones públicas de las sentencias definitivas absolutorias y condenatorias dictadas en las causas penales por el delito de contrabando de acuerdo al Expediente 2077/21, cuyo sujeto obligado era el Consejo de la Judicatura Federal. Se obtuvo como respuesta que los órganos jurisdiccionales tienen bajo su resguardo los expedientes judiciales; por lo tanto, no tiene facultades para entregar archivos en versión electrónica o digital de los documentos contenidos en expedientes. En la inconformidad, el Instituto Nacional de Acceso a la Información, determinó que debía realizarse una nueva búsqueda y entregar la versión pública de las sentencias requeridas.

La relevancia de la publicidad judicial radica en el impulso a la cultura de la transparencia y la efectiva rendición de cuentas como parte de los compromisos para contribuir en la promoción de sociedades justas, pacíficas e inclusivas para el desarrollo sostenible, facilitar el acceso a la justicia para todas las personas, y crear instituciones eficaces, responsables e inclusivas a todos los niveles, es decir, en el marco del Objetivo 16 de desarrollo Sostenible de la Agenda 2030 de la Organización de las Naciones Unidas, conforme al cual, no sólo la transparencia es mandatoria sino el que la misma se realice de forma eficaz[12]. La transparencia de las decisiones judiciales ayuda a cumplir tal objetivo pues el mismo reconoce que es una de las instituciones más afectadas por la corrupción y es por ello que una de las metas es la promoción del estado de derecho y garantiza la igualdad de

---

[10] *EQUIS Justicia para las mujeres*, Transparencia en la publicación de sentencias ¿Retrocesos a partir de la Ley General de Transparencia y Acceso a la Información Pública?, 2017, disponible: https://equis.org.mx/wp-content/uploads/2018/02/Informe_Transparencia_Sentencias.pdf.

[11] Ley General de Transparencia y Accesos a la Información Pública, publicada en el Diario Oficial de la Federación el 4.5.2015.

[12] *Organización Nacional de las Naciones Unidas* (ONU), Objetivos de Desarrollo Sostenible, disponible en: https://www.un.org/sustainabledevelopment/es/peace-justice/.

acceso a la justicia para todos. A fin de lograrlo, el Objetivo 9 es el camino por el cual se intersecta la meta estatal, puesto que, de acuerdo al mismo, la innovación y el progreso tecnológico son claves para descubrir soluciones duraderas a los desafíos y están en la primera línea de la respuesta a la COVID-19 en que se generó una crisis social que provocó la aceleración de la digitalización de los servicios, tal cual como sucedió en México.[13]

C. El impulso digital por COVID-19 en el Poder Judicial de México: Desvelando la desigualdad

Las actividades mecánicas institucionales dentro del poder judicial en México se han visto materializadas en el seguimiento de trámite procesal técnico y formal, aunque con poco avance en su automatización. La pandemia por COVID-19 puso de relieve esta carencia y trajo consigo que el Consejo de la Judicatura Federal dictara el 17 de marzo de 2020 el Acuerdo General 4/2020, en el que se restringió la actividad jurisdiccional a la atención de asuntos clasificados como urgentes de acuerdo al arbitrio de las y los juzgadores y sin lineamientos para identificarlos por lo que en algunos casos quedaron fuera de la protección judicial los de una importancia considerable, como los derechos de las víctimas a obtener medidas de asistencia y reparación.[14]

Podría parecer que el arbitrio judicial radica en la experiencia sensible de los casos de impacto social, sin embargo, al quedar fuera sólo uno de ellos, todos resultan importantes, es decir, que la urgencia la define el justiciable y no la Institución.

Fue por tal motivo que el juicio en línea fue la alternativa para iniciar juicios de amparo sobre casos "no urgentes" a través de la plataforma "servicios en línea",[15] por lo que quienes no pudieran acceder a medios digitales debían esperar a que se reanudaran actividades. Con el Juicio en línea se atendieron las necesidades tecnológicas requeridas en materia de juicios orales, mercantiles y penales en general a toda petición que se formulara ante el Poder Judicial de la Federación. La ventaja era evidente en cuanto a reducción de tiempos, desplazamientos

---

13   *Fundación para la Justicia y el Estado Democrático de Derecho* (coords.), El acceso a la justicia en México durante la pandemia de COVID-19. Análisis sobre la actuación del Poder Judicial de la Federación, 2021, p. 26, disponible en: https://imumi.org/wp-content/uploads/2021/08/el-acceso-a-la-justicia-en-mexico-durante-la-pandemia-de-covid-19.pdf.
14   *Fundación para la Justicia y el Estado Democrático de Derecho* (coords.) (nota al pie 13), p. 54.
15   *Poder Judicial de la Federación*, Portal de Servicios en Línea, disponible en: https://www.serviciosenlinea.pjf.gob.mx/juicioenlinea.

de personas y contacto humano para reducir contagios, aunque, por otra parte, la brecha digital también evidenciaría que no todas las personas tuvieran la oportunidad del acceso a este tipo de justicia. La premura del servicio en línea tuvo la principal deficiencia: el desconocimiento de la utilización del portal por el propio personal del Poder Judicial y de las y los litigantes. Tanto la brecha digital como el desconocimiento de la utilización de la plataforma por las personas usuarias provocó una reducción de demandas en un 44.81 %.[16] Así, los derechos de acceso a la justicia y a un recurso efectivo afectaron principalmente a quienes se encuentran en situación de vulnerabilidad. De todo ello se desprende que, en relación a la atención a violaciones a derechos humanos, muchas víctimas podrían haberse quedado sin protección, es decir, sin la oportunidad de remediar judicialmente su situación.

Por otro lado, existe la obligatoriedad de publicidad de las audiencias conforme a los art. 28 y 30 del Acuerdo General 12/2020 del Consejo de la Judicatura, pero realmente sólo es posible hallar sesiones de plenos y tribunales colegiados de circuito, pero no audiencias sustanciadas por jueces dentro del proceso penal "en la impugnación 2/2021, promovida por la Fundación para la Justicia ante el Centro de Justicia Penal Federal en el Estado de Tamaulipas, con residencia en Reynosa, referente al hallazgo de diecinueve cuerpos calcinados en Camargo, varios periodistas solicitaron estar presentes en la audiencia. No obstante, el juez señaló que no era posible su presencia porque la plataforma no soportaba la conexión de más de diez personas conectadas, por lo que se tuvieron que retirar."[17]

Resulta visible que la necesidad de digitalizar la administración de justicia requiere una evaluación previa de ser asequible a la totalidad de la población en todos los sectores de garantía de acceso a la justicia para el debido proceso. Si estas dos situaciones no son satisfechas, la implementación tecnológica es poco viable para la sociedad. La forma abrupta de aplicación en México tuvo el motivo COVID-19 para asegurar las medidas restrictivas para la salud, de otro modo y de forma ideal, el diseño tecnológico debe adaptarse a la sociedad de forma simple y normalizada con la costumbre de administración de justicia para la garantía de los derechos humanos, contrario a ello, el acceso a la justicia resulta un privilegio y se evidencia la brecha entre la realidad y la ley.

La mecanización de la administración de la justicia debe ser un reto para la tecnología, esto es distinto a suponer que las tareas humanas que no representan complejidad intelectual pueden ser sustituibles al grado de que la intervención humana deba ser mínima y por tanto innecesaria.[18] Por ello el avance de

---

[16]   *Fundación para la Justicia y el Estado Democrático de Derecho* (coords.) (nota al pie 13), p. 13.

[17]   *Fundación para la Justicia y el Estado Democrático de Derecho* (coords.) (nota al pie 13), p. 116.

[18]   *Sourdin*, UNSW Law Journal, Vol. 41, núm. 4, 2018, 1114 (XX), 1119.

perfeccionamiento tanto en la actividad mecánica y en el trabajo de razonamiento humano complejo es ya una realización práctica de las combinaciones algorítmicas. El aprendizaje profundo (*deep learning*), subcampo específico del aprendizaje automático (*machine learning*) que, a su vez, es un aprendizaje de capas sucesivas de más representaciones significativas), aspira a que se requiera menos la participación de ingenieros humanos con la aplicación de técnicas diferentes como la retropropagación *(backpropagation)*.[19] De esta forma se tendría la capacidad del razonamiento formal, algo parecido a AlphaGo que se desarrolla automáticamente en lugar de ser codificado por humanos. Mientras tanto, el aprendizaje profundo sigue siendo utilizado para reducir la carga cognitiva técnica, como lo ofrece el desarrollador.[20]

La intención de sustituir al humano por robot es que, a partir de cambiar las técnicas de aprendizaje profundo que sólo mapean insumos de formación a los objetivos de entrenamiento punto por punto, se trabaje con razonamiento y abstracción a partir de la intuición para lograr una argumentación lógica, minería y análisis de textos legales, donde se toman modelos de razonamiento y representación del conocimiento legal conforme a la teoría jurídica, interpretación legal y la incidencia de la dimensión epistémica de la política, modelos de razonamiento *A-BOX y T-BOX* son los que están desarrollando y el *GOLD standard Corpora* para el análisis sintético y semántico así como crear un corpus de normas multilingües.[21]

Por eso, las intersecciones valorativas de la justicia diferenciada son esenciales para la interpretación material y no violatoria de derechos humanos en la efectiva aplicación de la justicia como es la perspectiva de género, justicia para adolescentes, justicia restaurativa, usos y costumbres en comunidades indígenas, entre otras, que relacionen el caso con modelos teóricos o epistémicos de los que deriva la función del derecho, como la de colonialidad, teorías de violencias y de paz, feminismo, etc. Así, la publicidad de las sentencias evidenciaría el trabajo razonado de los jueces en perspectiva especializada para una mejor realización de sentencias además que se ayudaría de los datos faltantes y mostrados por el procesador sobre desigualdades particulares que devienen de fenómenos amplios. Suponiendo un caso de feminicidio, el cual se derivó de una violencia previa de género pero este término a su vez es interpretable socialmente por estereotipos y sobre todo en comunidades indígenas, son matizables por genealogías

---

[19] *Chollet*, Deep Learning with Python, 2018, pp. 8-332.
[20] Puede consultarse más sobre ello en: K Keras. Simple. Flexible. Powerful, disponible en: https://keras.io/.
[21] Puede encontrarse mayor referencia y detalle de los proyectos en: Mirel: Minining and reasoning with legal tex, disponible en: https://www.mirelproject.eu/ y Laboratorio de investigación y desarrollo de la Inteligencia Artificial-LIDIA, disponible en: http://lidia.cs.uns.edu.ar/home/.

antropológicas. En este caso, únicamente el juez humano podría comprender esta cadena tipológica de diferente forma que una máquina, pero sería de gran ayuda el filtro de datos y la combinación algorítmica. Por tanto, si se trata de un caso nuevo, el software no tendría elementos tipológicos para realizar la función predictiva por no tener ejemplos de datos anteriores con los cuales relacionarlo, pero la ayuda consistiría en que la máquina pudiera ofrecer una realidad múltiple que contribuya a la sensibilidad humana para empatizar con el caso. Esto sería más útil para el juez que si toma sesgo previo de los datos previos y lo perpetua.

D. La justicia penal digital ante la desigualdad social.

Tanto el sistema de justicia penal como la tecnología tienen en común la visión occidentalizada en su diseño e implementación en las sociedades, así como que no consideran la desigualdad y el impacto de afectación en los sectores vulnerados.

El sistema de justicia penal, por ejemplo, establece tipos penales que no conciben una cosmovisión originaria puesto que se trata de sistemas adaptados y adoptados, para las comunidades indígenas, la resolución de conflictos ocurre sin un catálogo especial de conductas delictivas y una medición de las mismas. A pesar de la *vacatio legis,* la interpretación de los delitos por los pueblos originarios tiene sesgos derivados de usos y costumbres que vale destacar como elementos diferenciadores de justicia; por ejemplo, opina *Felipe Pérez Hernández,* exagente auxiliar municipal del paraje Yanch'en, San Juan Cancuc sobre el delito de tráfico de drogas y consumo:

> El infractor es castigado solo cuando agrede a personas. Si alguien siembra marihuana no es castigado, porque no está haciendo nada y no nos compete. Aparte que no ha sucedido, tal vez cuando suceda, se le exhorte a no seguir y pague alguna multa al Juzgado...Compra de votos: No nos ha tocado el caso, ha habido problemas con los partidos, pero se resuelven mediante el diálogo y la conciliación.[22]

Por otro lado, la tecnología afirma la postura discriminatoria contra los sectores vulnerados puesto que la creación empresarial tiene desde el diseño una visión sesgada de la realidad por el grupo privilegiado de hombres blancos, con recursos procedentes del norte global que imponen sus propias perspectivas, derivado de lo cual la ONU se ha pronunciado por el llamado "bienestar digital",

---

[22] *López,* Análisis del modelo tradicional de justicia indígena en San Juan Cancuc, Chiapas, desde la perspectiva de los derechos humanos, 2015, p. 148.

sobre todo en el uso de la Inteligencia artificial advirtiendo sobre la desigualdad social y la desatención de la inteligencia artificial, cuyo único objetivo ha sido el mercado, que, de seguir así, los sesgos se exacerbarán y reproducirán.

El modo de contrarrestar la catástrofe social digital es garantizando los derechos humanos desde las prácticas en las que se basa la creación, la auditoria y el mantenimiento de los datos para luego ser sometidos a un escrutinio muy intenso.[23] Por eso es que los desarrolladores de softwares están haciendo esfuerzos para adaptarlos al enfoque teórico complejo de un Estado constitucional de derecho, es decir, de la aplicación de una justicia respetuosa de derechos humanos. De esta forma, los términos dignidad, libertad y transparencia serían valores medibles para que la complejidad que represente la autodeterminación algorítmica asegure el libre desarrollo de la personalidad.[24] La fuente principal para lograr lo anterior, son los datos fácticos sociales colectivos e individuales, similar a los estudios experimentales en el Tribunal Europeo de Derechos Humanos y en la Corte Interamericana de Derechos Humanos donde se descubrió que los elementos fácticos son de gran relevancia[25] los pesos que ciertas frases le otorgan al algoritmo de aprendizaje automático. Se requiere además que la combinación algorítmica tome en cuenta los algoritmos de verificación independientes que puedan cuantificar y certificar la capacidad de intuición, inteligibilidad, adaptabilidad y adecuación de los objetivos del robot. [26]De esta forma, la transparencia será la herramienta clave para el trabajo judicial de complejidad interpretativa en la toma de decisiones. Con ello se garantizarán los derechos humanos de las personas justiciables tanto en el razonamiento humano como en la combinación algorítmica. Las reflexiones sobre la autonomía de la voluntad deben ser permanentes y estar presentes en las desigualdades sociales para contribuir a su reducción como una de las responsabilidades estatales. Sin embargo, este objetivo se contradice con el del mercado que es la competencia para la obtención de ganancia y es para lo que la tecnología sigue siendo desarrollada por las empresas privadas.

Actualmente, los valores normativos verificables por las combinaciones algorítmicas más sofisticadas, son las normas y principios positivizados en el orden jurídico nacional e internacional, pero aún no es posible la interpretación algorítmica profunda que se une a la compleja incertidumbre de justicia, es decir

---

[23] *Asamblea General Naciones Unidas,* Informe especial sobre la extrema pobreza y los derechos humanos, 2019, disponible en: http://statements.unmeetings.org/media2/21999189/sr-extreme-poverty-ga-3rd-cttee-statement-f.pdf.

[24] *Gustavo Corvalán,* Revista de Investigações Constitucionais, Vol. 5, núm. 1, 2017, 295.

[25] *Medvedeva/Vols/Wieling,* Artificial Intelligence and Law, Vol. 28, 2020, 237.

[26] *Benanti,* La dignidad de la persona en la era de Máquina Sapiens, disponible en: https://thinkfide.com/la-dignidad-de-la-persona-en-la-era-de-maquina-sapiens-por-paolo-benanti/.

ponderaciones de derechos humanos conforme al caso y a la situación particular de las personas justiciables, lo cual hace que los sesgos de decisión potencien las desigualdades sociales.

Sobre ello, uno de los ejemplos más representativos fue el caso del procesador "Compas" (*Correctional Offender Management Profiling for Alternative Sanctions*) que ayuda al debate sobre la objetividad de los procesadores por el resultado de supuestos sesgos raciales y de género.[27] El procesador predictivo que calificaba a las personas con un número de riesgo correspondiente a la pena que debía imponerse, fue puesto en evidencia el 23 de mayo de 2016 por *ProPublica*, organización sin fines de lucro, en el artículo "Machine Bias",[28] que advierte sobre el sesgo racial del software tomando como referencia algunos casos, principalmente el de *Brisha Borden* y *Vernon Prater*; donde se evidenció en la sentencia de apelación la imposición de una pena incorrecta por recomendación del algoritmo. No hubo mayores detalles de la metodología de combinación de datos por justificación del secreto empresarial, aunque una razón más, pero sin ser mencionada, es que quedó fuera del control humano de la empresa por el aprendizaje automático, lo comúnmente llamado cajas negras.

A nivel global, en términos generales, la justicia digital ha sido asumida como una alternativa, que no puede sustituir a la posibilidad de iniciar procedimientos de forma presencial, sobre todo en países en los que la brecha digital — entendida como la desigualdad en el conocimiento y acceso a internet y a la tecnología — es tan amplia y afecta preponderantemente a los grupos en condición de vulnerabilidad, como la población migrante y en situación de pobreza.[29]

Según la Encuesta Nacional sobre Disponibilidad y Uso de Tecnologías de la Información en los Hogares (ENDUTIH) 2020, 78.3 % de la población urbana es usuaria de internet. En la zona rural la población usuaria se ubica en 50.4 %.[30] Esto refleja la desigualdad que, a pesar de que la brecha no es tan amplia, evidencia el acceso prioritario de la justicia al sector urbano y, como ya previo fue comentado, habría que considerar las vulnerabilidades extras que se insertan en las comunidades rurales para una espera de justicia pronta digital conforme a los instrumentos que suelen agruparse para favorecer el acceso a la justicia, al facilitar la transparencia, disminuir tiempos y agilizar la tramitación de los procesos,

---

[27] *Dieterich/Mendoza/Brennan*, COMPAS Risk Scales: Demonstrating Accuracy Equity and Predictive Parity, 2016, disponible en: https://bit.ly/2S4HRCC.

[28] *Angwin et al.*, Machine Bias, 2016, disponible en: https://www.propublica.org/article/machine-bias-risk-assessments-in-criminal-sentencing.

[29] *Fundación para la Justicia y el Estado Democrático de Derecho* (coords.) (nota al pie 13), p. 54.

[30] INEGI, Comunicado de Prensa Núm. 352/21, 2021, disponible en: https://www.inegi.org.mx/contenidos/saladeprensa/boletines/2021/OtrTemEcon/ENDUTIH_2020.pdf.

pero tomando en consideración esta brecha digital, siempre se les ha entendido como una alternativa que no sustituye a la justicia tradicional.

Es por tal motivo que la brecha digital entre distintas personas o grupos de personas puede volver ilusorio el acceso a recursos efectivos y el acceso a la justicia y ser un factor que acentúe diferencias entre ellos y perpetúe discriminaciones. Así, el Relator Especial sobre la independencia de jueces y abogados advirtió que, en el marco de la pandemia, estas diferencias podrían afectar gravemente el acceso a la justicia y que los Estados debían garantizar este derecho a través de la generación de políticas públicas adecuadas para el cierre de la brecha digital en el ámbito de la justicia. Lo anterior con el objeto de evitar que se torne en causal de ilegitimidad e ineficiencia.[31]

E. Conclusiones

Es indiscutible que la tecnología es parte de nuestra cotidianeidad y que las actividades humanas dependen cada vez más de ella, tanto en las funciones mecánicas como en las que implican razonamiento.

La impartición de justicia penal es una responsabilidad estatal para con la ciudadanía y es a partir de ahí que la transparencia es más que una obligación legal, una necesidad colectiva de bienestar.

Es por tal motivo que el Estado mexicano durante la pandemia, aceleró la mecanización procesal penal, lo cual evidenció que incluso en la administración de justicia, lo cotidiano y mecánico se une a lo racional y sensible que sólo el humano puede ofrecer. Se evidenció también, que la máquina proyecta los errores judiciales humanos al interpretar el caso, pero más aún, se evidenció un país desigual donde la tecnología sigue siendo un privilegio tanto de conocimiento como del medio para acceder a la justicia.

---

[31] *Naciones Unidas Derechos Humanos, Oficina del Alto Comisionado,* A/HRC/47/35: Pandemia de la enfermedad por coronavirus (COVID-19), impacto y retos para una justicia independiente - Informe del Relator Especial sobre la independencia de los magistrados y abogados, Diego García-Sayán.

List of authors / Listado de autores / Verzeichnis der Autorinnen und Autoren

Prof. Dr. Olufunmilayo B. Arewa: Temple University Beasley School of Law

Prof. Dr. Nadja Braun Binder: Universität Basel

Prof. Robin J. Effron, J. D.: Brooklyn Law School

Ayodeji O. Fakolade: Compleo Legal, Lagos

Prof. Dr. Arán García Sánchez: Tecnologico de Monterrey

Prof. Dr. Markus Ludwigs: Julius-Maximilians-Universität Würzburg

Prof. Michiyo Maeda: Keio University

Prof. Dr. José Hernán Muriel Ciceri, LL.M.: Tecnologico de Monterrey

Ass.-Prof. Dr. Ruben E. Rodriguez Samudio: Waseda University

Annika Velling, LL.M. (Oxford): Julius-Maximilians-Universität Würzburg

Prof. Dr. Juliana Vivar Vera: Tecnologico de Monterrey